Letters Along the Way

Letters Along the Way

A Novel of the Christian Life

D. A. CARSON

AND

JOHN D. WOODBRIDGE

CROSSWAY BOOKS

A DIVISION OF GOOD NEWS PUBLISHERS

WHEATON, ILLINOIS • NOTTINGHAM, ENGLAND

Letters Along the Way.

Published by Crossway Books
  A division of
  Good News Publishers
  1300 Crescent Street
  Wheaton, Illinois 60187.

Cover design/illustration: Dennis Hill

Art Direction: Mark Schramm

First printing, 1993

Printed in the United States of America

Library of Congress Cataloging-in-Publication Data
Carson, D. A.
 Letters along the way / D. A. Carson and John D. Woodbridge.
  p. cm.
 1. Evangelism. 2. Christian Life—1960- 3. Imaginary letters.
I. Woodbridge, John D., 1941- . II. Title.
BR1640.C37 1993 277.3'0825—dc20   92-40552
ISBN 0-89107-673-5

01	00	99	98	97	96	95	94	93
15	14	13	12	11	10	9	8	7	6	5	4	3	2	1

First British Edition 1993

ISBN 1 85684 075 1

Production and Printing in the United States of America for
CROSSWAY BOOKS
Norton Street, Nottingham, England NG7 3HR

This book
is gratefully dedicated to
Kenneth S. Kantzer

*"I admit that I worship
the God of our fathers,
as a follower of
the Way."*

—THE APOSTLE PAUL,
AS QUOTED IN ACTS 24:14

Preface

*I*n mid-1991 a former student of ours at Trinity Evangelical Divinity School, Timothy Journeyman, approached one of us to solicit advice about the wisdom of publishing a rather remarkable series of letters. These had been written to him over the past thirteen or fourteen years, covering the span from Timothy's conversion when he was a junior at Princeton, through further study and employment, to seminary training and the first years of pastoral ministry. As a pastor, Timothy could see that these letters contained not only a great deal of distilled wisdom that had helped him mature in his Christian faith, but also a fair bit of useful comment on the changing face of evangelicalism.

The writer of these letters is Dr. Paul Woodson, then Distinguished Professor of Systematic Theology here at Trinity. Naturally enough, Timothy approached Prof. Woodson about publishing them. Prof. Woodson did not think they were worth it, and in any case was loath to release time at his age from his more serious research, a multi-volume treatment of Calvin's doctrine of God. Still, he had no objection to Timothy seeing the letters through the press, with or without collaboration. That was why Timothy approached one of us for counsel. Since we have worked together on projects before, we decided to collaborate once again, edit the letters here and there, check facts, and generally prepare them for the press. We asked Timothy to reconstruct, as well as he could, the situation or correspondence that called forth each letter. Timothy's notes we have greatly reduced, leaving only enough material to enhance the reader's ability to appreciate the letters themselves. When we told him what we were doing, Dr. Woodson himself, we might add, seemed to be amused, but not displeased.

We should perhaps explain two or three of our editorial decisions. Not all the letters that Dr. Woodson wrote to Timothy Journeyman during this period have been included, but only those that deal with spiritual, moral, Biblical, or theological issues, or those that comment on the changing scene. Most pleasantries have been edited out. Where such deletions have affected the flow of the letter, we have noted them. In 1978 the letters were written by hand, with a fountain pen, and emphasis was achieved by underlining. Six years later, Dr. Woodson's letters were run off a computer printer, complete with italics. In 1978 Dr. Woodson used the male pronoun and adjective generically; gradually he changed his style to "gender-neutral" expressions or to complex expressions such as "he or she." Such distinctions we have tried to preserve in our editing because they provide a subtle feel for the changes the last decade or so has witnessed.

Rev. Timothy Journeyman joins us in wishing that these letters will prove enlightening, informative, and challenging to a wide circle of readers never envisaged when Woodson, hearing that Journeyman's father had died and that Journeyman himself had become a Christian in the wake of that tragedy, first picked up his fountain pen to write them.

—*The Editors*

1

*H*ow did this lengthy correspondence with Dr. Paul Woodson begin in the first place? I must confess that I dashed off my first letter to Dr. Woodson not really knowing much about him. I was simply paying a courtesy to one of my dad's friends from college days. It happened something like this.

In April of 1978, my junior year at Princeton was rushing madly to a frenzied conclusion. And what an eventful year it had been. My father had passed away in the fall. I did not even have a chance to say good-bye to him because I was in Princeton when he suffered his fatal heart attack at work in New York City. I loved him dearly and wished he had not driven himself so hard. But he was determined to provide a "good life" for his family. I would have preferred that he had spent more time with us even if that had meant a lower standard of living.

My mother did not soon get over the trauma of Dad's passing. And neither did any of us children. Sometimes when I dreamed, I found myself talking to my dad. I wished these dreams would never end. They always did.

Then again, Sarah, also a junior at Princeton who I had thought was the "love of my life," told me that she just wanted to be my friend. I knew immediately what she was really saying. It turned out that she was quite taken by a fellow on the basketball team. I played intramurals but was certainly not in this guy's league. I tried to say to myself, "So be it. This is Sarah's loss." But my bold attempt at self-deception did not actually assuage my heartache.

At least my grades held up through these traumas. I greatly enjoyed my history program at Princeton. The history of science was my personal forte. I wanted to write my senior paper on the reception of Darwinism at Princeton. Other people must have thought I was doing at least fairly well because the history department did not take my scholarship away from me.

The best thing that happened to me occurred in the early spring. One of my friends from the Princeton Evangelical Fellowship invited me to hear a speaker address the group about why Christianity is "true." As a kid I had gone to Sunday school, but by high school days, religion didn't mean much to me. I was working on my studies and preparing for the SATs so I could get into an Ivy League school. On weekends I partied with my friends, and I was not really interested in going to this meeting.

After trying to figure out an excuse, I finally yielded to my friend's polite insistence. The speaker was actually quite intelligent and very humorous. It was amazing. I heard the "gospel" (as some of the students in the group called it). That evening my friend asked me if I wanted to trust Christ as my Savior and Lord. Without fully understanding what this was all about, I did do that. Somehow I understood that Jesus had died on the cross for my sins; it did not take much to convince me that I was a "sinner." I sensed that I had done things that really were not ethical and good; even my "pagan" conscience had not been entirely seared. Without trying to be melodramatic, I must say that I had a sense of joy that evening after I committed my way to Christ.

One day early in May I decided to write a letter to Dr. Paul Woodson. He and my dad had been close friends at Princeton in those antediluvian years which, I am told, existed before I was born. My dad had told me that he had always admired Paul but thought he was a little too "religious." Paul had tried to tell Dad about Christ. Dad indicated to me that in college days he really did not want to hear anything about "religion." Be that as it may, I do remember that when I was a kid, our family visited the Woodson home. Apparently Dr. Woodson's faith in Christ had not created a barrier between the two men. My memories of Dr. Woodson were really vague, however, when I wrote to him.

He was teaching at Trinity Evangelical Divinity School, Deerfield, Illinois, when I dashed off a note to inform him of my father's death. I also mentioned that I had become a believer in Christ. To my amazement Dr. Woodson, in what was probably return mail, sent me the following letter.

Dear Tim,

Thank you for your good letter. Yes, I do remember you, but I must confess that the way your letter reads makes me believe that you have matured greatly since the last time we met. Then you were a small boy with a twinkle of mischief in your eyes. When you visited us with your parents, you scampered around our home quite full of yourself. Your mom and dad were so proud of you, and rightly so. I remember as if it were yesterday your dad saying to me that he hoped you would go to college, meet a young woman as wonderful as your mom, and then advance up the corporate ladder as he did. He wanted the very best for you.

And now the little boy has become a young man. How time flies! Your dad would be very proud knowing that you are a junior at old Nassau—and on a scholarship to boot. It pains me greatly that he is gone. But my personal loss obviously does not match that of yourself and your family.

I am very pleased that you took it upon yourself to write me even though we have not seen each other for years. I counted your dad one of my best friends when we were together at Princeton. Although we did not keep in touch as closely as we should have after college, I always cared for him. That his son would write to me is a genuine personal delight.

It is especially heartwarming to read that you have recently come to faith in Christ. Your dad, for one reason or another, never made such a commitment. He was very upright, one of the most honest men I have ever known. But he just could not see his way clear to become a Christian. He used to kid me about being too "religious," but he did so in a playful way, not in any malicious sense. That he told you I was a believer and that you might want to contact me sometime may mean that he was more open to the gospel in later life than we might surmise. Perhaps you could fill me in about any discussions you had with him about Christ. Did he seem to understand the gospel? I would love to know about this. He meant so much to me.

You asked me if I could recommend any books on growing in the Christian life. Christians in North America have remarkable access to an abundance of valuable materials about Christian spirituality. But realizing that you are a very busy student, I suggest only three books for you. The first is C. S. Lewis's *Mere Christianity,* a classic in its genre. A second is John Stott's *Basic Christianity*. A third is F. F. Bruce's *The New Testament Documents—Are They Reliable?* Should you read these books, might you be so kind as to give me your impressions of them? I would be interested in your reflections.

I should tell you that I am a bibliophile valiantly striving not to inundate you with titles. Because you and I have had no contact with each other since you have become an adult, I do not know what your interest level might be. Thus the shortness of the list.

In any case, whether you read these books or not, do write again. I am so pleased that you took the initiative to reestablish contact with a family friend. A few lines in your letter remind me of what your dad would say. Let's continue to keep in contact.

Again, thank you for your kind letter.

Cordially,
Paul Woodson

2

*A*lthough the reading list Dr. Woodson gave me proved very help-ful (its brevity was a boon), my comments on each book were unremarkable. So, too, were Dr. Woodson's letters back to me.

In my last year at Princeton, however, I found myself in what I thought then to be the most surprising quandary. Here I was, sev-eral months old as a Christian, but instead of feeling holier, I was beginning to feel more sinful. The more I learned of the Christian way, the more I discovered I could not live it. Far from easing my guilt, my fledgling faith was increasing it—and I didn't like it one bit.

Before long I wondered if I was really a Christian at all. How could a true Christian be so burdened with lust, envy, malice—sins I hadn't thought much about before? I wrote to Dr. Woodson just after Thanksgiving and frankly told him what I was going through. His letter was a wonderful Christmas present.

At the same time, his response marked a transition in his com-munication with me. In some ways, Prof. Woodson belongs to the nineteenth century when letters were not only personal but long and reflective. I doubt if many Christian leaders at the end of the twen-tieth century would take the time to answer a young Christian's ques-tions so fully.

December 15, 1978

Dear Tim,

It is almost inexcusable that I have delayed three weeks in reply-ing to your letter. It caught me near the end of term when papers and examinations completely fill the horizon of seminary professors. I thought of dashing off a quick note, but the candor with which you described your anguish forbade me from writing with glib brevity.

Unfortunately, by delaying until I could write with more balance and thought, I have undoubtedly contributed to your sense of dislocation. I apologize and will try to do better next time.

Before I set out some Biblical truths that bear on what you are going through, I must say that your experience is by no means unique. It is very common for new converts to Christ to pass through a stage of shame and guilt. Intuitively, we can see why this is so. Before you began to think seriously about Jesus Christ and His claims, not to mention His death and His resurrection, you probably lived your life with only those minimal ideas of right and wrong you had absorbed from your family and friends.

On becoming a Christian, all of that changed. Prayerlessness would not have made you feel guilty before; now it does. Resentment at some slight, real or imagined, never troubled you before; indeed, you may have nurtured it to safeguard your sense of moral superiority! Now you are appalled that such self-serving behavior is so deeply rooted in your personality. Doubtless you were already mature enough that you would never have wanted (at least in times of sober reflection!) to hurt a woman, but prolonged pandering to secret lust never struck you as evil—nor did barracks-room jokes or overt flirtation. Now you find you are far more chained to lust than you could have imagined. Worst of all, you are finding how impossibly difficult it is for poor sinners, like you and me, to love God with all our heart and soul and mind and strength, and to love our neighbors as ourselves.

But in one sense, this feeling that you are awash in guilt is a good sign. It means that you are taking sin seriously, and that is one of the marks of a true believer. I believe it was the Puritan theologian John Owen who wrote, "He that hath slight thoughts of sin never had great thoughts of God." Of course, if your consciousness of sin does not lead to a deeper awareness of the grace and power and love of God, it achieves little but a kind of repression that may keep you from some public offenses while churning you up inside. But rightly understood and handled, what you are facing can become a stepping stone to a deeper knowledge of God.

What is at issue is how you should apply to your own life what Christians have called the doctrine of assurance. Since you are studying history, perhaps the best introduction to this doctrine would be a survey of some historical turning points.

At the time of the Reformation, the Roman Catholic church, at least at the popular level, taught that it was a mortal sin for a person to claim he was sure he was saved. After all, the church argued, he will sin again; he might even sin seriously. That is why he has to keep going to confession and to mass; the sacrament of the mass was widely understood to be a further sacrifice of Jesus, a bloodless sacrifice, that could be applied to the lives of those who had confessed their sins. Put crudely, to the problem of continuing sin the church had a ready answer—a repeated sacrifice that atoned for the guilt that had accumulated since the Christian's previous attendance at mass. But suppose you died *after* committing some heinous sin, but *before* you had the opportunity of dealing with it in the confessional and at mass? Suppose the sin was not merely "venial"—something that could be paid off in the fires of purgatory—but "mortal"— something that threatened the soul with eternal ruin. From this perspective, to claim assurance of salvation sounded desperately presumptuous.

But with the insistence of Martin Luther and others that we are "justified"—that is, acquitted before the bar of God's justice, declared not guilty and received by God as entirely just—by God's grace, grace that is appropriated by faith in Jesus Christ and His unique sacrifice on our behalf, the place of assurance changed. Having died once, Christ dies no more (Hebrews 10:10-14). The Reformers could not accept the Catholic view of the mass. If a Christian sins, the sin is dealt with, they said, *not* by looking to a new sacrifice, but by confessing our sins *to God* and seeking His pardon on the basis of the atonement Jesus has already made for us. "If we confess our sins, [God] is faithful and just and will forgive us our sins and purify us from all unrighteousness" (1 John 1:9). (Incidentally, Tim, I am quoting from the NIV, the *New International Version,* just published. I read through the NIV New Testament when it came out a few years ago and resolved then that I would switch to the NIV when the whole Bible became available. It still feels very strange to me, but I am convinced we must use twentieth-century language to win twentieth-century people. I do not know what Bible you are using, but I do urge you to buy a modern translation.)

So for Luther and most of the other Reformers (Calvin did not go quite so far), assurance of salvation could never be based on whether or not you have just been to mass, but it is an essential part of living faith in Jesus Christ. In other words, if you really do *trust* Jesus, if you really do *believe* in Him, your assurance is already bound up with such faith. If you lack assurance that God has really saved you, it is because your faith in Jesus the Son of God is itself deficient. Only Christ, Christ crucified and risen and ascended to heaven, can save you; you receive His salvation by faith, and thus your assurance is as strong as your faith.

So I suppose that if the Reformers were alive today, they would say to you, Tim, that if you doubt you really are a Christian, you must check the foundations again. Do you really trust in Jesus? Does He not promise eternal life to all who hear His word and believe in the One who sent Him (John 5:24)? When you first trusted Christ, was it not clear to you that the ground of God's acceptance of you was Jesus' death on your behalf? Wasn't the assurance you then enjoyed based on what God had done in Christ Jesus on your behalf, and not on how holy or morally fit you felt at the time? So why should it be any different now? You began to walk your Christian life by faith; continue to walk by faith. No matter how guilty you may feel, your acceptance with God turns not on how you feel or how good you've been today, but on Jesus Christ and His powerful "cross-work" (as some early English Protestants called it) for you.

But by the time the Reformation reached the shores of England, this view of assurance, mediated through William Perkins, was significantly modified. Perkins and others noted with alarm how on the Continent the Reformation sometimes swept through entire regions without transforming people morally. Whole cantons could switch sides. People called themselves Lutherans, or said they now belonged to the "Reformed" church, and professed to espouse justification through faith without it making the slightest difference to their behavior. Of course, there were many wonderful conversions that thoroughly changed people. Even so, the more disappointing results were so common that many Christian thinkers were disturbed. This undeniable reality, combined with his reading of 1 John, convinced Perkins that Christian assurance should not be so tightly tied to profession of saving faith. After all, the Apostle John, writing to Christians, says, "I write these things to you who believe in the name of the Son of God so that you may know that you have eternal life" (1 John 5:13). John, then, clearly thinks it possible for Christians (those "who believe in the name of the Son of God") to need some grounds of assurance spelled out for them. Their assurance is not simply a component of their faith, or John would not have needed to write "these things."

And what are they? The "these things" John mentioned can be enumerated. We know we have eternal life, John says, if we obey God's Word (1 John 2:5-6, 29), if we love the Christian brothers (3:14, 19-20), if we confess certain truths about Jesus (2:22-23;

4:1-6)—if, in short, we have an "anointing" from the Holy Spirit (2:20, 26-27). I write "these things," John says, so that you Christians may know that you have eternal life.

Such assurance, then, is based on observable changes in our behavior; it is not simply an entailment of our faith. But how can these two strands of assurance be reconciled?

The answer, of course, is that just as the causes of doubt are varied, so are the Biblical antidotes. If someone who professes faith in Jesus is having doubts because he cannot quite believe he is good enough for salvation or because he is not certain that Christ's sufferings on the cross can atone for a pattern of life still painfully stained with sin, then Luther's approach is essential. We can never win God's favor ourselves. Apart from the Lord's mercies we shall all be consumed. And "if anybody does sin, we have one who speaks to the Father in our defense—Jesus Christ, the Righteous One. He is the atoning sacrifice for our sins, and not only for ours but also for the sins of the whole world" (1 John 2:1-2).

That is the only ground you will ever have for access into God's presence. If you lose sight of this truth, it is your faith that is weakening; and as your faith weakens, your assurance evaporates. Your faith, in this instance, is weakening because you are losing sight of that on which it rests, that which it trusts. A Christian's faith is powerful, not because it is intrinsically strong, but because its *object* is reliable—Jesus Christ, Jesus Christ crucified. So we may call Jesus and all He has done for us the *objective* ground of Christian assurance.

I guess, Tim, I am making three points. First, your experience is a common one for new Christians. Second, your wrestling with sin is not all bad—it is much, much better than *not* wrestling with it. The fact that you are concerned to fight is part of the subjective grounds that God Himself is working in you by His Spirit. And third, what you must do, what all Christians must do is return again and again to the cross of Christ. That is the *only* objective ground for forgiveness that will remove our real guilt and therefore ease the pain of our guilt feelings. That is what we poor sinners need, and not least *Christian* sinners who discover with gratitude and relief that "if we confess our sins, God is faithful and just [not sentimental and wishy-washy, but faithful and just—because He keeps His promises to His own children whom He bought at the cost of His Son!] and will forgive us our sins and purify us from all unrighteousness" (1 John 1:9).

If I write any more, you'll wish I had taken up my pen while I was still in the rush of term papers.

Warmly yours in
Christ Jesus,
Paul Woodson

3

Although my immediate response to Dr. Woodson's letter was immense relief, it did not last long. For a while my struggles seemed to get worse. I wondered what I would feel like in five years or in ten years. I had already met some people who assured me that I was simply going through a religious stage, a "born-again" phase. I'd get over it, they said; after all, one told me, he was an ex-Christian himself.

Probably none of this would have bothered me so much if I had not been wrestling with guilt at the same time. I could not see far into the future, but I could see far enough to be troubled. I did not think I was any stronger than my fellow student who had abandoned the faith. If God was keeping me, why was I struggling? If I was responsible to keep myself, how could my prospects be other than bleak?

In the first week of January I confided some of my troubled thoughts in a letter to Dr. Woodson. Strangely enough, although his reply was prompt, I had escaped that somber phase I was going through somewhat, and I doubt if I really grasped the wisdom of what he said. It was years later when I was reading through his letters again that the sane balance in his words struck me most forcefully. But I record them here, for this is when he wrote them to me.

January 12, 1979

Dear Tim,

You have no idea how much I appreciate the candor with which you write. At the risk of sounding like a man no longer young, I think I should tell you that I do not find many young men and women these days who actually wrestle and struggle with these kinds of questions. I am always encouraged to find *serious* Christians, those who want

21

to think and read and understand, Christians who want to be holy and grow in the knowledge of God and of the marvelous redemption He has provided.

When I wrote my last letter to you, I thought it had grown a little long. With your reply in hand, I now wonder if it was long enough! Because what I am now writing will build on what I said then, you might remind yourself of the distinction I made between *subjective* grounds of assurance before God and *objective* grounds of assurance. Above all, meditate on the Scriptures I cited.

If I understand you correctly, your present wrestling prompts you to wonder if you can really hang on to your Christian faith. Let's make this personal. Suppose you claim to be a Christian, walk with Christ and with Christians for a few years, and then gradually drift off into religious indifference. Let's say you have an affair or start cheating on your income tax. Then, vaguely troubled, you come to me and say, "Paul, I have to confess I have lost the assurance of my salvation." What should I say to you at that point?

Assuming I have been following you and know how you are living, I would still want to say that the only basis for being accepted by God is the person and work of Jesus Christ; the objective basis does not change. But at the same time I would tell you that you do not have the *right* to assurance before God if you habitually live in ways He condemns. Then I would take you through the sorts of verses in 1 John that I have already quoted: Believers have the right to assurance if they see that their lives are being transformed, but not otherwise. We may call such transformation the *subjective* ground of Christian assurance.

Indeed, there are still other approaches to assurance in the Bible, but these two will do for the moment. Which applies to you?

You need to be very careful at this point, and so does any Christian counselor or advisor (myself included!) who dares to tell you what to do. Just as a faulty diagnosis in medicine can issue in a catastrophically wrong prescription, so can a faulty diagnosis in the spiritual arena. For example, in the second scenario I gave, if the person increasingly playing around in sin were simply told to trust Christ and His cross-work, he would be confirmed in his sin; sin would have no bearing on whether he *ought* to enjoy assurance before God. On the other hand, toward the end of the Puritan period there were lots of rather sad examples of people who applied the lessons of 1 John to themselves so stringently and repeatedly that they could not bring themselves to believe that they had actually truly believed. Perhaps, they told themselves, their faith was spurious since so many sins still seemed to cling to them. They thus appealed to the *subjective* ground of assurance so ruthlessly that they lost any joy in their salvation; they lost sight of the *objective* ground of salvation.

So what are you telling me? If I read you rightly, you are far from saying that you do not care for God and His Word and His way. Rather you are saying that, since becoming a Christian, you have become more and more aware of the sin in your life, and you are discouraged by it. But what discourages you, I see as a sign of life—not the sin itself, but the fact that you *are* discouraged by it. If you professed faith in Christ and it did not make any difference to your values, personal ethics, and goals, I would begin to wonder if your profession of faith was spurious (there are certainly instances of spurious faith in the Bible—for instance, John 2:23-25; 8:31ff.).

But if you have come to trust Christ, then growth in Him is always attended by deepening realization that you are not as good as you once thought you were, that the human heart is frighteningly deceptive and capable of astonishing depths of selfishness and evil. As you discover these things about yourself, the objective ground of your assurance must always remain unfalteringly the same: "if anybody does sin, we have one who speaks to the Father in our defense—Jesus Christ, the Righteous One" (1 John 2:1). Let your confidence rest fully in that simple and profound truth.

What you will discover with time is that although you are not as holy as you would like to be or as blameless as you should be, by God's grace you are not what you were. You look back and regret things you have said and thought and done as a Christian; you are embarrassed perhaps by the things you *failed* to think and say and do. But you also look back and testify with gratitude that because of the grace of God in your life, you are not what you were. And thus, unobtrusively, the *subjective* grounds of assurance also lend their quiet support.

I must say something about another facet to this question of assurance. "Once saved, always saved"—if you have not yet heard the slogan, doubtless you will some day. It shares the fate of most slogans—it articulates truth and is in danger of distorting it. Christians have long been divided over it. But if I understand the Bible on this topic, there is an important truth in the slogan that must be preserved. Read, for instance, the unbroken chain in Paul's reasoning in Romans 8:29-30. Carefully think your way through John 6:37-40. There Jesus says that His God-given task is to preserve all those whom the Father gives to Him. The Father's will, He says, is that He should lose none of those the Father gives Him, but that He should raise them up on the last day. In other words, if Jesus were to lose one of those the Father had given Him, it would be because He is either unable or unwilling to perform the will of His Father, and that is unthinkable (see John 8:29). Jesus' "sheep" hear His voice, and they follow Him. He gives them eternal life, and they shall never perish; neither can anyone take them out of His hand (John 10:27-28). "Once saved, always saved"—not because we are so reliable, but because Jesus is so faithful.

But that does not mean that everyone who *professes* to be a believer truly is one. It does not mean that everyone who, let us say, makes a profession of faith at an evangelistic rally has necessarily become a Christian. Jesus Himself could distinguish between genuine and spurious belief (John 2:23-25). It is quite possible for someone to believe in Jesus (at least in some sense), join the church, and rise to positions of influence and prominence, without ever having truly trusted in Jesus. I do not know what else to make of another passage in John's first letter. Writing of some former church members who had now publicly gone over to the side of heresy, he says, "They went out from us, but they did not really belong to us. For if they had belonged to us, they would have remained with us; but their going showed that none of them belonged to us" (1 John 2:19).

The assumption John makes, then, is that the genuine believers will persevere in the Christian way. That is the same assumption other New Testament writers make. For instance, the writer of the epistle to the Hebrews insists, "We have come to share in Christ if we hold firmly till the end the confidence we had at first" (Hebrews 3:14). Jesus warned that only those who stand firm to the end will be saved (Matthew 24:12-13). He told the people of *His* day, "If you hold to my teaching, you are really my disciples" (John 8:31)—just as John writes in his second letter, "Anyone who runs ahead and does not continue in the teaching of Christ does not have God; whoever continues in the teaching has both the Father and the Son" (2 John 9).

Now if I try to put together these sorts of passages with those that promise Jesus will never let go of those the Father gives Him, I am left with a picture something like this: Jesus never lets go of His own, and, from the purely human side, the evidence that this is so is found in Christians who persevere to the end. That does not mean that such Christians never falter, never succumb to appalling acts of rebellion. Both Scripture and experience reveal how fickle all of us can be. It does mean that in the long haul the genuineness of my faith, the preserving power of Jesus, and my own perseverance in the Christian way stand or fall together.

But if I simply drift off into total disinterest, year in, year out, my perseverance is called into question. Since Jesus' keeping power over all those the Father gives Him cannot (for the believer) be called into question, then the genuineness of my initial profession of faith must be. But if I do persevere, it is not my perseverance that is keeping me. If I have to rely on my reliability, I am in big trouble! As responsible as I am to persevere, I soon have to recognize, with Paul, that my perseverance is nothing less than God working in me both to will and to do His good pleasure. Indeed, from Paul's perspective the assurance that God continues to work in His own people becomes an *incentive* to our own perseverance (Philippians 2:12-13).

The relevance of this to what I have said about assurance should now be clear. As long as you are trusting Christ, however falteringly, I have few fears for you. Your trust will work out in terms of growing understanding and obedience and perseverance, however challenging the way may be at times. Your faith must rest in Christ. He is the one who keeps you, as He is the one who saved you when you first trusted in Him. Your assurance should be as firm as the objective finality of Christ's work on your behalf, as steady as the promises of God to His own people, His own "new covenant" people (see 1 Corinthians 11:23-26). But if you drift from or rebel against Christ and His way, not in some painful lapse or temporary rage but in sustained defiance, then sooner or later you call into question the genuineness of the trust you claim to place in Christ.

Meditate on 1 Thessalonians 5:8-11, 23, 24; Jude 24, 25, if you would.

Warmly yours in
Christ Jesus,
Paul Woodson

4

In February of 1979, during my senior year at Princeton University, I wrote Dr. Paul Woodson a letter that brought a rather quick response. Looking back, I realize that I did not fully understand what he was saying, and I replied to him with a degree of self-righteousness I now find embarrassingly insufferable. Again he responded very quickly and presented a worldview so profoundly Christian it has shaped much of my thinking since then. I did think, however, that his letters were a touch preachy.

But I am getting ahead of myself. My conversion the year before took place in the context of the Princeton Evangelical Fellowship. This disciplined and conservative group provided me with all the early Christian nurture I received; doubtless I was also living off the early Sunday school lessons I had heard but had later rejected.

Then for the first time I met some Christians who strongly insisted that accepting Jesus as Savior was one thing, but accepting Him as Lord was another. Real discipleship and growth began with the latter; the former provided a kind of escape from judgment, but could leave me as a "carnal" Christian, a worldly Christian. I was told to study 1 Corinthians 3 where I would learn of worldly Christians who were saved in the end, "but only as one escaping through the flames," without reward and with no fruit. I wrote asking Dr. Woodson what he thought of this view.

February 8, 1979

Dear Tim,

Thank you so much for your thoughtful letter. I wish I could tell you that almost all Christians agree on almost everything, but that is simply not the case. Christians who read and think are invariably called upon to hear and evaluate strong competing views—including mutually exclusive interpretations of the Bible. Part of your spiritual growth (only a part, but an important part) depends on developing the ability, with God's help, of distinguishing a good argument from a bad argument, of approving and holding fast to what is good, and questioning and rejecting what is false and slippery.

Let me plunge right into 1 Corinthians 3. In fact, I had better begin with the word *carnal* that crops up in older versions in the first few verses of 1 Corinthians 3. The word *carnal* derives from the Latin *carne*, "flesh" (or, for that matter, "meat"). But Paul often uses "flesh" (in Greek, *sarx* and its derivatives) to refer to fallen man, sinful nature—not simply to flesh in the physical sense. Among an older generation of Christians, *carnal* still has this sense. However, outside the holy huddle of aging Christians, *carnal* in English usage has come to have a much more restrictive meaning. It has to do exclusively with sexual sin. "Carnal desire" is sexual lust; "carnal sins" refer to sexual sins. Quite clearly that is not what Paul means in the opening verses of 1 Corinthians 3. That is why the NIV renders the two Greek words found here as "worldly."

Using this terminology, then, the view to which you have been exposed holds that there are three kinds of men—the "natural man," those who have never been regenerate, who are alienated from God and still under His wrath; the "spiritual man," those who have not only become Christians but who characteristically follow Jesus with prompt obedience and observable godliness; and, between the two, the "carnal" or "worldly man," those who have become Christians by faith in Jesus but who still largely live like "the world, the flesh and the devil." This tripartite distinction is based almost exclusively on this chapter from Paul's letters. It is then frequently tied with the view that it is possible to accept Jesus as Savior without accepting Him as Lord. The natural man has not received Jesus at all; the worldly (or carnal) man has trusted Jesus as Savior; the spiritual man has received Him as Lord.

For you to follow what I shall now say, you will need to have your Bible open to 1 Corinthians 3. I am convinced that the construction I have just outlined distorts the text rather badly and is easily corrected by following Paul's line of thought more closely.

1 Corinthians 3 is set in the context of Paul's appeal for unity in the church in Corinth, a theme that occupies the first four chapters of his book. Some of Paul's readers identify themselves with Apollos, others with Cephas (the Apostle Peter), others with Paul, and still

others, probably the most sanctimonious of the lot, exclusively with Jesus (1 Corinthians 1:11-12). Paul is concerned to break this party spirit. That is still his concern at the end of chapter 3 (v. 22), where he mentions the same names again. Chapter 4 goes on to tell the Corinthians how they ought to view servants of Christ.

First Corinthians 3, then, is set in this context. In the first four verses, Paul berates his readers for being worldly. On what basis? There are three elements, and doubtless they are part of a pattern. First, Paul charges them with spiritual immaturity. They are not yet ready for "solid food" but can digest merely "milk." Probably the reference, as in Hebrews 5:12, is to elementary truths as opposed to deeper, more difficult and challenging truths. Second, the Corinthian believers are characterized by jealousy and quarreling; and third, these vices have crystallized in the factionalism that follows Paul or Apollos or some other Christian leader to the exclusion of others.

Now it is important to see what Paul does *not* say. He does not scold his readers for being indifferent to the claims of Christ, for living on every front like their pagan neighbors, for being indistinguishable from unbelievers. His readers come together as the church, confess Jesus as Lord, and hold in large measure to the apostolic gospel. Their worldliness (or carnality if you prefer) consists in this—they are not as mature as they should be by this time, and this immaturity manifests itself in a quarrelsome spirit and disturbing factionalism. In these regards the Corinthian believers are acting like the "world," like "mere men"—not like children of God and joint-heirs with Jesus Christ.

So how should Christian leaders be viewed? Where do Paul and Apollos fit into the scheme of things? How should the Corinthians think of their leaders? Paul begins to answer that question by resorting to an agricultural metaphor (3:6-9). Paul planted the seed, Apollos watered it, but God gives the increase. Only God is to be praised; Paul and Apollos are merely farmhands, farmhands with different tasks all leading to the same goal. In this metaphor, the church is the field (v. 9); the leaders are the farmhands; and God alone gives the increase. So for the purpose at hand, Paul distinguishes in his metaphor between the leaders and the rest of the church.

The same distinction is preserved in the next metaphor, drawn from the building trade. At the end of verse 9, Paul tells the Corinthians they are not only "God's field" but "God's building." This new metaphor is teased out in verses 10-15. Paul has laid the foundation, which is none other than Jesus Christ, and Apollos has started to build the superstructure. The foundation, Paul insists, cannot be altered. But successive builders may use good materials or bad—gold, silver, costly stones (such as marble or precious gems), or, alternatively, wood, hay, straw. What Paul calls "the Day" will show up what kind of materials were used. The test is with fire, and the wood, hay, and straw are consumed in the flame. Only quality building materials survive this final test. It is in this context, then, that Paul concludes, "If what he has built survives, he will receive his reward. If it is burned up, he will suffer loss; he himself will be saved, but only as one escaping through the flames" (vv. 14-15).

Who, then, is the "he" that will be saved "as one escaping through the flames"? In this context it is surely not the worldly Christian. Rather, it is the builder who has used shoddy materials—or, to escape the metaphor, it is the church leader who has been building the church with "materials" that do not endure the final test. Paul's readers are the building, the church itself. The warning, then, is that even Christian leaders, ostensibly faithful and fruitful, may be building the church with such poor materials—apparently spurious converts—that they have nothing to show for their work on the last day. Meanwhile the Christians who constitute the church, Paul's readers, are summoned implicitly to examine themselves as to whether they are genuine converts ("gold, silver, costly stones") or spurious ("wood, hay, straw").

This building metaphor continues in verses 16-17, with the additional factor that the building is now designated "God's temple." "Don't you know that you yourselves are God's temple," Paul rhetorically asks, "and that God's Spirit lives in you?" Elsewhere (1 Corinthians 6:19-20), the metaphor of God living in a temple is applied to the individual Christian, indeed to the individual Christian's body. Here, however, it is applied to the entire Church. The warning takes on the overtones of a threat: "If anyone destroys God's temple [that is, the church], God will destroy him; for God's temple is sacred, and you are that temple." Again, the primary warning is to builders who use shoddy materials or who are otherwise busily destroying the church with false teaching or self-love or a thousand other devices that detract from the gospel and its power. Implicitly, there is a warning to the members who constitute the church. They are to see themselves as one temple, God's temple, and do everything to make that temple holy. Otherwise they invite God's wrath.

The final verses of the chapter show that the root cause of the division in the Corinthian church was arrogance. Each faction thought its own "guru" was superior to the others, but in fact the criteria were appallingly selfish, boastful, wrong-headed. "So then, no more boasting about men!" (3:21). The wonderful truth is that all genuine Christian leaders are part of the Christian's heritage in Christ (3:21-23).

It should be clear by now that the tripartite division of the entire human race into three kinds of people—natural, carnal, and spiritual—based on this passage is *erroneous*. There are just two kinds— the natural and the spiritual, the regenerate and the unregenerate, the believer and the unbeliever, the justified and the unjustified. But within these two kinds are obvious gradations. Owing to the gifts of what many theologians call God's "common grace" (that is, grace that God gives "commonly" and not just to those who are justified), unbelievers do all sorts of good things and display a rich array of gifts. This no more makes them believers than the presence of a single sin proves a man to be an unbeliever. Among believers, there are different rates of growth, different levels of maturity, different displays of gifts, different attainments in disciplined holiness and self-sacrificing love. Where Christians are not living up to expectations on some point, Paul can berate them for living like "worldly" people, like "mere men," like the unregenerate; they are not living up to what they are called to be. But where the failures are chronic, repeated, and serious, Paul does not warn them that they are second-class Christians, a category qualitatively different from both non-Christians and first-class Christians. Rather, he tells them to check the foundations again. They may not be Christians at all. "Examine yourselves to see whether you are in the faith; test yourselves. Do you not realize that Christ Jesus is in you—unless, of course, you fail the test?" (2 Corinthians 13:5).

Here in 1 Corinthians 3, where things do not seem to have gone quite so far, he warns his readers that they are immature, acting like unbelievers so far as factionalism and quarreling go. He does not structure the human race into three mutually disjunctive divisions. Nor is there any other passage in all of Scripture that justifies the tripartite breakdown into natural man, carnal man, and spiritual man.

By now you can guess that I do not think that the distinction between accepting Jesus as Savior and accepting Him as Lord is a Biblical one. I think I understand how—and why—that view is defended; but it results in a schizophrenic Jesus and in millions of men and women who think that because they have made some confession of Jesus as Lord they are safe enough, even though there are no signs of grace in their lives, no indications that they have come to love holiness, fear God, pursue righteousness, confess sin, love their neighbors as themselves. I leave you to think about one text: "If you confess with your mouth, 'Jesus is Lord,' and believe in your heart that God raised him from the dead, you will be saved. For it is with your heart that you believe and are justified, and it is with your mouth that you confess and are saved" (Romans 10:9-10). Note: justification, belief, confession of Jesus as Lord, salvation—they are all part of a piece. What God has joined together, let no one put asunder.

With warm regards,
Paul Woodson

5

When I received this latest letter from Dr. Woodson, I thought it much too unbending. I wrote back in consternation that although I found his arguments convincing, this surely meant that the majority of what passed for Christianity in popular evangelicalism was pseudo-religion and that real Christianity was limited to very few. As I reread my letter to him today (I still have a photocopy), I am struck by the fact that, although I was trying to sound as prophetic and discerning as I then judged Dr. Woodson to be, in fact I came across as a young smart aleck ready to tell the church where to step off. Formally, my question to Dr. Woodson had to do with what it means to confess Jesus as Lord. In reality, I was just as interested in letting him know that I was on the side of the angels. Here is his reply.

February 20, 1979

Dear Tim,

(Ed. Note: Several paragraphs of this letter were devoted to pleasantries and to asking Tim how his studies were proceeding, whether he intended to pursue graduate education in the history and philosophy of science, and how proud Tim's dad would have been had he lived to see his son graduate from Princeton. There are also one or two inconsequential remarks on the way the presidential race was shaping up—remarks now hopelessly dated and mistaken. Then Woodson turned to the topic Tim Journeyman had raised.)

You asked what it means to confess Jesus as Lord. In my course on Christology at Trinity, I never devote fewer than eight hours to answering that question, and even then I barely scratch the surface.

It is one of the themes that holds the Bible together; it lies at the heart of all genuine Christianity.

To confess Jesus as Lord is to recognize who He is. He is the Lord, the Sovereign to whom all obeisance is due. But His Lordship is configured in several complementary ways in the Bible.

Sometimes when people in the Gospels address Jesus as "Lord," they do not mean much more than "Sir." The Greek word underlying "lord" (namely, *kyrios*) has a wide range of meanings, and only the context is sufficient to determine just what shading it carries in any particular case. The upper chamber in the British parliament is called the House of Lords. The chief civil officer of, say, London, may be referred to as the Lord Mayor of London. In neither case are there overtones of deity!

But the writers of the four Gospels understood that sometimes people addressed Jesus in ways that were deeper and truer than the original participants could have known. By the time they wrote, the Lordship of Jesus was a fixed point in the church's confession.

For example, in my last letter I referred to Romans 10:9-10—to be a Christian means to believe in one's heart and to confess with one's mouth that Jesus is Lord and that God raised Him from the dead. In this case, Lord certainly means more than Sir! The confession of Jesus as Lord was tied to His resurrection (Romans 1:3-4). But in fact Jesus' Lordship has other connections, even when the word *Lord* is not used. For instance, in Colossians 1:15-20, in what may have been an early hymn of the church, Paul confesses that Jesus is God's agent in Creation, that the universe was made by Him and for Him. He is also, more specifically, the head of the church and the first of this new humanity to be raised from the dead, "so that in everything he might have the supremacy." In 1 Corinthians 15, Paul insists that God now mediates all of His sovereignty through Jesus Christ. Some refer to this as Jesus' mediatorial Lordship or His mediatorial reign. According to Matthew, Jesus Himself claimed, after His resurrection, "All authority in heaven and on earth has been given to me" (Matthew 28:18).

There is more. Lord was the common way for Greek-speaking Jews to refer to the God who had revealed Himself in what we call the Old Testament Scriptures. Also it was clear to the earliest Christians that although Jesus could in some ways be differentiated from God (He prayed to God and addressed Him as His "Father"), He could nevertheless be identified with God. (Had He not said, "Anyone who has seen me has seen the Father" [John 14:9]?) Therefore, the application of Lord to Jesus became not only a confession of His supremacy but also of His deity. However imperfectly, Thomas grasped this point when he saw the resurrected Jesus and exclaimed, "My Lord and my God!" (John 20:28).

To confess Jesus as Lord, then, is to recognize who He is. But this can never be a mere credal formula. The essence of all sin in the Scripture is to think of myself as lord or to make something in the created universe lord. If, like sheep, we have all gone astray, it is in this—each of us has turned to his own way (Isaiah 53:6). We have not wanted God's way. The heart of idolatry is the worship of that which is not God (read Romans 1:18ff.). All of the individual sins that horrify us or titillate us—from genocide to secret lust, from drug pushing to greed, from murder to bitterness—are nothing more than facets of that fundamental rebellion. That is also why merely "religious" people can be the biggest sinners of all. They can make an idol of their own smug goodness, their own religion, their own rules, their own self-righteousness and never really worship the God who has revealed Himself supremely in Christ Jesus, never really confess that Jesus is Lord. Moreover, it is not simply that we have gone astray, but that in consequence of our rebellion we stand under God's wrath. Our self-love, our principal rebellion, does not merely alienate us from God; it dooms us.

What Christ achieved on the cross was nothing less than our pardon, our release, our cleansing, our freedom. But the entailment is a renewed life in which we are oriented toward God; we do confess Jesus as Lord. That is why Jesus says, "If anyone would come after me, he must deny himself and take up his cross and follow me. For whoever wants to save his life will lose it, but whoever loses his life for me and for the gospel will save it. What good is it for a man to gain the whole world, yet forfeit his soul? Or what can a man give in exchange for his soul? If anyone is ashamed of me and my words in this adulterous and sinful generation, the Son of Man will be ashamed of him when he comes in his Father's glory with the holy angels" (Mark 8:34-38).

In other words, it is necessarily characteristic of Jesus' followers that they renounce self-interest in favor of His interest. If they pursue their own interests, they are still lost in their sin; they will perish, they will lose their own soul. If they die to their own interests and live to His interest, they "find" themselves; they live. How could it be otherwise?

Incidentally, the expression "to take up one's cross" does not mean to put up with some inconvenience, like rheumatism or an irritating spouse or a hair lip. In the ancient world, those condemned to be crucified were usually forced to carry the crossbar of the cross on their shoulders out to the place of execution where the vertical pole was already fastened in the ground. Thus the person who "carried his cross" was beyond all hope. All personal prospects had vanished; there was only death to look forward to, a death of maximum shame and pain. So for Jesus to say that we have to take up our cross (elsewhere He says we have to take it "daily"!) is to say that we must renounce the very heart of our sin—self-interest, personal preference, self-promotion, self-congratulation, self-preservation, life lived around self. We die. Principally, repeatedly, we die and follow Jesus. Only then do we begin to live the way we were designed to live. And this is what is meant by confessing Jesus as Lord. This is the profound change of mind, of perspective, of values that is often summed up under the term repentance.

Some Christians, it must be admitted, find this very hard to reconcile with the fact that so many Biblical texts present salvation as God's free gift. And so they return by another path to the model of salvation you were asking about in an earlier letter. We receive our salvation by grace through faith, they say, but then the kind of Christianity depicted in these verses goes beyond that and is reserved, not for all Christians, but only for disciples, for those who call Jesus *Lord*.

But this is to force distinctions where the New Testament will not admit any. It is utter folly to introduce a sharp distinction between genuine Christians and genuine disciples, between believers and followers. Genuine belief in Jesus the Savior and Lord entails discipleship.

The Bible demands repentance; but if we repent, it is always because it is God working in us. The Bible demands discipleship; but if we follow Jesus, it is always because His Spirit is empowering us to follow the Master. The Bible demands faith, but we soon come to see that even faith is the gift of God. And all of these gifts are predicated on Christ's cross-work on our behalf. All of this stands or falls together.

Ah, someone says, this sounds as if you have to turn from sin and be pretty good before you can be a Christian, before you can accept Christ. No, that is quite wrong. If you think I have suggested any such thing, I have not made myself very clear. So let me offer an example.

Suppose someone were to approach you with a foul mouth, a lifelong vile temper, and ask you how to become a Christian. Suppose you ascertain that this person really has come to an end of himself, knows he is guilty before God, and wants to become a Christian. What would you say?

You should most certainly not say that he must clean up his act before becoming a Christian. You will not say, "First you must turn from your sin and accept that Jesus is your Lord. Then you can be a Christian." To respond in such a way would be to suggest that turning from sin and cleaning up one's life is something one does in one's own strength, before becoming a Christian and therefore apart from becoming a Christian.

Instead, you would be wiser to use, say, one of the formulas in the book of Acts. Then the gist of what you will say is, "Believe on the Lord Jesus Christ, and you will be saved," or "Repent and believe the gospel," or "Believe and be baptized for the remission of sins." In the New Testament, these are all roughly equivalent (though with slightly different emphases). Repentance toward God and faith in Jesus Christ go hand in hand. Indeed, in the New Testament, so does baptism go hand in hand with faith; those who believe are baptized. It is impossible truly to repent without believing in Jesus; it is impossible truly to trust Jesus without repenting. In any case, the Christian soon learns that even such repentance and faith stem from the antecedent work of God's Spirit in his life. That is why Christians sing:

> I sought the Lord, and afterward I knew
> He moved my heart to seek him, seeking me;
> It was not I that found, O Savior true;
> No, I was found of Thee.

So we proclaim the gospel of Jesus Christ and Him crucified and summon people to repentance and faith. But we are the first to recognize that if people are actually born again, if they actually do rest their confidence in Jesus, it is because God is powerfully at work in their lives.

What is inconceivable, however, from a New Testament perspective, is that someone could truly believe in Jesus and not change the course of his life. Jesus saves us not only from the doom of sin, but from enslavement to sin. According to Paul, confession of Jesus as Lord is bound up with our salvation; but it is meaningless to confess Jesus as Lord if we are so focused on ourselves that His way is meaningless to us, or secondary, or remote. The gospel reconciles us to God, not only by removing our guilt, but by removing our rebellion. Where we used to choose our own way, we now choose His way.

Small wonder that Paul conceives of his apostolic task as "[calling] people from among all the Gentiles to the obedience that comes from faith" (Romans 1:5).

We were created by God. We were created by Christ and for Christ. We cannot be what we were designed to be unless we live for Christ, unless all of our existence revolves around Him. The salvation He provides restores us to that center; it restores us to God Himself.

This central vision of the Bible determines what "the good life" really is. When Jesus promises the "abundant life" (to use the language of the *King James Version*), life "to the full" (John 10:10), He is talking about what it means to know God and Jesus Christ whom He has sent (John 17:3)—by what it means to confess Jesus as Lord and do His will.

In the fourth century, Augustine understood this well. In his *Confessions*, he addresses God and acknowledges that he had coveted power, but found that power merely corrupted him. He was learned in rhetoric, but discovered that rhetoric taught people to treat truth like a game. He searched for love, and seared his soul. "I panted after honours . . . and you laughed at me."

But when he became a Christian, the entire orientation of his life changed. The goals and values of his life were dictated by the God who has revealed Himself in Scripture, and supremely in Jesus Christ. Augustine came to see that pursuing moral probity and integrity was nothing less than the pursuit of the abundant life. To lead a good life meant to love God and to love neighbors. It was to withstand evil, suffering, death; it was to grow in character that displayed love, joy, peace, patience, kindness, goodness, faithfulness, gentleness and self-control. It was to imitate Paul, who in turn imitated Christ (1 Corinthians 11:1).

How different this is from much contemporary evangelicalism! Not a few of us think that the abundant life is having our own way, fulfilling ourselves, satiating our wildest fancies, growing in wealth and health and power and prestige. The goals are wrong; the very definition of an abundant life has been corrupted. The means are wrong; we now look for instant miracles or we barter with God, but know little about taking up the cross daily and denying ourselves. The center is wrong. "Jesus is Lord" has become a mere credal summary that I can wield as a magic formula to serve my passionate desire for self-fulfillment, rather than an expression of the very heart of all I hold dear, the sun around which all other worlds revolve.

Last autumn and again in January of this year, I found myself bedridden for two or three weeks—nothing serious, thank God, but disabling enough to give me time to think. One of the things I did was to watch quite a bit of religious television. Normally I hardly ever watch the "goggle-box," and I thought this would give me an opportunity to find out what was going on. I watched one or two programs that nurtured my soul; but they were very rare. Religious programming is a spectacle. The sets are often glamorous, perhaps with tropical foliage; the "performers" are in expensive suits or glittering dresses; the choirs are choreographed in complex routines. There is almost no Bible teaching—a verse here and there, usually out of context. With a few exceptions the educational potential of television has not been taken up by religious broadcasters. There is a great deal of folksy smiling and touching, liberally larded with doses of three-minute expressions of compassion. There is an emphasis on healing, happiness, victory, and joy, and almost nothing about the cross of Jesus or His empty tomb. Not a few preachers roundly condemn alcohol, drugs, lust, Communists, and secular humanists, but never say anything about materialism, greed, pride, violence, prayerlessness, Biblical illiteracy, self-centeredness, or the idolatry of sport. Often what little gospel there is—and in two or three well-known TV preachers, I could not detect any—is so tied to the resurgence of American self-esteem that I shuddered to think of how this programming would appear in other countries. Mercifully, few Christians in Bolivia or Nigeria (or even England) will ever see these distorted pictures of the faith. But I tremble at the prospect of the future, when technology has advanced and these programs are aired, complete with subtitles, all over the world. And I still haven't mentioned the fantastic emphasis on money in most of these programs.

And yet there is another side to American evangelicalism that must not be overlooked. I first started serving as pastor of a church in 1952. The number of American evangelicals with bona fide doctorates in Biblical studies was not more than five or six. Although there were a lot of conservative congregations, the national leadership of many denominations had abdicated any serious Biblical constraints. Many of the upstart evangelical groups were on the periphery of American culture, of American discourse. Evangelicalism was leaner and more disciplined, but it was a day of small things. Fuller Seminary was just five years old; Billy Graham had only recently become known.

I must not bore you with the turning points in the phenomenal growth of evangelicalism since then. I hope we'll be able to sit down and talk about these things at length. But my point is that with this extraordinary growth, growth for which to thank God, there has also come a certain dissipation, a broadening and distorting of what *evangelical* means, a certain assimilation into the surrounding culture.

Yet millions of people have been genuinely transformed by this movement. They are not the coiffured singers on a television show, but the humble folk who people our churches, organize young people's meetings, seldom miss a prayer meeting, and like to read their Bibles every day. A lot of very ordinary men serve as faithful pastors of small churches across the country, seeing three or four genuine converts in a good year. There are enormously fruitful meetings for women associated with the Bible Study Fellowship, several immensely productive campus ministries winning students to Jesus Christ, and rising numbers intent on evangelizing and transforming our inner cities.

Some of our problems, in other words, are the problems of growth. Doubtless many conversions are spurious; but it is not always easy to see, especially at first, which professions of faith are insincere and which issue in genuine but rather slow and truncated growth.

There are huge geographical variations. Spiritual poverty pervades the New England states. Countless towns of twenty or thirty thousand people have no church where the gospel proclaimed in Scripture is unashamedly believed and lived and preached. But in the South, where there is much more access to the gospel, that gospel is so often attenuated by cultural compromise that it cannot (and should not) be exported. What a strange and complex world!

I guess what I am saying is that while you cultivate a perceptive and discerning mind, you must also cultivate compassion and eyes that see the little people, the little people who hear Jesus gladly. You said you have been reading some of the books of Francis Schaeffer. His writings have helped to stabilize the faith of countless college students. Whether his analyses are right or wrong on this or that detail, one of the things you must learn from him is his compassion. Even when he calls the church to re-examine the foundations again, he never writes out of spite or wrath. One always hears the overtone of empathy, the catch in the throat that is transparent and a vital part of the man's witness. By and large his imitators and detractors fail precisely at this point; they sound more like angry young men than like prophets. In this area, Schaeffer joins Isaiah who, as he saw God more clearly, declared, "Woe to me! . . . I am ruined! For I am a man of unclean lips, and I live among a people of unclean lips, and my eyes have seen the King, the LORD Almighty" (Isaiah 6:5). If there are times to stand with Jesus in the terrible denunciations of Matthew 23, we must end up where Jesus ends up at the conclusion of that chapter—weeping over the city on the way to a cross.

Three years ago last summer, Mrs. Woodson and I enjoyed a holiday in Wales. One rainy afternoon, we explored an old castle near Tenby. As we left the grounds, we noticed an old Methodist church that was offering tea and crumpets to tourists like us. We went in and found an elderly lady ready to serve us. I walked around the small building, and from the posters, Sunday school material, and other clues, I concluded that this was probably one of the many Welsh churches that had forfeited the powerful gospel of Christ crucified to a more liberal tradition largely melded of equal parts of good works and unbelief.

But in chatting with the woman, I soon discovered she was eighty-five years old and had always lived in this valley. I reflected to myself that she probably remembered the Welsh revival of 1904-05, a mighty movement of the Spirit of God. I asked her, a bit out of the blue, what she remembered of the Welsh revival. She jerked her head around to look at me, and her eyes danced. What did I know about that, she wanted to know. I told her I had read a few books about it, but that was all. I asked her if it was true that in some districts the pit ponies in the mines would no longer obey their masters; they had been accustomed (I had read) to cursing and swearing and rough handling and could not at first get used to the change in their handlers, whose conversions were so dramatic that not a few lost a third of their vocabulary overnight. Her eyes filled with tears, and she told me of the night her father—just one such miner—was converted, and that the reports of the pit ponies were true. She was ten years old herself when she became a Christian.

I asked her how this little Methodist church was getting on now. Very loyally, if in vague terms, she defended the minister, a young man who seemed very energetic and keen to help. I asked her (I confess I was a bit bold) if he preached the Bible. She replied that he sometimes did and that he was a very good man. I asked her where she found most of her help in understanding God's Word and applying it to her own life. She smiled and said she didn't know what she would have done if it had not been for the Bible teaching on Trans World Radio, broadcast out of Monaco.

What I am saying, Tim, is that God has many ways of preserving his people. You and I, finally, do not know the hearts of people. While we seek to be prophetic, to be faithful to Scripture, to think through what it means to confess Jesus as Lord in our culture, and to witness faithfully to the Savior who loved us and gave Himself for us, we also need to learn that it is Jesus Himself who builds His church; it is Jesus alone who is the final judge; and He has ways of sanctifying His people and calling them back to Himself, in the quiet corners of this nation and the world, that utterly transcend all our assessments and evaluations.

Keep the faith—not only its creed, but its life.

A fellow servant of
Jesus Christ,
Paul Woodson

6

When I received Dr. Woodson's letter, I was quite taken back. Why would he have spent so much time writing a minor treatise on the meaning of the Lordship of Christ? I could only surmise that he felt very strongly about the question—one that continues to be debated in evangelical circles. I am not certain that I agreed with all his points; but many of them did strike home at a personal level. Perhaps that is the reason I felt uncomfortable with his letter. In any case, I immediately penned a thank-you note in which I indicated that the ramifications of what he had proposed were too significant for me to take in quickly.

In passing, I also mentioned that a number of my fellow students in the history of science were accepting uncritically the premise that "matter is all there is." Over the years I have learned that certain subjects can be counted on to "press Dr. Woodson's button," and this was one of them. Within a week my comment had elicited the following letter.

March 25, 1979

Dear Tim,

You certainly have your hands full fending off the jibes of students who treat your belief in the existence of spirit beyond matter as folly. If I could misdirect the point of a song's poignant question and ask them, "Is this all there is?" they would probably reply, "Yes, matter is all there is. What we know is what we can see, taste, touch, and measure 'scientifically.'"

The Bible gives a categorically different response to this question.

It affirms that a spiritual world exists beyond matter (Colossians 1:16).

Please don't think yourself alone in arguing that there is an unseen but very real spiritual world. The company of those who do is enormous. It includes many non-Christians as well as Christians. Secularization theories that posited a spreading wave of atheism throughout the world are not as compelling as they once were. The vast majority of this world's people are theists of one kind or another.

Many distinguished philosophers have disputed the claims of materialism. Plato (one wag declaimed that all philosophy after him is but a footnote) argued that the material world is ephemeral, whereas the real world is the world of forms or ideas. Even if Plato's specific adherence to a belief in God is much debated, Christians have often found Platonism and its variants an attractive bridge across which to walk to the true faith—witness the experience of Augustine. In fact, Augustine's *Confessions* provides a splendid account of his pilgrimage to Christianity, neo-Platonism being one of the last way stations along the journey.

Other great minds like Descartes (d. 1650) have wrestled mightily with the relationship between mind and body. Descartes concluded that the mind does exist and is not identical with body; he could not doubt that he, the thinking self, existed. By the way, have you ever noticed that in his *Discourse on Method* (1637), he develops the ontological argument for God's existence? This is sometimes a surprising discovery for students who might have otherwise assumed Descartes to be a non-theist, and perhaps even a materialist.

The most excruciating dilemma for the materialist who denies the reality of spirit is to account for life's origins. If God did not create life and if matter is all there is, then one must come up with an account for life's origins with matter being its source. By the middle of the eighteenth century, materialists were becoming more numerous and bold. La Mettrie, a French materialist and physician, wrote an important work entitled *L'homme machine* ("Man Machine") in which he posited the thesis that those elements of existence which we assume to be reflective of the spiritual side of man can be explained by assuming that man is simply a machine. Another French *philosophe*, Denis Diderot, tried to drive home the point in a literary *tour de force* entitled *D'Alembert's Dream*. He related how a marble statue could become a living man. It is difficult to know if Diderot, who had formerly trained for the priesthood and had a remarkable intellect, was genuinely satisfied with his own explanation of life's origins. Even the materialist often has the lingering hope (or perhaps it is better to say dread) that death does not end it all.

Another galling problem for the materialist is the difficulty of defending his own personal "freedom." La Mettrie and Diderot, especially the latter, wanted to argue that humankind is "free" to do as it wishes; but if matter determines what each of us will be, wherein lies our freedom? The materialist cannot reconcile his personal quest for meaningful "freedom" with the central tenet that matter is all there is. On the contrary, matter determines everything.

But my guess is that your friends are not really concerned about the personal struggles of La Mettrie and Diderot. The more proximate cause for their conviction probably finds its roots in the late nineteenth century when large numbers of individuals in Christendom began to assume that "science's" description of the natural world explains all there is. In his book *What Is Darwinism?* (1874), Charles Hodge complained against the quarantining of religion and metaphysics into a quaint nonverifiable upper story of thought. He worried that many people would believe that science could *really* explain all there is, and all there is does not include a spiritual side to mankind or the world. Hodge went so far as to claim that Darwinism was atheistic in impulse because it explained life's origins by excluding God as the Creator. He supposed that Darwinism's chief propagandists had atheistic intentions by attempting to overthrow the argument from design—an argument used apologetically in the nineteenth century to defend God's existence.

Interestingly enough, at the end of the twentieth century, a fair number of defenders of God's existence remain in the scientific community. In addition, the argument from design is making a notable comeback among natural scientists. To be sure, the basic paradigm of the West is Darwinistic, and many laypersons have been led to believe that the theory of evolution is more than that—an established fact. But if I am not mistaken, we will see in the near future a good number of nonevangelical nonevolutionary scientists become emboldened to speak out against the alleged established dogmas of the dominant paradigm. Part of their unease stems from the "evolutionary" nature of evolutionary theory itself. I recently stumbled upon an interesting essay by Stephen Gould of Harvard. In it he observed that he had been forced to abandon the version of evolutionary theory he had learned in graduate school. He is now proposing a new form of evolutionary theory which I have not yet had the time to study.

My point is a simple one. This is not the time to be overly

impressed by materialistic explanations of life. My guess is that some of the students you are encountering have more confidence in the "fixed truths of evolution" (i.e., dogma) than some of the leading scientific practitioners who write professionally on the topic.

But I have written too much—again. Perhaps we can enter into a longer discussion of this important subject at a later time. I do want to do more reading in the area. If some of your student friends use particular books in making their case, I would be pleased to know what they are. This topic genuinely interests me.

As ever,
Paul Woodson

7

*B*ecause of my own fascination with the history of science, Dr.
Woodson's comments about science in his last letter stimulated
my interest. I began to sense that he had studied European intellectual history at one time or another in his career.

His "discourse" did seem a little quaint, however. He did not
indulge in the scientific jargon that peppered the rhetoric of my professors and assigned readings at Princeton. On the one hand, I did
not gainsay what he had proposed, but on the other, I was working
on the reception of evolution at Princeton in the nineteenth century
and sensed that on this topic I knew far more than he did. I am not
saying this in a prideful way. It simply was the case.

Back in the late 1970s I was not certain where I stood on questions about the origins of man and the earth. I assumed that the naturalistic theories of evolution and the Biblical accounts of Creation
genuinely clashed. Carl Sagan's popularized versions of evolutionary
theory had no appeal for me. I thought Sagan's defense of atheism
to be a rank dogmatism based on a priori naturalistic assumptions.
Sagan seemed unwilling to listen to arguments that might contradict
his stance—as is the case with many ideologues.

What an irony! The Bible teaches that a fool says in his heart there
is no God (Psalm 14:1). And yet Carl Sagan, an atheist, was
adjudged to be brilliant by many in the American public. A wrench-
ing irony indeed.

Obviously I was not an atheist, and I did not buy Sagan's atheistic assumptions. But were there not a few evangelical Christians who
were evolutionists? Had not B. B. Warfield, an evangelical if there
ever was one, espoused theistic evolution? Had he not tried to meld
belief in a Creator God with theories of evolution?

I tried to talk about this "melding" option with some of my
Christian friends at Princeton. A few drew back in horror. They cau-
tioned me not to share my musings with other Christians on cam-

pus. I was shocked. I began to ask myself if some of my Christian friends were too conservative in their intellectual outlook. Is it not possible for honest believers to differ regarding evolution and other matters? Are there not many ways to interpret the texts of Scripture? I decided to write to Dr. Woodson to get his perspective.

April 30, 1979

Dear Tim,

(A few pleasantries have been deleted from this letter. Dr. Woodson bantered about the winning and losing tendencies of a number of professional athletic teams which he knew Tim admired. Woodson was obviously trying to be personal and provocative in a playful way.)

Your description of your friends' reactions to a Christian holding a belief in theistic evolution gave me pause. I should tell you up front that I myself do not believe arguments for theistic evolution are persuasive. On the other hand, I do think that one has the obligation to set forth what those arguments are; it does not help much to squelch discussion, particularly among students in a university setting.

If I may, I would like to set aside the evolution question for the time being. But don't worry. After what I just said, I know I am obligated to expound the reasons why I believe theistic evolution is untenable.

Rather I would like to comment briefly on the problem of Christians as individuals or as participants in groups who believe that they alone understand the faith properly.

When I was a teenager, I belonged to a parachurch organization that literally captured my imagination. Its leaders were dynamic and skilled at what they did so well—youth ministries. How they viewed the world was the way I viewed the world. If they said that Mr. Smith was a true friend of the gospel, then that person was indeed a fine believer.

Now my readiness to adopt their perspectives may at first seem naive to you. But let me explain. I was genuinely impressed by the godliness of these people. Moreover a fish does not take much notice of the water in which it swims. I did not fully understand that there were other believers "of good faith" in other ponds who might think about their Christian beliefs a little differently. In addition, the leadership of my group seemed to imply that the "ponds" of other Christians were foreboding and dangerous.

You are probably guessing what I am going to argue. The Apostle Paul warns us not to be "tossed back and forth by the waves, and blown here and there by every wind of teaching and by the cunning and craftiness of men in their deceitful scheming" (Ephesians 4:14). Moreover he urges us to speak "the truth in love" (Ephesians 4:15) as if there is indeed "the truth." We are to hold firmly to the central teachings of the faith—such as the deity of Christ, the Trinity, justification by faith alone, the utter truthfulness of Scripture, and other doctrines. In the Early Church, for example, Christians frequently gave allegiance to what was known as a "rule of faith" (a list of principal beliefs). You might study Tertullian's famous version of this rule. Its list of beliefs strikingly resembles a list evangelical Protestants of today would draw up. Tertullian indicated that if a person deviated in belief from the rule, Christians would perceive that the individual had become heretical.

What I am suggesting is this—throughout the history of the church Christians have established sets of beliefs or creeds that they believe represent the essential tenets of the faith. This is certainly a worthy enterprise. Churches, schools, and Christian organizations are wise to draw up their own "rules of faith" with great care and much prayer. Believers have defended these creeds. If someone no longer upholds a creed to which he has given a commitment, then in all integrity he should leave the group. I admire the integrity of people who do this even if I mourn their straying from a well-crafted evangelical "rule of faith."

But what happens when you encounter Christians whose list of "central beliefs" aligns with yours but whose "less-than-central beliefs" do not so mesh? At a divinity school like Trinity I meet many wonderful students—not to say faculty!—who do not share all of my beliefs. We agree to disagree on what might be called less important points of doctrine (sometimes called *adiaphora*). I may sometimes attempt to persuade them to see the merits of my position. On occasion they will take it upon themselves to be missionaries to me. At the same time, together we recognize that we share a basic commitment to the truths of the Christian faith; our dispute is one among family members. And I assume that my brother in Christ would join me shoulder to shoulder in resisting the attacks of a third party against the central tenets of the faith.

Given this way of evaluating things, you can see why I try to have as open an attitude as possible in working with other Christians who uphold the central doctrines of the faith but who may differ with me on other points. I feel much more at ease with that person than I do with someone who professes to uphold a statement of faith (perhaps one similar to or identical with my own) but then casts aspersions upon it for the sake of being academically acceptable.

I can imagine your rejoinder to this line of thought. It might run like this: Paul Woodson simply misunderstands my predicament. I want to assess the merits of theistic evolution as a Christian, but some of my friends are criticizing me for even undertaking this enterprise. For them "theistic evolution" constitutes a central belief. For me it is no such thing. To my mind whether a person believes in theistic evolution or not has no bearing on his commitment to the gospel.

Now if you are thinking along these lines, you may have little sympathy for your brothers and sisters in Christ who gave you this warning. You may think them more than a touch reactionary. But a more sympathetic posture is possible. You might understand that sometimes Christians become edgy about certain beliefs owing to the entailments they perceive to flow from a particular position. Your friends may sincerely believe that the advocacy of theistic evolution will somehow undermine the central tenets of the faith. Whether or not you agree with them, you might demonstrate the same forbearance to them that you hope they will demonstrate to you. After all, you are both on the same team. They have just included a larger list of beliefs among their central tenets than you have.

I will write on another occasion about my own reasons for rejecting theistic evolution. But for now, I hope that the Lord will give you the grace to understand where your "Christian critics" are coming from. They are trying to protect the faith. Moreover, a few may not have perceived yet that "orthodox" Christians sometimes talk about the faith in different ways. We may hope that the Lord will give them the grace to understand your desire to study your subject matter more fully.

I feel as if I have left so many threads of arguments dangling. I did not really answer your question very well, for we have said little about the Bible's own teaching about "separation" from the world. In Fundamentalist circles such discussions are commonplace. I surmise that some day we will need to air out these issues carefully.

But I should end this letter. I need to take a little rest now. When you get to be my age, you will be amazed at how alluring an afternoon nap becomes. I even slept through the second half of a Bulls game last Saturday afternoon.

Trust all is well.

Cordially,

Paul Woodson

8

At the beginning of October 1979, I arrived in Cambridge to begin a M.Phil. in history. It was an extraordinary year—both the time I spent in Cambridge and the month or so I spent in France.

Cambridge University had about 10,000 students. Five hundred of them met on Saturday evenings for a Bible Reading, an exposition of Scripture. Hundreds more were affiliated with CICCU (Cambridge Inter-Collegiate Christian Union) through Bible studies in the individual colleges. The majority of them were Anglicans— something I was completely unprepared for, since most American Episcopalians I had met were as interested in Bible studies, preaching, evangelical life, and evangelism as in joining the Mormons or the Amish. Many of these students went to The Round, an Anglican church so packed out on Sundays it had an overflow unit served by TV monitors. Canon Mark Rushton was no orator. He simply preached straightforward Biblical messages and developed a personal relationship with hundreds of individuals, the integrity of his own Christian faith winning them to Jesus Christ.

Eventually I settled into Eden Baptist Church. Its new minister, Dr. Roy Clements, never preached less than forty-five minutes, and he gave me enough to think about and pray over for a whole month every time he preached. At the time I could not compare him with others; I was still far too young a Christian. But not only did I feel I was getting to know God better, I felt I was getting a course on Biblical theology every time I went to church, and I was learning how to apply the Bible to every area of life and thought. Several families invited me to their homes. Gradually I became aware of a set of assumptions and mores rather different from anything with which I was familiar.

Prof. C. F. D. Moule had retired from the Faculty of Divinity, but he was still lecturing in Ridley College, the Anglican theological college loosely connected with some other theological colleges in town

(I never did get the connections sorted out). A friend at Ridley invited me along to listen to some of his lectures. What I could follow of his material on Christology, the doctrine of Christ, was careful and reverent and often made me want to go and worship.

My first months in England were thus exhilarating, stimulating. They were also disconcerting, for many of the categories I had accepted as an American evangelical seemed to be exploding all around me. The line between conservative and liberal was blurred; the distinction between evangelical and nonevangelical denominations was obliterated. I wasn't quite sure how to integrate these new experiences with what I thought I knew. Just before Christmas I wrote a long letter to Dr. Woodson trying to convey my sense of joy and freedom, my happy discoveries, but also my scarcely articulated hesitations. His reply was prompt.

January 1, 1980

Dear Tim,

I thought I would use the quietness of this first day of a new decade to reply to your thoughtful letter. I am delighted to learn how much you are enjoying your year in Europe.

Since I have never studied in England, I need to be careful what I say! As you know, in 1951-52 I did a year of post-doctoral work at Marburg, largely focusing on Calvin studies. During that year, I spent a lot of time in France and a little time in England (which was when I came to appreciate the powerful pulpit ministry of Martyn Lloyd-Jones at Westminster Chapel). I would give you a letter of introduction, but I gather his health is none too good. Incidentally, I believe that one of his daughters and her family now worship at Eden.

Since that memorable year, I have enjoyed innumerable visits to the United Kingdom, mostly to England. Not a few of my students have gone to the U.K. for doctoral study. So although I claim no special knowledge of the strength of Christianity in Britain, for what it's worth, I'll pass on some of my impressions.

First, the history of the resurgence of evangelical Christianity in the U.S. is very different from the superficially similar resurgence in England. One of the hardest things for American evangelicals to come to grips with in English church life is the place of the established church. It is hard for us to realize that the Church of England is in some respects the strongest evangelical voice in the country and the source of the most notorious heresies. It embraces John Stott and John Robinson (of *Honest to God* fame—or infamy, as some would have it! [Ed. note: This little book, published in 1963, was a popularization of existentialist theology. Robinson's "God" was an impersonal "ground of being."]).

The theological education delivery systems are entirely different. Although there are a few Bible institutes and Bible colleges in England (London Bible College is the best of them), there are no graduate seminaries. The Church of England runs many theological training colleges, but most courses are operated at a fairly basic level, and those interested in exclusively pastoral ministry often finish their work in two years. Only the best of these students simultaneously enroll in university faculties of divinity. Here the standards are still reasonable (though they are now falling apart on language requirements). Most of those committed to a serious theological education eventually study in university departments. Some of the oldest and most prestigious chairs in English universities are tied up with the Church of England, but the pluralistic university environment and the diversity within the state church ensure that theological subjects are not commonly treated out of any confessional stance. Here in the U.S., of course, the overwhelming majority of serious theological students study at seminaries.

These educational factors meant that when concerned evangelical leaders wanted to revitalize evangelical thought in Britain in the 1940s, they tried to think of ways of infiltrating the universities. One of the results was the founding of Tyndale House in Cambridge, of which by now you have doubtless heard and may have visited. This residential Biblical research library was conceived and developed as a place where a community of evangelical scholars might encourage one another and help to sort out one another's intellectual challenges, with the aim of preparing competent evangelical Biblical scholars for posts in the universities. From these small beginnings also came the Tyndale Fellowship for Biblical Research with its annual lectures and study groups. British Inter-Varsity Press and Paternoster Press played important roles in the revitalization of British Biblical scholarship. In the late thirties virtually no university posts in Biblical subjects were held by evangelicals of any description; today, although I have no figures, the scene is very different. And this does not begin to account for the influence of Tyndale House and Tyndale Fellowship around the world, largely effected by the hundreds of doctoral and post-doctoral students from abroad who have studied in the U.K. Meanwhile, the British equivalent of Inter-Varsity Christian Fellowship (of which CICCU is a part—indeed, early CICCU gave birth to IVCF and related bodies around the world) wielded enormous influence in many universities, so that today there are scarcely any evangelical leaders, whether pastors or academics, who have not had some connection with IVCF (Ed. note: Woodson seems unaware that at the time of his writing British IVCF had recently changed its name to UCCF—Universities and Colleges Christian Fellowship).

Contrast the United States. There was no state church, so evangelicals saw no advantage, at least in the early days of the resurgence, in trying to recapture decaying denominations. They simply built new ones. As part of this process, they built countless Bible colleges and eventually graduate seminaries. The Presbyterians led the way with Westminster Theological Seminary in 1929. Fuller was founded in 1947. The Southern Baptists had long been operating their own seminaries, and at the midpoint in the century, these were not afflicted with the controversies that now surround them. Their academic standards were not renowned, but they produced pastors and missionaries with evangelistic zeal. Though unaccredited, Dallas Theological Seminary was a bulwark of evangelicalism throughout the period, with its own theological distinctives. Now there are many seminaries, including the one where I teach. Trinity was organized as a graduate institution as recently as 1963. Meanwhile, a plethora of campus ministries has attempted to evangelize college and university campuses—organizations such as Campus Crusade, the Navigators, IVCF, and many relatively independent groups such as the one in which you came to faith at Princeton.

Now what are the outcomes of these two quite separate developments? At the risk of generalization slipping into caricature, there are some pluses and minuses on each side.

The U.K. (especially England, to some extent Scotland) has contributed enormously to the worldwide resurgence of intellectual leadership in evangelicalism. Just see how many faculty members in Biblical and theological studies in our best seminaries have their doctorates from some university or other in the U.K. The U.K. has exercised similar influence in a number of countries. The focus on rigorous exegesis has led to the writing of many, many excellent commentaries. Moreover, the push to infiltrate universities and to expand evangelical influence in the state church has meant that evangelicals in Britain have been less confrontational than their counterparts in the U.S., and frequently they are more in touch with the most recent topics of debate in intellectual circles.

On the other hand, only 4 or 5 percent of the British population goes to church regularly. Even though there is a state church, the influence of Biblical truth and Biblical values (as opposed to ecclesiastical politics) in the national discourse is declining. British society is still far more stratified than American society; correspondingly, British evangelicalism is largely middle class or upper middle class and largely located in a large, fuzzy ring around London. Huge areas of the back country, of the northern coal fields, and of the working-class population are completely turned off by religion and are rarely exposed to any evangelical brand of Christianity.

Do not make the mistake of judging the state of the church in England by the state of the church in Cambridge. A former student of mine, already an ordained minister, studied four years in Cambridge in the early seventies, but spent many of his Sundays preaching in village chapels around East Anglia. Quite regularly his congregations numbered ten or fifteen in buildings designed to seat four hundred. The average age was perhaps sixty or sixty-five. And that is within twenty or thirty miles of Cambridge. Wait till you visit many towns in the north!

Moreover, the price of a nonconfrontational approach has not been cheap. One or two British evangelical academics have told me that they would not contribute essays on, say, the doctrine of Scripture because they were a little nervous that such essays listed in a resume might compromise the chances of promotion. The classical heritage that turns many British scholars into competent commentators turns very few of them into theologians (Ed. note: Woodson means "theologians" in the sense dictated by primary American usage, i.e., systematicians. In Britain, "theologians" more commonly refers to all those working in the field of Biblical and cognate subjects, so that a commentator is necessarily a "theologian."), though of course there are remarkable exceptions such as J. I. Packer and Bruce Milne. Most English efforts at (systematic) theology never get beyond historical theology or the endless discussion of method; they never produce syntheses of what is to be believed and performed. And although the still elitist system of British education (only a fraction of the percentage of students that go on for tertiary education in the U.S. goes on in Britain) produces some marvelous leaders, the level of theological and Biblical competence in the average clergyman, both inside and outside the state church, is abysmally low.

The converse strengths and weaknesses characterize America. Close to 40 percent of the population attends church. Although there are huge differences from region to region, American society is not nearly as stratified as English society. It is more mobile both geographically and socially. The result is that evangelicalism is not restricted to a single American stratum of society. The establishment of many independent Bible colleges and seminaries has fostered a confrontationalism that has often been harsh and uninformed; it has also helped to preserve the integrity of the gospel. The danger of seduction by academic advancement, though serious in the U.S., has been far less than in the U.K.

In England, the evangelical wing of the state church, after years of rapid growth and increasing influence, is now dissipating its strength in controversies that relativize the gospel and tend to put Anglican loyalty above loyalty to either the gospel or the Scriptures. Though still growing, the evangelical wing will, I predict, shortly become so broad that it will lose its cutting edge and settle down to establishment respectability. Some similar forces are at work here, too, of course; but because of the possibility of being eclipsed by a new, independent evangelistic witness, and because of the emphasis in seminaries on training people for *ministry*, for *servant-leadership*, for *evangelism*, and *mission*, not only the curricula but the tone of the theological training are more likely to be constrained by the gospel than by the pressures of academic preferment.

For several decades, the academic standards of evangelical seminaries were nothing to write home about. But the best of the seminaries are now responsible. From the perspective of maintaining a classical approach to understanding the Biblical text through the Biblical languages, they are far superior both to the "liberal" seminaries of North America (which are shrinking in numbers of students) and to the divinity faculties of most British universities, where most students take either little or no Greek and less Hebrew. I am referring to the level of the first theological degree. At doctoral level, evangelical institutions are still exceedingly weak. Even at the doctoral level, however, I predict that in another twenty or thirty years intellectual leadership in Biblical exegesis will pass out of British hands. And because evangelical seminaries are committed (in theory at least) to living and thinking under the authority of the Word, they retain a place for holistic thinking that makes systematic theology not only possible but necessary, and with it the possibility of addressing contemporary issues on a large scale.

With some shame and embarrassment (since I am professor of systematic theology), I think I should add that we evangelicals, myself included, have not even begun to live up to our potential in this regard. Of course, this means that in America we have not infiltrated the university faculties of divinity and the university religious studies departments as well as our counterparts have in England, and this accounts for some of the mutual suspicion and hostility. But when I try to tot up all the gains and losses, I do not think that ours has been the weaker path, even though we have made many mistakes. Our greater freedoms—outside the parameters of a state church and a university system—have nurtured much greater growth and vitality, but they have also fostered empire-builders, schism, and shoddy showmanship. At very least, it must be said that both sides have enough to repent of to keep us in tears a long time, and enough challenges and dangers and opportunities to keep us pressing on.

The second thing I'd say is that coming to grips with the categories used by Christians in another culture can be a liberating experience. You have been a Christian less than two years—though of course you were exposed to American values in your home, and in your case many of these values borrowed hugely from the Judeo-Christian heritage on which some strands of American culture depend. From this background you forge a set of expectations, of do's and don'ts. Then you go elsewhere and discover the pattern is a little different. If you handle yourself wisely, such experiences will help you ask what aspects of your faith are *essential* to Biblically-based Christianity and what aspects are merely local cultural accretions.

But do not kid yourself—you must not decide such issues on the basis of personal preference, but on the basis of thoughtful reading and re-reading of Scripture, discussion with other informed Christians, prayer, and a fair bit of rigorous self-criticism . The grass on the other side of the fence always looks greener. If British evangelicalism relieves you of some of the cultural "taboos" you have inherited, believe me when I say that if you stay there long enough, you will discover sets of taboos you haven't even thought of!

Moreover, travel and study of the kind you are undertaking will force you to think through theological labels. Conservative/liberal, low church /high church, evangelical/catholic—they are like rules in language learning. You learn the rules, construct countless sentences, and then, when you attain a certain degree of proficiency, you start learning the exceptions—and in some cases, there are more exceptions than there are rules. So you may have learned the distinction between "liberal" and "conservative" in the theological arena, only to find out, now that you are in Cambridge, that the categories don't quite fit the realities—that is, there are many "exceptions." John O'Neill, at Westminster College in Cambridge and always present at Prof. Hooker's seminar, is so "liberal" on questions of authorship that he does not think the Apostle Paul wrote more than about two-thirds of Galatians and Romans, even though virtually everyone else right across the theological spectrum insists that Paul wrote both. But O'Neill will defend, in a fashion, substitutionary atonement—something most "liberals" will deny. I have already mentioned John Robinson. He is so "liberal" his God is not a theistic God at all—that is, a personal but transcendent deity; but when it comes to questions of authorship and the dating of New Testament books, his work *Redating the New Testament* shows him to be more "conservative" than I am, more conservative, I suspect, than anyone in our New Testament department.

There are a lot of other examples. The lesson to be learned, however, is not that the labels have no meaning, but that life is very complicated. The "exceptions" to the labels, or the footnotes, the caveats, the shadings, are very complex. If you simply throw your arms up in despair and decide all labels are useless, you will end up denying the truth; alternatively, if you batten down the hatches and simply stick by your own biases without constantly assessing things in the light of Scripture, you will become what the press nowadays means by "Fundamentalist." The term has become a sociological category that defines an attitude, not a theological category that defines a belief system. In the popular press, there are Muslim Fundamentalists (not least since the mess in Iran—and the "fundamentalism" won't go away even if the hostages are released when Carter steps down), Christian Fundamentalists, Mormon Fundamentalists, and so forth. As far as the media are concerned, "Fundamentalist" is a pejorative label attached to religious conservatives of any description who are motivated by rigid dogma that never listens and is always vituperative. But there is a third alternative. If you think through these areas carefully, you will grow in discernment and understanding, and your study in Europe will bring you back with greater depth and enlarged horizons.

Incidentally, that is why the most "dangerous" graduate supervisors are never those who are cheerfully or viciously opposed to your historic Christianity, but those who embrace most of it while holding parts of it at arm's length. If such a supervisor is also gracious, pious, and prayerful, he will prove to be simultaneously enormously helpful and exasperatingly dangerous to an evangelical research student. In fact, when students ask me if they should undertake doctoral study under Prof. Such-and-such because his views are most sympathetic to their own, I almost always counsel them, at least initially, to find someone who will give them a stiffer ride.

Allow me to warn you that your re-entry into the United States next summer will probably not be smooth. You are enjoying England because you have braced yourself for the cultural differences, and you are finding the experience delightful. When you come home, you will expect to fit right in, and your guard will not be up. You will not realize how much you have changed. Idiosyncrasies and eccentricities in Britain you will judge delightful; corresponding idiosyncrasies and eccentricities in the U.S. you will find narrow and bigoted. Reverse culture shock is always the worst because you do not brace yourself for it. Be warned! I speak from sad experience after my year in Germany. When I started to pastor a church in 1952, it was several months before I could look at myself in the mirror and say, "Paul, if you were called to minister in Jamaica or India, wouldn't you make the effort to accommodate yourself to the people you are called to serve? So why can't you make the same effort when you serve your own people? Isn't the real reason a kind of arrogance—you expect them to be just like you and are frustrated because they are not?" If you become so cosmopolitan and sophisticated that you can more or less fit in anywhere, but you cannot serve Christ and His people with empathy and understanding anywhere, you have wasted your year.

And, yes, Roy Clements is a remarkable preacher. I heard him several times in Nairobi where he served Nairobi Baptist Church. Pay special attention to the way his sermons follow the flow of argument in a text and to the thought and care and freshness he brings to the application of the Scripture to all of life and thought.

I am sending this to your new address in Paris, as I think it will be delayed finding you if I send it to Cambridge.

As ever,
Paul Woodson

9

*D*r. Woodson's letter about England made me appreciate all the more the wonderful opportunity I had in studying at Cambridge. But because I had taken provocative courses on the French Enlightenment from Professor Robert Darnton at Princeton, I could not shake the allure of paying at least one visit to Paris. Consequently, at Christmas break I headed for France with the intention of spending a month there.

At least a few doubts crossed my mind. My French was très rusty, and I had heard horror stories about the alleged rudeness of Parisians toward Americans. Refusing to be intimidated, I took the London to Paris boat-train, arriving late in the afternoon in the city made famous by Abelard and Aquinas during the Middle Ages. Grabbing a taxi, I went to a small two-star hotel on the Left Bank not too far off Boulevard Saint Michel. The next days I was utterly beguiled. What museums!—especially the Impressionist collection. Can anyone not be overwhelmed by the beauty of Notre Dame viewed at night when the remarkable edifice is clothed with light? And who could not be both a little amused and intimidated in watching people parade down the Champs Elysées as if they owned the world? I wrote to Dr. Woodson and told him about my fascination for this remarkable lady, Paris. I had no idea that Professor Woodson was a Francophile himself. I had found another of his "buttons."

January 10, 1980

Dear Tim,

Envy is obviously a sin to be confessed. And thus I begin this letter with a confession. I can identify with the sheer delight you experienced wandering down the Champs Elysées from l'Arc de

Triomphe to the Louvre after a storm has just passed by. You are right. When the sun bursts forth, having shaken the bondage of deep, dark clouds, the boulevard and buildings glisten with newly fallen rain drops. My own favorite walk in Paris is down tiny side streets where one might discover an otherwise hidden bookstore. Oh Paris, with your rush and clatter, monuments and museums, and irresistible smells issuing from family-owned bakeries and restaurants on the Left Bank—what a remarkable city you are!

After this gush of words, you will understand perfectly that my envy is genuine, but it is at least confessed.

But the question you raised concerns what is transpiring religiously in France. You have noticed that many French and many Europeans in general seem preoccupied with the pursuit of material things. But is this not true of Americans as well? The quest for enjoyment and "self-fulfillment" seems to be a transatlantic, if not a pan-world, phenomenon.

It is striking, however, how churches have emptied in France whereas Americans still attend church on a given Sunday in surprising numbers. From an aesthetic point of view one might suppose that attendance would be higher in France, given the beautiful church buildings that grace both the large and small cities. I remember attending Notre Dame Cathedral for a Sunday afternoon organ recital. On that day, too, a storm had just passed over the city. When the clouds parted, shafts of light from a setting sun pierced red and blue stained-glass windows, only to be refracted by them into gorgeous colors dispersed on the high upper walls of the cathedral. The combination of sight and sound lifted one up into a genuine spirit of worship.

If an abundance of pleasurable aesthetic experiences were sufficient to draw people to churches in France, then the churches would be very crowded. But they are not. Something is missing. It would be too long a detour to try to explain fully what has caused this situation. Historians of religion sometimes chart various phases of a powerful "dechristianization" movement that has rolled over France. One of the explicit phases of dechristianization was launched in 1793-1794 during the French Revolution. The dechristianizers wanted to abolish all vestiges of the Christian religion. Sundays were eliminated; Roman Catholic and Protestant clergy were ordered to abdicate their ministries, and churches by the hundreds were closed. So-called priestesses of "Reason" (i.e., local prostitutes) danced on the altar in Notre Dame before Robespierre called for another religion to replace the "Cult of Reason." He proposed as the new national religion the "Cult of the Supreme Being," which of course denied the divinity of Christ.

Although freedom of religion was ultimately restored, secularization has continued and perhaps has reached its zenith. Two years ago, I received a letter from a historian friend of mine who was doing archival work in France. He said that he belonged to a group of Roman Catholic historians who teach at secular universities (Ed. note: the separation of church and state took place in 1905). At the group's summer retreat in a convent not far from Dijon, members discussed contemporary approaches to the teaching of history at a state university. In dismay one scholar in his forties turned to his colleagues and reminded them that they were in the last generation of professors to be catechized as children in the Roman Catholic church. Another professor said that in his medieval history class he had found students so ignorant of the basic Christian doctrines that he had drawn up a handout of vocabulary with definitions. The list included words such as *Trinity, Holy Spirit,* the *Fall*—and this in a country that was once the principal daughter of the church at Rome. My friend said he felt as if he were present with the last dinosaurs who suddenly realized that they would become extinct with no progeny to follow them. The next generation would be pagan.

What you have noticed, then, is a hardness to the gospel in France. This hardness is particularly evident in university circles where orthodox Christianity has not had a hearing for one hundred years. Evangelical missionaries often say that France is one of the hardest places in the world to plant a Christian witness. They seldom find university-trained French people in their churches.

But we should not despair. The same Holy Spirit who moved through France in earlier days can do so once again. If you have some time, you might visit the Free Faculty of Theology at Vaux-sur-Seine. John Winston and Henri Blocher with their colleagues are busily preparing young French people and foreigners from French-speaking lands for ministry.

Do not be surprised if some day in the not-too-distant future the French in large numbers turn to the Lord. This would be wonderful. Sometimes God delights to take on the most unpromising soil. Although Americans often think of the French as impervious to friendship and difficult to get to know, and then read these social perceptions into their spiritual assessments, my own experience has been that they are simply much more careful in selecting friends. Americans tend to have a good number of superficial friendships, but relatively few have deep ones. The French will often have deep personal friendships with a few people and with family members. One of my best friends is a Frenchman who took an interest in me nearly twenty years ago. His name is Jacques. Although we seldom see each other, I know he remains a fast friend to this day.

Well, enough for pop comparisons of national character. I do hope you will see beyond the physical beauty of Paris to the wonderful people there who so desperately need to hear the gospel of Jesus Christ. Though they seem hardened to the gospel, my guess is that in the decade ahead the French will become more "spiritually" oriented. The question is: What forms of "spirituality" will they espouse? Our hearts have a God-shaped vacuum that must be filled—a sentiment expressed by Pascal, a Frenchman. We need to be available to French people who come to that conclusion, as I am certain many of them do. But to whom can they turn if we are intimidated by them and if French Christians are intimidated by their fellow citizens as well?

Please write again. As you can see, your letter prompted me to relive other days and to struggle with the sin of envy. The envy may not be admirable, but I do enjoy reliving days gone by.

Cordially,
Paul Woodson

10

*M*y head was spinning from the rush, the noises, the smells, the sights—the general effervescence of Paris. I quickly jotted a second letter to Dr. Woodson just before returning to England. I don't really remember why I felt a compulsion to write again. Whatever the reason, I mailed the letter at a small bureau de poste near Gare St. Lazare before I caught the boat-train back to London.

In my letter I described the splendors of churches and museums, but I also mentioned my horrible feelings of claustrophobia in a metro car. It was the evening rush hour, and I was trying to make my way down to my small hotel on the Left Bank from an area around the Gare du Nord on the Right Bank. In my metro car a surging wave of humanity swayed back and forth, struggling to keep their balance by holding onto seats, center poles, or anything else that would give support. Their bodies pressed against each other and against me. The train lurched and rattled like a caravan of incandescent sardine cans through darkened underground tunnels below Paris. Glued to each other during the frenetic voyage, we tried to avoid our neighbors' eyes by staring blankly ahead. The trip seemed interminable. At each metro stop a few of my fellow passengers made their escape, only to be replaced by still larger numbers of victims anxiously pushing their way through the car's automatic doors. Squashing us even further, the newcomers undoubtedly had a death wish to suffocate, for I was certain I would soon do just that. If I were asked for a nonreligious definition of purgatory, I would describe it as a thousand-year nonstop ride on a Parisian metro at rush hour.

Still, my enthusiasm for Paris did not diminish; my desire to stay above ground and to see the city on foot, however, increased considerably.

I did say (rather piously and hypocritically, as will soon become evident) to Dr. Woodson that I had noticed that any vibrant evangelical Protestant presence in Paris seemed quite restricted. I asked him if he knew why this was so. Had the French people ever contemplated becoming a Protestant nation? I did not recall hearing much about French Protestantism or the Huguenots in my history classes at Princeton.

Much of my letter to Dr. Woodson, I now realize, covered up my own misery. At the time I simply could not confide to him that the temptations of Paris had been plucking at me in a disastrous fashion. I tried to keep up a spiritual facade in my letter, and I pretended to be interested in evangelicalism's fate in France. In fact, I did not really care a whit. When I wrote the letter, I was overcome by feelings of guilt for my sin. I felt spiritually dirty.

After I returned to Cambridge, I received the following letter from Dr. Woodson. He had not picked up in my letter that something was desperately wrong. In one sense I had deceived him.

February 2, 1980

Dear Tim,

It indeed surprised me that a second letter postmarked Paris followed so rapidly on the heels of the first. I did respond to the first letter and sent it to Cambridge, not your temporary quarters in Paris. I hope it arrived safely. Please pardon the delay in my writing the second. Winter quarter has set in, and I am teaching a new course. I have been feeling more than a little overwhelmed by the work load. This letter will of necessity be brief.

(Ed. note: Several paragraphs have been deleted. In them Dr. Woodson once again flew his Francophile colors very high. Moreover, he empathetically attempted to describe how uncomfortable he had felt when he was once trapped in an elevator between floors.)

As you could discern in my last letter, I, too, have been struck by the lack of a strong evangelical presence in Paris and for that matter throughout France. But I do not want to denigrate the fine work of certain members of the Reformed Churches of France, of the Baptists, the Moravians, and other evangelical Christians. Various missionaries have served the Lord faithfully in France. Their courage in witness has been outstanding.

Nonetheless, evangelical Christians constitute a very small minority of the general public. Please pardon an excursus on how this situation emerged. By your question, I assume that your history classes did not concentrate on the history of Protestantism in France. This topic is generally neglected by historians.

As early as 1520, evangelical Protestants in Paris were opprobriously called Lutherans. The first Protestant martyr, a weaver, was burned to death in 1524. By the 1560s Reformed believers known as Huguenots assumed that they represented the triumphant way of the future. Encouraged by none other than John Calvin himself and the approximately one hundred pastors who slipped over the border from Switzerland, their ranks increased until they represented perhaps 10 percent of the population. A number thought that France would become Protestant. But the Saint Bartholomew's Day Massacre of 1572 slaughtered at least 10,000 Huguenots, including the flower of the Protestant nobility. Eight distinct wars of religion followed (often enmeshed with political machinations), fought out between Roman Catholics and Protestants. In 1598 Henry IV, who had recently converted from Protestantism to Roman Catholicism, granted his former co-religionists freedom of conscience in what was known as the Edict of Nantes. Nonetheless fighting eventually broke out again, and the Protestants were roundly defeated. One of the last Protestant enclaves, the city of La Rochelle, fell in 1628. The next year, the Treaty of Alès (1629) gave Protestants important rights, but it also signaled their demise as a serious military challenge to the crown.

When Louis XIV became king in 1661, he launched an anti-Protestant campaign culminating in the Revocation of the Edict of Nantes in 1685. On his deathbed in 1715, His Majesty created the legal fiction that there were no longer any Protestants in France because Roman Catholicism was the only religion allowed. From 1685 until the Edict of Toleration in 1787, the Huguenot faith was essentially outlawed in France.

But the Huguenots' desire to worship God freely could not be extinguished. A few very bold young pastors, such as Antoine Court and later Paul Rabaut, organized and directed an underground church known as The Church of the Desert. Huguenot pastors led services for the Reformed churches in open-air meetings held in the ravines of the Cévennes Mountains or any other place that might escape the prying eyes of governmental spies and troops. Some thirty to forty of these pastors were killed for leading Protestant worship services. If arrested, the laymen who attended their services could spend the rest of their days rowing on the king's galleys; the women could be consigned to a convent or prison for life. The late

Protestant historian, Samuel Mours, a dear pastor with whom I once corresponded, researched the human toll of this persecution: 219 men and 32 women executed; 635 killed by gunfire and other means; 3,484 men and 3,493 women taken prisoner; and 1,940 sentenced to serve on the galleys.

Not until the late 1750s did the Huguenots begin to enjoy a *de facto* toleration. By that date, their minority status seemed irreversibly established; they numbered about 600,000, but the French population ranged between 26,000,000 and 28,000,000. Then in 1762 Voltaire came to the aid of the Protestant Calas family of Toulouse. Jean Calas, the father, had been put to death by the Parlement of Toulouse for having allegedly killed his son, Marc Antoine. Voltaire waged a three-year letter-writing campaign to win back the good name of the Calas family; he believed Jean Calas innocent. In 1765 the highest court in France exculpated the Calas name from all guilt. This was the famous Calas case, a *cause célèbre* of eighteenth-century France.

Voltaire's actions on behalf of the Calas family and other Huguenots won for him the deep gratitude of the Protestant community. The rascally Voltaire had ulterior motives. He made the point this way, "One good deed is worth a hundred dogmas." Eventually, a number of Protestant pastors became so impressed by the activities of Voltaire and his "philosophic" colleagues that they let down their guard against Voltaire's anti-Christian ideas. In fact, more than a few began to assume a "philosophic" perspective in their own preaching and ministry. Once again we have an illustration of how unbelievers gain leverage over believers by acting the way we would expect Christians to act in the social arena.

I hope some day to write a book on the Church of the Desert in eighteenth-century France. The experience of these Calvinists affords a remarkable illustration of what may happen when the leadership of churches accommodates itself too much to the culture. When the dechristianization movement swept through France in 1793-1794, the Reformed pastoral corps was not prepared to resist the onslaught. Threatened by the decrees of radical revolutionaries, the majority of the Reformed clergy abdicated their ministries. Sadly, a small number said explicitly that they were abdicating because they only wanted to follow the dictates of "Reason," not the teachings of superstition (by inference orthodox Christianity).

In the very last years of the eighteenth century and the early years of the nineteenth, the Reformed churches regrouped. Indeed some experienced the benefits of a wonderful revival. But later in the nineteenth century and during a portion of the twentieth, many fell under the spell of Protestant liberalism and lost their evangelistic zeal. For this reason members of the Reformed churches have not witnessed extensive growth in this century. The minority is becoming even smaller before the pressures of secularism and enervating theological minimalism.

To be sure, a number of twentieth-century "Huguenots" have accomplished heroic deeds. During World War II, for example, many mothers and fathers and boys and girls risked everything by hiding Jews from the Gestapo. French Protestants have had a remarkable history of resisting those who have tried to violate their consciences. Their history is a proud one, but from an evangelical point of view, it is often a tragic tale.

In a word, Huguenot history is the history of a minority. It began this way as far back as the last third of the sixteenth century, and it has never transcended this limitation.

Again, I must ask your indulgence. I said at the beginning of this letter that it would be brief. In fact, it has become a historical minisurvey. I got carried away by a topic dear to my heart. Moreover, you will recognize that I am not very knowledgeable about French Protestant history in the nineteenth and twentieth centuries. But these comments may give you some perspective. I should add parenthetically that the number of Protestants among the political and industrial elites of France is disproportionate to the shrinking number of Protestants in the general population.

Enough of this. I really must get back to my class preparations. I am so pleased that you had a wonderful time in Paris. It sounds to me as if your vacation jaunt was a smashing success from all points of view. Do take care.

Yours in Christ's fellowship,
Paul Woodson

11

After my shameful moral lapse in Paris, I finally wrote to Dr. Woodson, merely hinting at what had happened. I was still too ashamed to go into details. He must have guessed pretty closely, judging by his response.

At the same time, I wanted to know where that left me. I had often been told that all sins are the same in God's eyes. They are simply sins, and all sins are black, not shades of gray. The idea was to prevent us from being arrogant or condescending toward those who did "worse" things than we did. But now I realized that the same argument could cut the other way. Now that I had fallen into one of the "worse" things myself, maybe I should conclude that it was no worse than other things I had done. Or if distinctions in the seriousness of sin should be made, was this just a little sin that didn't count for too much, or was it like the blasphemy against the Holy Spirit for which there is no forgiveness?

Looking back a decade later, I realize of course that I was less interested in the answers to these questions than in coping with my sense of guilt and shame. That episode came back to haunt me a year or two later, precisely because I did not deal with it very well at the time. I don't think I was quite ready to come to terms with the letter Dr. Woodson sent me.

March 20, 1980

Dear Tim,

Thank you for writing so frankly. Many would have hidden their sin entirely. Hide it, repress the memory of it, pretend it didn't happen, and you will either become relatively indifferent to sin—an extraordinarily dangerous situation from the Bible's perspective—or you will find your guilt erupting months, even years later, in subtle and corrupting ways that can warp your personality and strip you of quiet confidence before the Lord. So what you do now—I cannot say this strongly enough—is of utmost importance.

So how shall we assess any sin we have committed? Those who insist that all sins are equally heinous before God, that sexual sin, say, is no different from the sin of malicious gossip usually resort to James 2:10, "For whoever keeps the whole law and yet stumbles at just one point is guilty of breaking all of it." Perhaps James's point is clarified by what he says next, "For he who said, 'Do not commit adultery,' also said, 'Do not murder.' If you do not commit adultery but do commit murder, you have become a lawbreaker" (James 2:11). The earlier context makes it clear that showing favoritism in the Christian community is lawbreaking (James 2:8-9).

This way of looking at law exhibits its *personal* nature. He who said such-and-such is the same *person* who said something else. Thus lawbreaking, from God's perspective, is never merely a matter of transgressing discrete statutes. It is a matter of rebellion against God. So the person who obeys God on many points, but who disobeys Him where it is in his personal interest to do so, is still a rebel. Whether you crack a mirror in half or smash it to a trillion pieces, you can still quite legitimately think of it as a broken mirror. So it is with contravening God's demands—break one, and you have broken "the whole law"—not in the sense that you have transgressed each statute, but in the sense that you have defied God Himself and therefore stand under His judgment as a lawbreaker. You cannot contravene God's will at any point without becoming a rebel, a lawbreaker.

The practical entailment of this perspective for the Christian is that you cannot pursue selective holiness. The struggle against sin must be waged on all fronts, or you will lose. "Therefore get rid of all moral filth and the evil that is so prevalent, and humbly accept the word planted in you, which can save you" (James 1:21).

For example, if you lead an outwardly spotless life, all the while allowing bitterness or envy to fester away inside you, not only will such inward corruption ultimately erupt in some pathetic outward display, but all the while you will not really be walking with God. The deep-seated rebellion will be there. You cannot walk with God unless you pursue holiness on every front.

Similarly in the sexual arena, unless by God's Spirit you learn increasingly to discipline your mind, then all the time you are nurturing lust you are rebelling against God. Not only may that quietly pampered lust explode in acts of sexual sin, but it also impedes any significant growth in spiritual maturity. A short poem called "Temptation" (Ed. note: It was by G. Studdert Kennedy. We have corrected Woodson's letter at one point where his memory failed him.) captures the point exactly. The poem begins with protestation and slides toward grim honesty:

> Pray! Have I prayed! When I'm worn with all my praying!
> When I've bored the blessed angels with my battery of prayer!
> It's the proper thing to say—but it's only saying, saying,
> And I cannot get to Jesus for the glory of her hair.

Tim, I do not pretend any of this is easy. None of us escapes the pull of temptation. But you must be aware of the nature of the fight, or you will not really struggle. You will feel yourself victorious over all the sins that do not really tempt you and never really grapple with the sins that do. Part of what it means to confess Jesus as Lord is that we are committed to pursuing His will, His ways, on *every* front.

The earliest Christians were described as those who followed the Way, who belonged to the Way (Acts 9:2; 19:9, 23; 22:4; 24:14, 22), that is, the way of the Lord (Acts 18:25, 26), the way of salvation (16:17). The expression is flexible enough to describe simultaneously the *means* of salvation (God has appointed the way of salvation, Mark 12:14; Jesus Himself is the way, John 14:6) and the *course* or *path* Christians take, indeed Christianity itself, broadly conceived. All of us stray from the way. But Christianity is not simply about pardon when we stray; it is about new birth and power and God's fatherly discipline to keep us on it or to bring us back to it. Psalm 1 (which you should read) makes it clear there are only two ways. One is based on God's Word and ultimately yields fruit; the other adheres to the counsel of this fallen world, the patterns of a lost humanity, and ultimately perishes. That is why all sin is simply sin.

But that does not mean that all sins have exactly the same effects in every respect or receive the same punishment or are viewed by God in exactly the same way. That inference, commonly made, will simply not stand up to the scrutiny of Scripture. Under the Old Testament law, the covenant connected with Moses and Mount Sinai, there were different punishments for different sins. Jesus insists that on the last day, some will be beaten with more stripes and some with fewer. In Matthew 11:20-24 Jesus warns the cities of Galilee that had heard Him preach and had witnessed His miracles that their plight on the day of judgment would be much more severe than that of Sodom and Gomorrah, proverbial for wickedness, or of Tyre and

Sidon, pagan cities up the coast. Jesus' argument is not that the cities of Galilee were indulging in practices that a detached, human observer would have classed as more vile than those of the pagan cities, but that their privileges were so great—having not only been taught the Scriptures, but having also observed Jesus and listened to His words—that their failure to repent represented a deeper moral failure than socially "worse" sins. In other words, God takes into account our heritage, our background, our advantages when He judges us. The Jesus who pronounces a bleaker woe on Capernaum than on Sodom is the Jesus who may well pronounce a bleaker woe on New York or London than on Beijing or Kabul. But my point, in any case, is simple—the Bible does not treat all sins as exactly the same.

And sexual sins, it must be said, the Bible sometimes treats with special attention. Consider Paul: "Flee from sexual immorality. All other sins a man commits are outside his body, but he who sins sexually sins against his own body. Do you not know that your body is a temple of the Holy Spirit, who is in you, whom you have received from God? You are not your own; you were bought at a price. Therefore honor God with your body" (1 Corinthians 6:18-20). Precisely *why* Paul treats sexual sins this way is disputed. After all, chronic alcohol abuse, for instance, is also a sin against one's own body. But in the context, the idea is not that by sinning against your body you may *damage* your body, but that you may *violate* it. The Spirit indwells the believer; you—every part of you, not least your body, which is slated for the renewal of the resurrection—belong to another, to Jesus Christ, who bought you at such great cost. How dare you, then, give *yourself*, in the deepest act of giving of which any human being is capable, to another in violation of Jesus' claim on your life, on your body (see Romans 12:1-2)? From a Christian perspective, this is grotesque.

And there are practical consequences. Within marriage, few sins destroy trust as savagely as fornication. Moreover, whereas all sins have the potential for becoming bad habits, few sins are as addictive as promiscuity. Few sins are as efficient at destroying a Christian's reputation for probity and integrity as sexual sins. I suspect it is the snicker factor.

When we remember that here in America the entire culture is becoming saturated with sexual innuendo, we have every reason to be alarmed. I do not know if you read *Christianity Today*. Probably Tyndale House subscribes to it. Go and peruse the first few issues of this year. *CT* commissioned a comprehensive poll of Americans

72

through the Gallup organization to find out just what is and is not believed, and the results are spelled out in several issues. Some of the results are surprising; many would have been predictable. But one of the most important is that the connection between religious belief and personal conduct, between doctrine and morality, between religious experience and moral integrity is dissolving. Despite the resurgence of many elements of formal evangelical belief, we are drifting toward a twentieth-century brand of ancient paganism where, as in some ancient pagan belief systems, there is no necessary link between belief and conduct.

But the Christianity of the New Testament will not let you off so easily. Read 1 John—doctrine, obedience, and love go together. Read Galatians and Romans—Christology, justification by faith, and the obedience of faith stand or fall together. Read 1 Corinthians—the gifts of the Spirit, the doctrine of the resurrection, transparent love, and moral probity stand or fall together. Jesus is Lord.

I do not for a moment want to convey the impression that Christians simply do not sin. Here, too, 1 John is of enormous help. Writing to Christians, John says that, on the one hand, if anyone claims he does not sin or has not sinned, he is a liar, self-deceived, guilty of calling God a liar (since God says we are all sinners—1 John 1:6, 8, 10). On the other hand, John insists that Christians do not go on sinning, that they obey Christ and love the brothers (see especially 1 John 3:7-10). How can both emphases be true?

In fact, unless you hold both emphases strongly and *simultaneously*, you will go seriously astray. Stress the former, and you will become lackadaisical about sin; stress the latter, and you may gravitate toward some version of Christian perfectionism where you hold you have already attained perfection when all your colleagues (and especially your family!) can see you are deluded. The fact is that until Jesus' return, we will sin. As we grow in holiness, we will become aware of inconsistencies and taints we had not even spotted before. Most of us will sometimes stumble and drift, at times rather seriously. There will be different rates of progress, different degrees of spiritual maturity; all of us will have to return to Jesus for renewed cleansing and forgiveness. But at the same time, if we are Christians, we will insist that there is never any excuse for sin. In no case do we *have* to sin. Though in our lives as a whole, we may ruefully recognize we will sin, in any particular instance we do not *have* to sin, and that particular sin is therefore without excuse. Sinning is simply not allowed in the Christian way. No provision must be permitted to encourage it; no excuse ever justifies it.

You and I live in this tension. The only solution is not a theoretical one, but a practical one, an existential one. "If we claim to be without sin, we deceive ourselves and the truth is not in us. If we confess our sins, [God] is faithful and just and will forgive us our sins and purify us from all unrighteousness" (1 John 1:8-9).

That, Tim, is God's answer to your sin and your only hope. And it is enough. Never, never treat God's forgiveness lightly, as if you may sin with impunity because God is there to forgive you; but never, never wallow in the guilt of some sin you have committed in the fear that God is not merciful enough or gracious enough to forgive you. Learn not to flirt with sin; and when you fall, learn to beg God's forgiveness for Jesus' sake and press on. That is the only way you can live with a clean conscience; it is the only way that your confession of Jesus as Lord will have any bite in your life.

I write as a fellow sinner, forgiven and pressing on.

In the love of Jesus Christ,
Paul Woodson

12

*D*r. Woodson's letter was both reassuring and alarming. I acted on his advice. I called upon the Lord to forgive my sins and claimed 1 John 1:9. I had already asked Him a thousand times to forgive me as I had tossed and turned during a sleepless night in Paris. This time, as I thought through the promises and character of God, a genuine sense of peace did come over my heart.

My alarm came, however, from the way Dr. Woodson signed off his letter: "I write as a fellow sinner, forgiven and pressing on." Could it be that Dr. Woodson himself still struggled with these temptations? I admired him so much I could scarcely imagine that he too faced such spiritual battles. Before you dismiss me for utterly naive, please remember I was a relatively young Christian in 1980. I had somehow convinced myself that I was a strong Christian, and I was still so immature that I failed to see that this misapprehension put me in great danger. My moral lapse in Paris did at least deal a stunning blow to that vain delusion. But did senior Christians feel similarly crushed?

In this context another dreadful thought gripped me. If I were ever in a similar situation again, would I yield to the same temptation? I had repented of the sin, but it still haunted my mind in technicolor. What kind of Christian was I anyway? Did anybody else feel this way—trapped by memories of the past? I didn't want to raise such troubling concerns with Dr. Woodson. They were too painful and personal. When I wrote to him the next time, I thanked him profusely for his letter. I indicated that I had profited immensely from it. That, at least, was the truth. His words had allowed me to understand better that the Christian life sometimes resembles a battle zone.

To deflect Dr. Woodson from further discussing these sensitive matters (at least they were sensitive to me), I commented about the surprising strength of the Communist Party in France. By this time I had gathered that Dr. Woodson was so enamored with France that *an issue like this would steer him away from my worries over guilt, forgiveness, and true repentance.*

While sipping a café noir in a small restaurant located near Notre Dame, I had read an article on the activities of Georges Marchais, the head of the Communist Party in France. The reporter for Le Monde treated Marchais as a legitimate political voice whose political and social programs deserved commentary and consideration. A genuinely naive American, I could not understand why a Communist like Marchais deserved front-page coverage. I did not recall reading many articles on the front page of the New York Times about the political programs of the American Communist movement.

I compared the status of the Communist Party in France with the Communist Party in the United States in my letter to Dr. Woodson. He rose to the bait and wrote the following letter.

April 13, 1980

Dear Tim,

Your amazement at the prominent place a Communist leader like Georges Marchais holds in French political life is understandable. Many Americans have a hard time perceiving the wide spectrum of political options that greet the French when they go to the polls. They can vote for the radical rightists like Le Pen at one end of the spectrum or for Maoists at the other end, or for Communists, Socialists, centrists, Gaulists, and others tucked in between. The French know very well which point of view each of the major newspapers espouses; moreover, even the news analysts on the state-run television are in tow to the powers that control the government. It certainly is a different world than ours.

For decades communism has appealed to many French people—about 10 to 20 percent of the population. For example, the Communists played a well-known and heroic role in the Resistance during World War II and thereby gained admirers. Moreover, they have repeatedly claimed that they really do represent the workers' interests. Many of France's most notable intellectuals are devoted to the causes of the political Left (*la gauche*).

But appearances can be deceiving. The Left in France includes, in addition to a tightly disciplined Communist Party, a dynamic Socialist Party led by the President of the République, Francois Mitterand. On occasion the Socialists will team up with the

Communists in elections, but, remember, the Socialists are generally non-Communist. Unwilling to bow to the dictates of Washington, they will often cut their own deals with the Communists or others if this serves their purposes. Mitterand sometimes drives our government and the leadership of NATO to distraction. But the French are the French. There is an independent streak in them.

But why should communism in the year 1980 retain its appeal? Do not the French know about the Gulags in Russia, the stifling of liberties in geographical areas under Soviet control? Are not these defenders of personal liberties savvy enough to see the specter of totalitarianism behind George Marchais's siren rhetoric? Do they not know that he is very loyal to Moscow, and not one of those "moderate" Euro Communist types? How can the Communist faithful still support such leaders?

I think I got a taste of the appeal of communism's projected idealism when I happened to be in Strasbourg, France, during the Student Revolution in May and June 1968. I was on sabbatical during the spring quarter and working on a book on theology. My wife and I had chosen to stay in Strasbourg. As you may know, it is a beautiful city coiffed by a gorgeous cathedral. John Calvin spent time there in exile.

When the revolt broke out, the students seized the building housing the Protestant and Catholic Faculties of Theology of the University of Strasbourg. Whether it was foolish or not, I gained access to some of their planning sessions.

What a seething sense of excitement gripped the students that day! They did not know if and when the police (*les flics*) might launch a counterattack and storm their blockaded doors. I was struck by the seriousness of the dialogue. Many students were Marxists who stood ready to shed their blood if the police attacked. They saw themselves as defenders of the lower classes unjustly exploited by French capitalists. Their great concern was to figure out a means to awaken "the workers" from their passive slumber so that they might join the students in the revolution. They sensed only too well that the deep-seated suspicions of the workers against students (often considered a privileged class in France) had to be overcome in order to detonate the revolution.

I will never forget one of the student meetings. A speaker was encouraging his colleagues to join a march towards the center of Strasbourg. Militants among the marchers, he said, should throw rocks at the windows of the stores they passed. With shards of glass raining down upon their heads, the capitalistic store owners would become enraged and summon the police. The police would overreact, a melée would break out, and the workers would finally grasp that the students had generously taken up the workers' grievances and were getting beaten up in consequence. Traditional antagonisms between workers and students would melt away. A pro-Communist revolutionary force of students and workers would be born.

The logic of the student speaker's address begged for analysis. Heads spun by the effervescence of the moment were not inclined to such cerebral activity. The crowd wanted action, not careful reflection. Justice and fraternity and an end to the bourgeoisie's pillage of the workers' labor and goods now seemed attainable. It would take swift and decisive acts to throw reactionary capitalists of the city off balance. The young revolutionaries saw themselves as *engagés*— "engaged" and doing good for their neighbors. I could not but be impressed by their apparent willingness to suffer personal pain for the larger causes.

What I am trying to say is this. Americans sometimes have difficulty sensing the appeal of communism to people of other lands, either in Europe or in the Third World. We assume that the obvious lack of notable economic successes in Communist lands, the infliction of enormous physical pain on millions, and the outrageous suppression of human rights would inoculate other members of the world community against communism. My experience during the overly charged days of May and June 1968 in Strasbourg helped me to grasp that one of the faces communism presents to the young is very idealistic and attractive, even if a hollow facade.

Moreover, on occasion some young Communists exhibit a greater concern for the welfare of their neighbors than do Christians whose Lord said, "Love your neighbor as yourself." Dr. Herb Kane, one of my colleagues here at Trinity, has argued that the threat of world communism is what Christians have earned for their failure to follow through on the social implications of the gospel. That may be an exaggeration, but it does drive home a point of no small magnitude.

Again, my pen seems to flow when I write about French topics. I become much too prolix. Hopefully, I have not bored you. Trust that all is well. You are in my prayers.

Cordially,
Paul Woodson

13

*P*artly because I still had not completely dealt with how sinful I saw myself to be—the result of my experience in Paris—my questions at this time, though important, continued to be cast in theoretical frameworks. I wanted intellectual resolutions, not advice on how to think "Christianly."

The challenge to my faith engaged me on many fronts when I started dating a Scottish lass whom I shall call Laura—Laura of the dimples, Laura of the deep-throated laugh that welled up inside and burst forth in joy, Laura of the clear complexion and the wind-blown hair, especially as she cycled around Cambridge at nothing under top speed. I met her at some history lectures; afterward we talked for about two hours, and it seemed like ten minutes. She had a first-class mind, genuine compassion for people (especially the underdog), strong moral resolution (her grandfather was a Church of Scotland minister), and an intensity that seemed to drain the last drop of life out of each experience. And she was an agnostic.

By this time I had been a Christian long enough, in three different university settings, that I had talked about my faith with scores of agnostics. But Laura was different, not only because I was immensely drawn to her and wanted her to think well of me, but also because she was an aggressive agnostic. She did not try to convince me that my Christian beliefs were wrong or intellectually suspect. She was more faithful to a genuinely agnostic position than anyone I had ever met. Perhaps, she said, I had had some sort of experience she knew nothing about, an experience that configured the pieces in my thinking in a way she could not manage. Most agnostics I had met were, paradoxically, dogmatic—they didn't know anything about God, and they insisted I couldn't know either. But not Laura. She didn't know anything about God and couldn't tell whether I did or didn't. She was an agnostic's agnostic.

But on one point she was dogmatic. Granted the numbers of people who did not know anything about God, and the still greater numbers of people who thought they did but who could not agree what God was like, how did I find the nerve to suggest that if they did not come to see things as I did, they were lost, damned, going to Hell? That, she insisted, was the worst form of obscurantist arrogance.

After a while, any serious conversation we had always returned to that subject. I had no satisfying answer for her, and I knew it; pretty soon I wasn't even sure I had one for myself. My letter to Prof. Woodson toward the end of May elicited this response, briefer than some of his missives.

June 2, 1980

Dear Tim,

Although I am once again approaching the end of term, I decided that a quick response would be more helpful than a lengthy one. You are twice blessed—for once, the grace of speed unites with the grace of brevity.

I wish I could meet your Laura of the dimples. I much prefer a woman who has some starch and sparkle than one who agrees with everything I say. I once knew a middle-aged minister who insisted that he and his wife had never had a serious disagreement. I was sorely tempted to ask him which one of them had given up thinking. Your Laura, as you describe her, reminds me of Petrarch's Laura who bedazzled the man for life.

To keep myself from rambling, I shall restrict what I say to six points.

First, there are different forms of universalism, the view that all (or most) will finally be saved or turn out to be all right. Some hold that everyone is "saved" (I'll use that as a generic word; the opinions as to what "salvation" consists in widely differ) except for those who explicitly drop out. Others hold that all will be saved even if their religion is a lot of bunkum, because God is merciful. Still others think that all will be saved if they hold with sincerity and faith to their own understanding of religion (or irreligion)—which of course reduces to claiming that you are saved on the basis of your good-faith sincerity. Others think that all will be saved because at heart all religions really are saying the same thing.

80

Doubtless there are half a dozen other forms; I'm no specialist in the field. Some of what I'll say in this letter applies to some brands of universalism but not to others. Laura's brand, so far as I can guess it from your letter, I'll say more about farther on. There is quite an extensive literature, but much of it is designed for the theological student or pastor. If you'd like to read more, I'll be happy to give you a bibliography. At a popular level, I can't do better than recommend that you read the third chapter of the little book by Paul Little, *How to Give Away Your Faith*.

Second, before you as a Christian can comfortably address the question of universalism, you have to resolve in your own mind the question of revelation. Has God revealed himself to us or not? If so, where? If not, the discussion is futile. I do not mean that Laura is then right. I mean that her position and your position are then both equally arrogant. If God has not disclosed Himself to us, perhaps He doesn't exist. Or perhaps He does exist and is entirely arbitrary, capricious, even cruel. Or perhaps He is impersonal. But how can you possibly know?

What Christianity claims is that God has revealed Himself to us—in Creation (His existence, creative power, something of His providence), in discrete acts in space/time history as attested by witnesses, in Scripture which He has mediated to us by His Holy Spirit, and supremely through His Son Jesus Christ, the incarnate Word—that is, His "infleshed Self-Expression." Has God spoken or not? Again, the Christian claims that God has not only revealed Himself through deeds, but through words: God is a speaking God. Just as this personal/transcendent God undertakes to disclose Himself in deeds locked into space/time history, so He condescends to reveal Himself in words that are culturally conditioned, yet meaningful and reliable. Has Jesus Christ risen from the dead? How many witnesses saw Him? How good are the records that relate their witness?

You have been a Christian for enough time now to know what sorts of answers I would give to such questions. Moreover, you have probably done enough reading and been exposed to enough good teaching that your own faith is relatively stable. If at your deepest level of conviction you know that Jesus died and rose again, that both He and His immediate followers made all sorts of claims about His exclusive role in mediating salvation to a lost world, then the question becomes how to respond to Laura on the basis of these "givens." I will assume this is where you are. In that case, you might try giving Laura the little book by Bruce that I mentioned in one of my earlier letters—the more so since she is studying history (Ed. note:

Woodson is here referring to F. F. Bruce, *The New Testament Documents—Are They Reliable?*).

Third, it is essential to see that Laura's view, as "open" and "tolerant" as it seems, may in fact be narrower and far more culturally enslaved than she thinks. Alexis de Tocqueville, in his famous *Democracy in America,* wrote:

> I know of no country in which there is so little independence of mind and real freedom of discussion as in America. In America, the majority raises formidable barriers around the liberty of opinion: within these barriers, an author may write what he pleases; but woe to him if he goes beyond them. Not that he is in danger of an *auto-da-fé,* but he is exposed to continued obloquy and persecution. . . . The master no longer says, "You shall think as I do, or you shall die"; but he says, "You are free to think differently from me, and to retain your life, your property, and all that you possess; but you are henceforth a stranger among your people. You may retain your civil rights, but they will be useless to you, for you will never be chosen by your fellow citizens. . . ." The ruling power [read "opinion"] in the United States is not to be made game of. . . . No writer, whatever be his eminence, can escape this tribute of adulation to his fellow citizens. The majority lives in the perpetual utterance of self-applause; and there are certain truths which the Americans can only learn from strangers or from experience.

Like much of de Tocqueville, this is both penetrating and too harsh. But that it is close to the mark is suggested by the baccalaureate address of Aleksandr Solzhenitsyn at Harvard two years ago. He said, in part:

> There is yet another surprise for someone coming from the East where the press is rigorously unified; one gradually discovers a common trend of preferences within the Western press as a whole. It is a fashion; there are generally accepted patterns of judgment and there may be common corporate interests, the sum effect being not competition but unification. Enormous freedom exists for the press, but not for the readership, because newspapers mostly give emphasis to those opinions that do not too openly contradict their own and the general trend. Without any censorship in the West, fashionable trends of thought are carefully separated from those that are not fashionable. Nothing is forbidden, but what is not fashionable will hardly ever find its way into periodicals or books or be heard in colleges. . . .

That Solzhenitsyn was almost universally vilified for his address rather confirms his judgment.

Now Laura's position would have seemed preposterous to most people in Europe in, say, the sixteenth century. Why? Is it because we have become more enlightened? Or is it because Laura is (dare I say it?) parroting the biases of the late twentieth-century North Atlantic liberal press? Does she have an independent mind willing to think hard, or is she far more enslaved to current fads than she can imagine?

Fourth, if you assume the truth of the gospel as presented in Scripture, how does her charge against you appear? Well, to start with, it seems painfully inconsistent. She claims to be an agnostic, even a "pure" agnostic. But if she is truly an agnostic, she cannot in conscience say you are arrogant if you claim you have found the truth and Him who is truth incarnate. The most she can claim is that she has not (yet) made any similar discovery. Her insistence that you are the one who is arrogant shows she is not really an agnostic at all. She is, in fact, deeply committed to pluralism, which is a philosophical commitment (even if she does not recognize it).

You must insist that it is not a question of coming to see things as you do, as if you are setting yourself up as the criterion of truth. Rather, it is a question of truth, of revelation. If God has shown Himself to be such-and-such, then it is an act of defiance or rebellion that tries to make Him out to be something else. From a Christian perspective, her attitude is not more broad-minded than yours; it is, sadly, more ignorant and more rebellious. At their best, Christians do not say, "Believe this because I am right." They say, "I am a poor beggar who by the grace of another has found bread. Let me share this good fortune with all other poor beggars." At the turn of this century, G. K. Chesterton wryly remarked that if a man comes to a cliff and keeps walking, he will not break the law of gravity, he will prove it. We will all give an account to God, the God who has revealed Himself. It is not more open to deny this; and we will still give an account.

From this perspective, she is not inviting you to be less arrogant, but to deny what you have found to be true. She may say that your beliefs in Jesus may be right, but what she gives with the right hand, she takes away with the left, if she also insists you abandon any exclusiveness the Biblical writers set out. She wants, in short, a tame Jesus, a domesticated Jesus, a gospel that demands little instead of a gospel that demands everything, a god who will not offend her sensibilities instead of a God whom she has offended and to whom she must give an account.

I believe it was Goethe who wrote:

> *Sage mir, mit wem du streitest,*
> *Und ich sage dir, wer du bist.*
>
> *("Tell me with whom you are contending,*
> *And I'll tell you who you are.")*

Fifth, lest she be under any misapprehensions, insist that you would be the last person to want to legislate your understanding of God and His ways, forcing those who do not agree to conform. The church is a pilgrim body, perpetually to some degree at odds with the "world." This is a theme you and I probably need to take up at some point. The only reason I mention it is that Laura may in part be reacting against some form of Presbyterianism that includes in its vision a legislated Christian nation. In my view, the strong forms of this view betray serious mistakes, both from the perspective of Biblical theology and from the perspective of evangelistic and pastoral strategy.

Finally, be careful. I would not be so bold as to say this to you if your own father were alive, but my conscience will not allow me to be silent. I am certainly not imposing some artificial rule that says it is always wrong for a Christian to date a non-Christian. But the tugs of love are very powerful. You must frankly ask yourself, as a Christian, whether the deep division in worldview between you will nurture your spiritual growth, benefit your children, breed unity in the home, foster intimacy, encourage evangelism, benefit your prayer life, bring glory to God. It is not for nothing that the Bible warns us against being "unequally yoked" with unbelievers—and though the warning is not restricted to the marriage relationship, it certainly applies there. Try not to hurt her; do not simply drop her; but I beg you, be very, very careful.

With love and prayers,
Paul Woodson

14

I must confess that Dr. Woodson's letter stunned me. In fact, I read three-fourths of it, simply laid it down on my desk, and walked out of my quarters into the cool air of a foggy night in Cambridge. It wasn't that I was really angry. As I said, I was stunned and a little saddened. Why did Dr. Woodson have to load up on me about universalism and arguments against such? Certainly I had written him about Laura and her penchant for agnosticism. But could he not have given me a little leeway rather than hitting me with a theological treatise on the intricacies of her misconceived arguments? These were the kinds of thoughts that filled my mind as I plunged down a side street without any real destination in mind. Perhaps I liked Laura more than I had ever admitted—even to myself. And the very thought that my faith might get in the way of our relationship turned my stomach into knots.

When I returned to my quarters after my pilgrimage to nowhere, I had regained my mental equilibrium—somewhat. I finished reading Dr. Woodson's letter and realized that he was painfully worried that my relationship with Laura might be more serious than I had let on in my letter. He was, in fact, right.

I did appreciate his analysis of universalism's pitfalls. However, I did not think it appropriate that he targeted Laura so directly, given my tender feelings about her. Laura and I did discuss some of the points Dr. Woodson raised. At first I did not mention my source. She asked in a teasing way who or what had provided my new ammunition against her arguments. I told her about Dr. Woodson. I fear that she saw him as a distant foe who gave me an unfair advantage in our exchanges. I regret to say that Laura did not seem to understand the spiritual dimensions of our discussion. Our talks on universalism were more like verbal chess matches with each of us trying to checkmate the other.

I wrote to Dr. Woodson and told him that I understood his concern about my fascination for Laura. In my heart of hearts I knew my relationship with her could not last. For one thing I was soon to return to the United States. For another, I was coming to the conviction that Laura and I really were incompatible because she had such a hard time believing that my faith meant much to me. On one occasion she mused about the future and said that we got along so well we could simply ignore our differences in "matters of religion." For a day or two, I actually saw her suggestion as a reasonable way out of the impasse. It is amazing how emotions can make something appear reasonable when it isn't.

In my letter to Dr. Woodson I hinted that I thought his own letter had been a little overbearing. Undoubtedly my less-than-veiled criticism affected him more than I had anticipated. He wrote the following letter to me, which essentially moved our exchanges to another topic. For this I was grateful.

Please do not misunderstand. I counted it a genuine privilege to correspond with Dr. Woodson. His Biblical insights and personal compassion were remarkable. But sometimes his comments stung and almost appeared meddlesome. On occasion I felt indignant. I was not so sure that I wanted to receive any more of his "counsel." I feared that he might be correct on more than a few observations. As best as I can recollect these were my feelings in the late spring of 1980.

June 12, 1980

Dear Tim,

I must apologize for having perhaps been too forthright in my last letter. I had no intention of offending you. I am certain that Laura is a wonderful person. Otherwise, you would not have spent so much time with her and spoken so highly of her. To speak with conviction and to do so with love sometimes eludes me. You probably sense my problem with this more than I do. In any case, my sincere apologies.

But now I am trapped in a dilemma. You said in your last letter that you are not convinced that you have the right as a believer to raise questions of religion with a nonbeliever unless he or she initiates this kind of conversation. It is not especially civil to invite oneself into the world of another's belief system. Religious beliefs in particular are personal and should not be subject to intrusive scrutiny by others.

My dilemma is this. I have just apologized for coming on too strongly in my discussion of universalism, but now I sense that you may not have grasped how serious the matters are that you and Laura have discussed. What to do? At the risk of offending you again, I feel obliged to make at least a few comments. I really do so with fear and trembling because I know you may begin to believe that I am an old theological windbag, that I have no heart, that I have no idea of what it is like to be in love.

Christians ought to be civil towards each other and towards non-believers. Jesus tells us that we are to love our neighbors as ourselves. We should be courteous, generous, and genuinely interested in the well-being of others whether they be believers or not.

But the question remains: Is it uncivil to present the claims of Christ to unbelievers if they have not asked about our own faith? Certain social conventions lead us to believe that religion and matters of conscience are private affairs. I would argue that a Christian must break with these conventions if they hinder evangelism. Believers have received a commission from their Lord to preach the gospel and to make disciples. This appears to be a non-negotiable directive. To neglect this commission in the name of a social convention may signify that a person has not counted the cost of what it means to be a disciple of Jesus Christ. Such a person may fear potential reproach from friends or colleagues more than the Lord's disapproval.

Before you think I have again climbed on my high horse and ridden into the orthodox sunset, let me assure you I struggle with the same social pressure. It leads me to say to myself: I do not have the right to bother my neighbors with the claims of Christ upon their lives. Their religious beliefs are their own affair. I hope they will ask me about the faith. I am not going to take the first step in this matter. They may find me offensive and a busybody. Then years pass by, my neighbors have not asked me about Christ, and I begin to wonder if I will ever talk to them about the Lord.

A few related thoughts spring to mind. First, think of the literally millions of people who are so grateful that someone presented the gospel to them. In other words, many people are very thankful that a person took the initiative to share Christ with them. You wrote to me in one of your first letters about the person who politely badgered you to come to a Christian meeting at Princeton. Are you not very grateful that this person overcame any fear that you might reject him?

Second, a Christian does not need to be "uncivil" in presenting the gospel to someone. As I already noted, believers are called to love their neighbors as themselves. There is an offense to the cross all right, but we do not need to add to the offense by being offensive. One of the things that has taken the pressure off me personally in witnessing is the realization that I cannot convert anyone. That is the task of the Holy Spirit. I am called to be loving and faithful and to leave the rest to the Lord.

Third, I may say to myself that only those Christians who are called to evangelism should witness. I may muff things up if I try to share my faith. In reality, some of the most effective witnesses for Christ are laypeople who have not received formal theological education. Whether lay or cleric, we will find the Lord with us when we falter or trip over our words or do not know exactly how to respond to a question. I can relax as I witness for Christ.

Fourth, returning to my previous discussion of universalism, if I really believe that people are lost apart from Jesus Christ, I will feel compelled to speak to my neighbor about Christ. We are talking about a life and death matter. I ask this question of myself on occasion: Do I really believe that people are lost apart from Christ, or do I mouth these sentiments as dry creed without any genuine sense of the enormous entailments?

Finally, my guess is that we will also break the social convention when we are in love with Christ. It is very difficult not to tell our friends about a person we love—just as you very graciously told me about Laura. Owing to our love for Christ, we will want to tell others about Him, despite our often highly exaggerated fears that our friends will scorn our efforts to present the gospel.

I am a fellow wayfarer with you, Tim. I do apologize for being so preachy if that is what you have thought I have been. As you can see in this letter, I struggle with many of the same things you do. Your good letters have caused me to pause more than once and think about the coldness of my own heart and my own hypocrisy. I am rooting for you. Be assured of that. We are on the way together.

Sincerely,
Paul Woodson

15

I returned to the United States in the summer of 1980 and found a good job. (Ed. note: Journeyman found this job through the services of some friends of his deceased father. The job and the abundant income it provided become the focus of a later letter—Seventeen.) Partly owing to the shock of returning to America (New York City at that!), partly owing to my continuing sense of shame, and partly owing to the ambivalence I felt at leaving Laura behind—that friendship, as I had foreseen, never went anywhere—I felt emotionally whipsawed during the closing months of 1980 and the first part of 1981. I was feeling a bit tender, and my letters to Prof. Woodson were brief to the point of curtness. Sensing my mood, he replied with kindness but without sermons or counsel.

My exposure to cultural diversity freed me from some taboos associated with the evangelicalism of my youth. This apparent "freedom" was reinforced by meeting a number of young evangelicals about my own age who openly rejected the restraints of their parents' generation. On the other hand, the expectations of older evangelical leaders and my own desire to know the Lord in a real and vital way pressed me toward tighter discipline. The whipsaw left me tired, alternately wondering what I could get away with and what I needed to do to become genuinely holy.

I had earlier developed the habit of being frank with Dr. Woodson, and I now decided it was time to improve our lines of communication again. In July of 1981, after I had been home for about a year, I tried to express my uncertainties candidly. I have sometimes wondered if I would have developed this correspondence with him had my own father lived. Probably not. Yet ironically, it is doubtful I ever would have been as frank with Dad as I was with Dr. Woodson. In retrospect, I have come to thank God that out of the incalculable loss of my own father (a loss no other friendship could *retrieve), He gave me this means of stimulating my spiritual growth and checking my hesitant trips down various byways.*

August 5, 1981

Dear Tim,

I often wonder how you are finding your new job now that you have been at it a year; and I am always especially eager to learn how you are progressing in your Christian discipleship. My wife and I invite you to come and stay with us for a few days, perhaps at the Christmas break. Of course, we understand that now that you are out of an academic environment, it is not always possible to schedule several days off. Nevertheless we would dearly love to see you.

Part of the tension you feel is bound up with living in a world that, by and large, does not know God. But the tension, I think, is manageable if we keep in mind a number of factors, a couple of which are peculiar to Western culture at the end of the twentieth century.

First, in the welter of ambiguous or at least disputed things, never overlook the things that are absolute. I am referring not only to truths, but to ethical standards. It is always wrong, for instance, to be puffed up in arrogance; it is always wrong to make money a god; it is always wrong to nurture bitterness; it is always wrong to foster malice and hate; it is always wrong to fornicate. Start by reading and re-reading Scripture for the certainties. They will give you plenty to work on! Indeed, two or three of these immovable points will turn out to resolve many of the more difficult cases. Can there be any doubt, for instance, that the Bible says we are to love God with heart and soul and mind and strength, and our neighbors as ourselves? Or that we are to be holy, as God is holy? When in doubt, emphasize the certainties.

Second, although the ambiguities arising from cultural diversity are considerable, it is vital to distinguish two common approaches to such problems. The first is an unexpressed but scarcely disguised, "What can I get away with?"—or, more winsomely, "What am I permitted to do?" The second is a defensive, "How shall I protect myself from the dangers of the world at this point? What barrier can I put around myself to keep out this sin? How shall I distinctively separate myself from the world at this juncture?"—or, more winsomely, "How can I avoid giving the appearance of participating in evil?"

In their most winsome versions, both stances have their merit. But neither is radical enough. "What am I permitted to do?" is a fair question, but it is cast in a form that suggests Christianity is a system of prohibitions, and once you have systematized and categorized the prohibitions and learned to follow these rules, you are reasonably safe. Alternatively, "How can I avoid giving the appearance of participating in evil?" is a fair question, but if it is made the final criterion of right and wrong behavior, Jesus Himself will fall under it. He was the friend of public sinners, corrupt civil servants, the morally and the ceremonially unclean, and did not worry if His reputation suffered accordingly (Matthew 11:19). One always has to consider where the criticisms are coming from! Endless concern for one's reputation may have a great deal less to do with a desire for holiness and outreach than with a wretchedly sanctimonious spirit.

Both of these suspect attitudes are mirrored in Paul's readers, so far as we are able to reconstruct them, in 1 Corinthians 8. The issue there is eating meat offered to idols. However the details are construed, certain points are clear. The conservative group, those who think it is wrong to eat meat that has been offered to idols, are viewed as the "weaker" brothers. They are "weaker" because their conscience is "weaker"—that is, Paul holds that a conscience is "weak" if it makes one think something is wrong when in fact that thing is not itself objectively wrong, wrong in God's eyes. By implication, however, the person who holds that fornication is a sin would never be accused of having a "weak" conscience, because fornication is a sin. But even where the proposed action—in this case, eating meat offered to idols—is not itself evil, Paul insists that the person who thinks of it as evil, the person with the weak conscience, should not indulge. Contravening one's conscience is always risky. A damaged conscience can no longer protect a person.

By implication, increasing Christian maturity should reform the conscience, a point Paul makes clear elsewhere. Eventually, the Christian's conscience should be shaped by the Word—free wherever the Word of God does not mandate or prohibit, and joyfully obeying where it does.

But perhaps the most intriguing emphasis in 1 Corinthians 8 is that those who have already attained such maturity are exhorted to curb their liberties to avoid damaging those who have not yet come so far. The question therefore becomes, not "What am I free to do?", but, "How can I best serve the church of Christ? How can I best edify my fellow Christians, including those with very sensitive consciences?" The mandates of Christian love must always be weighed.

I hasten to say that those who insist that something or other be prohibited if anyone is to be a Christian, where that thing is not clearly prohibited by Scripture, must be gently opposed. That is not what Paul is dealing with here.

Let me offer an illustration. Suppose I am working with a conservative group where the consensus is that drinking alcohol is wrong. Quite frankly, the Bible makes no prohibition in the matter. Jesus Himself, after all, changed water to wine. Drunkenness is forbidden, and a case can be made for the view that strong drink is frowned upon—probably uncut wine, since most table wines in Jesus' day were cut between three to one and ten to one. But absolute prohibition cannot be found in Scripture. There may be all sorts of good reasons for being a teetotaler—better health, cheaper insurance, in some contexts a better witness, fewer calories, and much more. Still, one cannot legitimately appeal to the Scripture for a blanket prohibition.

So what shall I do? While working with those for whom alcohol is offensive or dangerous, I shall not touch it. While working among Christians in, say France, I shall sometimes partake of it (even though, quite frankly, I don't much like the stuff—except for port!). If I am on my own, I prefer not to indulge, partly as a matter of personal preference, partly because I have worked with enough alcoholics that I have learned to be wary, partly because I believe that personal discipline helps to reinforce Christian discipline (meditate on 1 Corinthians 9:24-27). But if I find someone who insists that if I drink I cannot possibly be a Christian, I am tempted to ask for a glass of port. I want to make clear to all that my salvation turns on Christ alone, not on arbitrary rules, and that as Christ's redeemed saint, I am at liberty to do whatever Scripture, mediated through the new covenant, leaves me free to do.

I am a free man. But that also means I am free to serve, to become all things to all men so that by all possible means I might save some—as Paul insists in the same chapter (1 Corinthians 9:19-23). Answers framed merely in terms of what may or may not be done are always sterile, and usually miss the point. There are relationships to be considered, the advance of the kingdom, the winning of men and women to Jesus Christ. Ethical decisions that do not deeply weigh such matters are already hopelessly compromised, profoundly sub-Christian.

Third, you must come to grips with the fact that Western culture generally, and American culture in particular, is at many points profoundly apostate. I use the word advisedly. We have self-consciously thrown off the heritage of Christian values passed down to us. Millions do not think of themselves as standing before a sovereign and holy God to whom they must give an account. Such a society, through the media, snickers and sneers at the notion of moral accountability before a sovereign God as outmoded at best, certainly repressive and dangerous, and fanatical at worst. Our society makes temptation a convenience. Enticement to arrogance becomes the incentive to use some credit cards; enticement to sexual sin becomes the standard of the advertising industry; enticement to pleasure and self-interest becomes the siren pull in politics, economics, and entertainment.

We Christians are not immune from such blandishments. We participate in the sins of our age. It takes constant meditation on the Word and repeated decisions of the will, empowered by God Himself (see Philippians 2:12-13), to set ourselves to serve God with joy, to *delight* in the Lordship of Jesus Christ. In large measure that is true in every generation; it is peculiarly urgent in ours.

As I have suggested, two other factors peculiar to our culture and place in history make these considerations more urgent. The first is the shape of the new conservatism emerging in the Reagan years. When I was pastoring a church through most of the '50s, people wanted to work hard, gather a little nest egg, buy a house, press on to a better job, get a better education. Most adults lived under the shadow of the Great Depression and World War II; the cold war was omnipresent.

Then came the assassination of President Kennedy, the Viet Nam years, Woodstock. It is hard for me to realize that these are things that you and your generation read about in history books. We lived them. The brutal loss of confidence and direction gave impetus to a further reaction. The flower children of the '60s are wearing pin-stripe suits and clamoring for MBAs. Many applaud the rising conservatism, the commitment to work, the number of women having babies again.

But it is not the same conservatism. The conservatism of the '50s had many weaknesses. It was jingoistic, too nationalistic, too arrogant. But at least it was building for the future. Parents who remembered the depression wanted to build a secure future for their children. In that sense, even the hard work was undertaken for the next generation. And all of this was within an inherited culture that still largely defended the absoluteness of some moral values.

Not the new conservatism. Now people want to make a lot of money for themselves; their children place a distant third or fourth, somewhere after career, self-fulfillment, and profound commitment to materialism. Education is not something to be valued in itself; it is a means to an end—namely, more money and power. The heroes are not the manufacturers, those who make things, but the money barons, those who manipulate stocks. The yuppie generation, conservative in some respects, is the most discouragingly selfish I have seen anywhere. Such selfishness and covetousness is the very essence of idolatry.

What I am saying, Tim, is that you must understand your own times *in the light of God's Word,* or you will probably be seduced by your times. Now that our generation has so frenetically set about to live exclusively for material things, it will probably generate a backlash, some kind of weird search for "spirituality." There are signs of it already. But the concerns of this new "spirituality" have to do with self-fulfillment. The New Age will become more popular than the new birth.

Who will take up His cross and confess that Jesus is Lord?

Finally, in the growing (though late) evangelical resurgence for issues of public morality, there is, strangely, a loss of concern for private morality and personal and spiritual integrity. Rightly, we are becoming more and more sensitized to issues such as abortion, abuse of power, the spoiling of the world God has entrusted to us, the abused and the downtrodden. We are merely recapturing one of the mainstreams in our own evangelical heritage, a stream largely eclipsed as we tried to emerge from the devastating blows of classic liberalism. The "liberals" emphasized good deeds, so we emphasized justification; they stressed service to the poor, so we stressed evangelism; they underlined conduct in the public arena, so we underlined doctrine and personal piety. To recapture moral resolve in the public arena is therefore a healthy return to the prophetic calls of the Biblical writers.

But what concerns me is that at least some contemporary evangelical drum-beating on social issues seems to come at the *expense* of personal morality and private devotion. I hope I am wrong. But if not, the flimsy base will not long sustain the superstructure. Believe me, I am far from advocating a merely personal and pietistic devotion. But pursuing the faddish is always easy. As soon as it becomes popular to support certain issues, I want to ask what is being left out, what is being ignored or even despised. If the Scriptures demand that we be concerned with justice, they also demand that we earnestly pray that we may increasingly grasp the limitless dimensions of the love of God (Ephesians 3:14ff.) and learn to delight ourselves in Him.

I have come a long way from your questions about legalism and freedom, discipline and libertinism. If I have not made myself clear, let me sum up my understanding of what the Bible says. The issues you are thinking about can never find resolution if examined in isolation. You must set yourself to know God, to love God, to obey God and Jesus Christ whom He has sent. With such goals as your burning lodestar, you will find yourself better equipped to deal with these issues.

Your fellow servant,
Paul Woodson

16

To be frank, I found this latest letter from Dr. Woodson to be once again a little heavy. Doubtless this owed something to the pressures of my job, the scant time I reserved for reading, thinking, praying, and perhaps also to a kind of coldness or, more accurately, apathy that had settled over my Christian life. I began to conclude that one of the greatest causes of deadness in the church was the heavy emphasis in many conservative circles on doctrine. What I wanted was life, vitality, experience, reality.

When I shared these perceptions with Dr. Woodson, I thought he would agree since I knew he was no defender of apathetic Christianity. And so I was unprepared for his response.

September 18, 1981

Dear Tim,

You offer me strange alternatives—cold, moribund, doctrinal, boring Christianity, or bright, experiential, exciting, nondoctrinal Christianity. Am I allowed no other?

At the risk of sounding like an old man, I would guess that part of your perspective is the result of moving into the "real world" of the everyday worker. I'm sure your bank expects you to be on your toes, and, with your "arts" background, doubtless you are taking courses to enable you to compete in the financial industry. Your life is regulated, harried, pressured. You find you have little time for reading, and when you do read, if it is not the *Wall Street Journal* or an accounting textbook, you want some light entertainment, not something cold, arid, and stale like *doctrine!* Am I close? If I am misjudging the situation, please set me straight.

Another factor may bear on the disjunctives you offer me. Truth to tell, I (and those like me who teach in seminaries) am partly responsible for it. At the risk of caricature, evangelical preachers (whom I help to train!) have tended to gravitate to one of two extremes. On the one hand, some find frightfully relevant topics and exciting modes of delivery. They may coat their message in up-to-date psychobabble and press for exciting, upbeat, self-help "worship" services. They are thin on doctrine; they are usually thin on basic Bible, but most of their parishioners cannot isolate the problem because these preachers liberally gloss their presentations with religious buzz words.

On the other hand, not a few preachers, not least those who are trained in conservative seminaries like this one, ploddingly plough their way through Biblical passage after Biblical passage, pedantically explaining each participle, carefully unpacking the significance of the Greek genitive absolute or the Hebrew construct infinitive (as if the elderly woman in the congregation who has just lost her husband cares for such niceties), habitually deploying as many eight-cylinder theological words as possible. If people do not respond, it is because we live in perilous times when people will not put up with sound doctrine. This graceless presentation is often labeled "expository preaching."

Of course, I have resorted to crude caricature. Yet although most preachers fit into neither camp but belong to some mediating position influenced by all sorts of other pressures, it is easy to think of preachers who fit the caricature.

The first type of preacher builds a shallow church. It may be a wonderfully exciting place to be for a short time, but such works tend to have a lot of people moving through them. Such preachers are always hostage to passing fads. Few of these are heretical; most are relatively frivolous. They tend to package the latest psychobabble in religious language and parrot it back to the world as if it were profound Biblical insight. Among the ill-informed, they gain a reputation for relevance, for being "with it." I remember a ditty said to be composed by an old preacher in protest against such clerics:

> You say I am not with it.
> My friend, I do not doubt it.
> But when I see what I'm not with
> I'd rather be without it.

Sadly, the first type of preacher is all too often reinforced by the bad example set by the second type of preacher. What the second offers is not expository preaching. At best, it is expository lecturing; at worst, it is a string of random grammatical and historical and theological thoughts roughly based on a set text. Worst of all, it is desperately boring and nurtures almost no one. I do not know the minister of the church you are now attending; but if you have come under such preaching for a few months, especially after a year's exposure to the ministry of Roy Clements in Cambridge, I can understand your frustration.

Of course, preachers cannot take all the blame. Christian radio and TV often provide quick-fix sloganeering theology. Christian magazines, under pressure from competition, so focus on the bottom line that the number of subscribers is the only thing that matters. To keep that number high, you have to be "with it" and cater to the spiritual fast-food industry. Some of these magazines are losing their prophetic voice; and they have never been so popular. But I suspect that in time they will crumble on the demand for constant entertainment. Meanwhile, there are very few voices in America that have taken the high road, and fewer still have a national audience. If preachers are at fault, so are congregations and readers. Like the churches in Revelation 2 and 3, we have drunk deeply from the wellsprings of our own culture and scarcely recognize that the well is polluted.

But enough criticism. How *should* things be? Hard cases, they say, make bad law. They also make bad theology. We should begin with principle and move outward.

From a Biblical perspective, then, it is of paramount importance to observe how strongly Christian maturity is tied to an ever-deepening knowledge of the Word of God. The Christians addressed by the epistle to the Hebrews are told, "We have much to say about this [that is, about the priesthood of Melchizedek and related topics], but it is hard to explain because you are slow to learn. In fact, though by this time you ought to be teachers, you need someone to teach you the elementary truths of God's word all over again. You need milk, not solid food! . . . But solid food is for the mature, who by constant use have trained themselves to distinguish good from evil" (Hebrews 5:11-14; cf. 1 Corinthians 3:1ff.). Human beings and all their opinions and fads "are like the grass, and all their glory is like the flowers of the field; the grass withers and the flowers fall, but the word of the Lord stands forever" (1 Peter 1:24-25; Isaiah 40:6-8). Before you read any further in this letter, it would be wonderful if you would take the time to sit down and read slowly and meditatively Psalms 19 and 119 and 2 Timothy. It is not for nothing that the Old

Testament repeatedly views the *absence* of the Word of God as a sign of profound judgment. Conversely, Jesus prays to His Father, "Sanctify them by the truth; your word is truth" (John 17:17)—the implication being that there is no sanctification apart from the truth, the truth conveyed by God's Word.

If the Bible is right about Heaven and Hell, the nature of God, the way of salvation, the destination toward which we are rushing, the multifarious forms of idolatry, the utter importance of Jesus Christ and His death and resurrection, the person and presence and power of the Spirit, the love of God, the importance of thinking with eternity's values in view, the corrosive nature of self-centeredness, the corrupting effect of sin, the beauty of holiness, the privilege of knowing God, the nature of the church, and much more, then clearly the Scriptures and the doctrine they contain are relevant to the real world. The question is whether or not men and women are prepared to listen. Sometimes when people complain that doctrine is irrelevant, they are betraying their own enslavement to the priorities of a lost and frenetic world.

Because you are a Christian, I assume you will agree with what I've just said. The question then becomes why such doctrine so frequently *seems* irrelevant.

The answers are many; but as I've already hinted, I lay a great deal of the blame at the feet of preachers. Expository preaching is much more than lecturing. Ideally, it is the re-presentation of the initial Word of God to a new generation. It is mediated through a preacher, and his entire personality should be shaped by the truth he is conveying. He must not only think through the texts he is expounding, but must ruthlessly eliminate comment on arcane technical points that fascinate the specialist but do little to capture the driving message. Up to this point his work is only half done; for the preacher must also think through in a controlled, Spirit-empowered manner just how this passage ought to make an impact on the way people live and think.

A chief reason why so much of what passes for evangelical expository or doctrinal preaching is so boring and irrelevant is that the preacher has spent a vastly disproportionate amount of preparation time in exegesis and outlines, and so little in thinking through how the Word of God is to wound and heal (to use the language of Hosea). Another is the merely professional stance of some preachers. Far better to take Peter's line: "If anyone speaks, he should do it as one speaking the very words of God" (1 Peter 4:11).

That means, for instance, that any treatment of, say, the atonement, must also say some practical things about how we are to approach God when we sin. Examples must be concrete. If sin is introduced, it must not be an abstract entity that largely pertains to sinners out there—the shape and nature of sin must so be teased out that church members discover their *own* sin and learn to deal with it. If sin is discussed purely in the categories of personal alienation, then the "answer" to sin will rest in personal relationships and self-fulfillment. If sin is discussed exclusively in the categories of legal justification, then our own penchant for sin may be lightly skirted. If sin is treated solely with respect to its bearing on our guilty conscience, then the objectivity of our offense before God will not be recognized—even though from the Biblical perspective the problem of sin is not simply the guilt we feel, but the objective guilt we incur before God and therefore the doom we deserve.

How you think about sin affects how you think about sin's remedy, about what is wrong with you and with the world, about what is important or unimportant in a world under God's curse and God's love. *There is no area of doctrine whatsoever that does not have enormous ramifications for the way we think and live.* Indeed, even leaving out some major component of a Biblical topic may have the unsolicited effect of introducing a "wobble" into our discipleship that may prove troublesome later or call forth an unforeseen backlash.

Similarly, if the preacher talks about Jesus as, say, the incarnate Word of God, the "so what" question must be firmly broached and answered in concrete terms that call us to worship, to obedience, to repentance, to faith, to understanding, to reflection, to discipleship, or the like.

If you are in a church that is merely frivolous in its preaching, get involved in a good Bible study where you are fed. Put some energy into it. Do some reading in advance and pray your way through the passage to be studied before you show up for the meeting. If you are in a church where the preaching is formally Biblical but depressingly boring, ask yourself the application questions as you hear the preacher work through the text. Instead of tuning out, ask yourself: If this is what the passage says, what difference should it make to the way I live, think, and work? What is God saying to me here?

If all else fails, find a church where you will be fed and where you will have an opportunity to start exercising your growing grasp of Scripture in leading others in Bible study. The best Bible students are almost always those who try hard to help others understand the Bible and put its message into practice.

If you still doubt the relevance of doctrine to life, start reading some books that are doctrinal in content but written with warmth and a deep concern to bring about spiritual growth. Read John Bunyan's *The Pilgrim's Progress* and J. I. Packer's *Knowing God*. Start working your way through the published volumes of "The Bible Speaks Today" series—sort of halfway between commentary and sermon. For instance, you might start with J. Alec Motyer, *The Day of the Lion* (on Amos); John R. W. Stott, *Only One Way* (on Galatians) or his *Guard the Gospel* (on 2 Timothy). Read the two volumes of F. Derek Kidner on the Psalms in the Tyndale Old Testament commentary series. With your interest in history, you ought to work your way through the two-volume biography *George Whitefield* by Arnold Dallimore. I challenge you to remain dry and lifeless through this reading list!

Finally, ask yourself if you have shared your faith with anyone recently. If you have no outlet, then like the Dead Sea you will only take in and, as a result, simply die. If you regularly talk to others about your faith, questions will come up that demand answers, and the relevance of doctrine and of Biblical knowledge will be forced on you. And pray—alone and with others—that the truths you learn will shape your thinking and values and enable you to respond with joy to the God of your salvation.

Warmly yours in
Christ Jesus,
Paul Woodson

17

I enjoyed learning about Dr. Woodson's perception of the components of good expository preaching. His letter even provoked a
radically new idea to dance through my mind—perhaps I could be
a pastor someday. To open up the Word of God and preach it the
way Dr. Woodson suggested would be a great thrill. What could be
a better life work than that? At the time I did not realize that pastors do far more than preach.

After my return from Cambridge, I had found a remarkably well-
paying job in New York City, essentially due to my father's connections in the insurance industry. I was making more money than I
should have and relishing the work just as my father had before me.
I especially enjoyed the toys (in particular a new car) I had recently
purchased. The restaurants and theaters in New York City had welcomed me once I flashed a thick wallet larded with multicolored
credit cards.

But the toys and my moderate social life of casual dating (partly
to get Laura off my mind) were rapidly paling. I wondered to
myself: Is this the way I want to live the rest of my life, trying to
make money and finding innumerable ways to spend it? My own
father had literally worked himself to death on the money treadmill.
Perhaps I could become a pastor. Surely this would please God. And
what could be more important than helping others think God's
thoughts after Him?

As soon as I thought these things, my head would begin to spin.
You hypocrite, Tim, *my conscience seemed to scream.* You still battle with selfish thoughts and sins on every front—from years gone by
and from immediate temptations. How could you ever talk to others about victory in Christ when on occasion you fail so miserably
yourself?

With these thoughts chasing around in my mind, I wrote Dr.

Woodson that although I had appreciated his discussion on preach-
ing and theology, his observations had lost some of their pungency
for me because I was disheartened by my continuing battles against
old-fashioned foes—the lust of the flesh, the lust of the eyes, and the
pride of life.

I doubted at the time that Dr. Woodson would say anything new
in response. After all, had he not already addressed these matters?
To my considerable relief, he wrote the following letter—one that
discloses his patience with this "disciple" of Christ who sometimes
seems to follow from so far off.

November 22, 1981

Dear Tim,

I covet God's peace for you in these days. Your recognition that
the struggles of the Christian life continue to bedevil the believer even
years after conversion is an important one. You may recall that we
discussed these matters earlier.

That you are experiencing rounds of temptation is not as unusual
as you might suppose. From the inception of the Church believers
have found this pilgrim way to be strewn with multiple temptations.
You recall the words of James, "Consider it pure joy, my brothers,
whenever you face trials of many kinds, because you know that the
testing of your faith develops perseverance" (James 1:2-3). Peter
indicates that the Lord can deliver us from temptations, ". . . the
Lord knows how to rescue godly men from trials and to hold the
unrighteous for the day of judgment" (2 Peter 2:9). Martin Luther
warned, "Don't argue with the Devil. He has had five thousand years
of experience. He has tried out all his tricks on Adam, Abraham, and
David, and he knows exactly the weak spots." The Puritan John
Cotton commented that temptation is like a beast that scares the
Christian off the road from time to time. But the true Christian will
get back on the road. In other words, if a person is tempted, commits sin, and stays off the road, that may mean that the person really
does not know Christ. But the fact that you are concerned about the
temptations is a good sign.

Or to put it another way—if the temptations are such that they
become the doors through which you are marching in a headstrong
way toward more sin, stoking your addictions with wanton exuber-
ance, then you should fall on your knees and cry out for God's mercy

and deliverance. If, on the other hand, you are resisting temptations, you should fall on your knees and ask for God's continued protection.

Do not be surprised. Persons who are living for the Lord represent prime targets for the evil one because they are doing damage to his dismal interests. Others he does not particularly need to disturb; they are already out of commission as effective Christians because they are egotistic, have high tolerance levels for sin, and are quite satisfied with their "no-risk" Christianity. Christians who know the Lord well are often more aware of their sin and spirit of rebellion than people who make no effort to submit to God's will. As he approached death, John Calvin, of all people, complained that his heart had been cold towards the Lord during his life and asked for forgiveness. If Calvin's heart was cold, my own heart must be arctic.

We often think of Martin Luther as a person whom God used in a remarkable way. But he was more than once overwhelmed by the evil one. Listen to his lament: "For more than a week [in 1527] I was close to the gates of death and hell. I trembled in all my members. Christ was wholly lost. I was shaken by desperation and blasphemy of God." He saw the evil one as a very personal figure, determined to undo him. This sensitivity helps explain the lyrics of Luther's wonderful hymn, "A Mighty Fortress Is Our God":

> *And though this world, with devils filled,*
> *Should threaten to undo us;*
> *We will not fear, for God hath willed*
> *His truth to triumph through us:*
> *The Prince of Darkness grim,*
> *We tremble not for him;*
> *His rage we can endure,*
> *For lo, his doom is sure,*
> *One little word shall fell him.*

The reason Luther had the confidence to pen these lyrics is that he knew that the devil had been defeated at the cross. Christ's name could defeat him.

And yet the devil, already defeated, still tries to make us believe that he has power over us. But Luther believed that the devil's machinations can be turned into a positive good. We begin the better to understand our faith, the power of the gospel, and the love of God— after we have been beset by temptations. Luther wrote, "If I live longer, I would like to write a book about *Anfechtungen* [assaults upon the soul], for without them no man can understand Scripture, faith, the fear or the love of God. He does not know the meaning of hope who was never subject to temptations." Luther also argued that a person should expect to be tempted after having devotions. Apparently, the devil is especially worried when we have communed with the Lord.

In another passage Luther associates these challenges with the cross that Christians must bear: "For them [Christians] the holy cross serves for learning the faith, for [learning] the power of the word, and for subduing whatever sin and pride remain. Indeed, a Christian can no more do without the cross than without food or drink."

I must say that I became intrigued by the spiritual counsel of Martin Luther once I read comments like these. Luther seemed to have experienced the same kinds of temptations and struggles that I have personally encountered. His counsel regarding how to deal with them is so refreshing even though it is nearly five hundred years old.

Tim, there is so much more I would like to say about this topic. But there are some pressing school matters to which I must attend. Please do not be discouraged by the fact that you are becoming more aware of your own sin. On the other hand, if the allusions you were making in your letter refer to sins that you are not willing to forsake, then please be very careful.

Moreover, the cross that Christians carry is not too heavy. Jesus said, "My burden is light." He gives believers the power to overcome temptations. Temptations are not to lead to a life of sin and depression. In this regard another comment of Martin Luther comes to mind: "A Christian should and must be a cheerful person. If he isn't, the devil is tempting him. I have sometimes been grievously tempted while bathing in my garden, and then I have sung the hymn 'Let us now praise Christ.' Otherwise I would have been lost then and there. Accordingly, when you notice that you have some such thoughts say, 'This isn't Christ.' . . . Christ knows that our hearts are troubled, and it is for this reason that he says and commands, 'Let not your heart be troubled.'"

Tim, I will be praying for you. Please remember Peter's admonition: "Dear friends, I urge you, as aliens and strangers in the world, to abstain from sinful desires, which war against your soul" (1 Peter 2:11).

Cordially,
Paul Woodson

P.S. Please pardon the disjointed quality of this letter. I wrote it hastily, and one thought simply piled up on another as I rushed to complete it.

P.P.S. Have you decided whether or not you can visit us at Christmas?

18

Early in the spring of 1981, before the latest couple of letters from Prof. Woodson and while I was still feeling depressed, I had consulted a psychiatrist two or three times. I came away somewhat frustrated. By the end of the summer I was in any case gradually emerging from this "dark night of the soul." Doubtless, renewed efforts at serious Christian reading played a part, as did readjustment to America, increasing distance from Laura, and fellowship with other Christians.

Nevertheless my brief encounter with psychiatry prompted me to raise some questions. Toward Christmas, taking care that my letter would reach him after his end-of-term examinations and marking, I asked Dr. Woodson what he thought of the relation between psychology/psychiatry and the Christian faith.

December 21, 1981

Dear Tim,

(Ed. note: The letter begins with some complaints about the amount of marking to do at TEDS and then comments on Tim's report that he felt his Christian life was going a little better. Woodson's tone is encouraging, perhaps slightly relieved. Woodson also alludes to a phone call from Journeyman in which the latter regretfully declined the Woodsons' invitation to spend part of the Christmas season with them. He then turns to the new topic.)

At their best, psychology and psychiatry accomplish an enormous amount of good. Psychiatry, with its roots in traditional medicine, holds special promise. How many conditions loosely labeled "mental illness" or the like find their roots in some chemical imbalance or genetic disorder? I certainly know a number of people who have been helped through illness, depression, alcoholism, and many other debilitating conditions by means of regular visits to a psychologist or psychiatrist. Rightly utilized, such skills evince God's goodness in "common grace."

But there is another side to consider. One of the most consistent and ruthless critics of psychotherapy is Thomas Szasz, himself medically trained. Among his many books are three that you might like to scan: *Myth of Mental Illness; Ideology and Insanity: Essays on Psychiatric Dehumanization of Man;* and *Myth of Psychotherapy: Mental Healing as Religion, Rhetoric and Repression.* From within the evangelical camp, about a decade or so ago Jay Adams published his influential book, *Competent to Counsel.* His thesis, in brief, is that psychology and psychiatry have wrongly taken over areas of influence and counseling that rightly belong to pastors and have given the impression that anyone who has not been through their schools and adopted their frameworks is incompetent. Adams is concerned to blow smoke on this posturing and to assure pastors that they are "competent to counsel." In the course of his book, Adams, in my view, occasionally resorts to reductionistic arguments and sometimes lacks any shading in gray; but at the time it was a breath of fresh air that helped not a few pastors gain the confidence and effectiveness out of which they had previously been intimidated.

I fear that since then a number of pastors have followed Adams relentlessly and have sometimes done a fair bit of damage. In one sense, that is not Adams's fault. You cannot be held responsible for all the actions of your followers. But I have seen some pastors who follow Adams's technique and priorities who do not have Adams's skill, maturity, and compassion. Adams would be the first to insist that his emphases must never be taken as justification for a ruthless technique devoid of empathy, compassion, a listening ear, Christian love; but some who profess to follow him make all of these mistakes and justify their omissions on the ground that they are resorting to "Biblical" counseling.

But I digress. You asked about current psychology and psychiatry, not the state of Christian counseling. I make no pretense of specialist knowledge, but I do not mind sharing my impressions, so long as you take them for what they are—the musings of a theologian, not a psychologist. The first (but not the most important) criticism I would level is that most counselors (I shall use this generic term to embrace those trained in either psychology or psychiatry and who are engaged in counseling—as opposed to those engaged in theoretical research), especially in America, are reductionistic in their controlling models. So far as I can tell, this is less so in Europe where synthetic approaches are more common. But here counselors tend to gravitate to one or more of the major schools of thought. They are Freudians, or they are behaviorists, or they are Jungians, or whatever. In each case, whatever valid insights they bring to the task, the narrowness of their controlling model means they are overlooking important dimensions of human personality.

Suppose, then, someone has engaged in fornication once or twice and feels so terribly guilty about it that it is affecting his sleep, his eating, his equilibrium. He goes to see a counselor. What will the counselor say?

If the counselor is a follower of Jung, and sensitive as well, he or she might pick up on the religious background and ingrained moral standards of the "patient" and try to get the "patient" (some counselors now prefer "client"!) to talk it out. There will doubtless be some sort of cathartic release in this approach. It does not usually help to repress one's feelings, and the act of talking it out may help to restore a sense of proportion.

If the counselor is a follower of Freud, he or she will view this as a classic case of sexual repression. The counselor will not only encourage the "patient" to talk it out, but will gently try to get the "patient" to cast this episode into the framework of breaking out of inherited sexual repressions. In one case I knew in Toronto, a young woman was eventually told by a Freudian psychiatrist that she ought to go out and fornicate frequently for a while in order to liberate herself from these false moral inhibitions. Of course, that was an extreme case; most counselors would be more circumspect than that. But it does follow the logic of the model to an (admittedly) extreme conclusion.

If the counselor is a behaviorist, it is hard to predict what advice will be given. But one thing is sure—if the counselor is a strict behaviorist, in the line of B. F. Skinner, "moral" questions as you and I understand morality do not come into play. Morality, like every other part of our belief system and personality development, is solely the product of genes and environment. Any notion of right and wrong is therefore *necessarily* relative—completely independent of distinctively Christian concepts of morality, which are tied to the character of God. *Right* is what God approves; *wrong* is what He disapproves. Right and wrong take on their deep significance, what I would define as their *moral* significance, by virtue of their connection with the character of an eternal God who has so graciously (if not exhaustively) revealed Himself to a race of rebels.

This is not to say there is nothing to be learned from behaviorists. I know a Christian psychologist who uses behavior modification techniques, along with the articulation of Christian truth, in helping homosexuals who wish to leave that pattern of behavior. But it is to say that the counselor who is a committed behaviorist will not even begin to address the problem that Christians judge to be fundamental in such a case.

By contrast, a knowledgeable and sensitive Christian counselor, after listening at length and after gentle probing into the counselee's background, will conclude that the reason for the sense of guilt is that there is real moral guilt before a holy God (assuming the counselor concludes this is not an instance of fantasy or the like). Doubtless the guilt has been precipitated by factors in the individual's background. But from the Christian perspective, the critical question is not whether the background has exerted influence (that is surely a given), but whether or not that background has reinforced Biblical truth, warped it, or denied it. I have myself in such instances gently tried to make the connection between feelings of guilt and real objective guilt, and then I have said that the latter is far worse and far greater than the counselee can imagine. That certainly gets people's attention! But it is no more than elementary truth. What it does is open the door to talking about God, the nature of right and wrong, and *the only way that real guilt can be relieved.*

If in some measure guilt feelings are the by-product of real guilt, it is the real guilt that must be dealt with first. Handling the guilt feelings is a derivative question, and it finally turns on how to apply the doctrine of Christian assurance. If in several sessions such a counselee comes up against the gospel and will not frankly close with Christ, sooner or later I say that there is nothing further I can do to help. I am happy to remain a friend, to be available, to direct the counselee to someone else. But I am above all a minister of the gospel and refuse to be sidetracked into some other vocation.

My most serious charge against most contemporary psychology and psychiatry is that they constitute a false religion. It is not that the branches are themselves reductionistic; it is that, root and branch, they are, by and large, profoundly indebted to ideological roots they only barely discern. Or, to put the matter more charitably, most practitioners of psychology and psychiatry operate out of the matrix of ideological roots that are profoundly unbiblical.

I know this charge can sound a bit much; so let me explain what I mean. I think that much modern psychology has become a kind of religion, in the sense that it has a god, a goal (an "eschatology"), a set of values. It is a branch of secular humanism; its god is the self; its worship is the service of self. Its goal is self-love, self-esteem, self-realization; its values are pragmatic provided they revolve around the idealization of self, the realization of self's potential.

The cost is incalculable. Psychology and psychiatry claim to explain everything. They offer good techniques, even good drugs. But they destroy meaning. Everything is explainable; nothing is meaningful.

Contrast how God looks at things. The Bible insists that human beings are extremely important. We were made in the image of God and face an eternal destiny. Our choices are important, our character is important, our words and thoughts are important—precisely because they are all related to God, who is all-important. But the Bible also insists we are rebels, sinners, whose moral pretensions cannot gloss over the deep-seated root of our malaise—a fallen nature that revolves around self instead of around the God who made us and for whom we were made.

So along comes psychology and tells us to serve ourselves! In the process, it destroys any concept of sin, but simultaneously destroys any justifiable concept of human dignity. We have merely arisen from the primordial muck, and to muck we will return. Sin is replaced by behavior patterns, by electrical discharges across synapses in the brain—no more. By dismissing sin, psychology destroys meaning; the cost of relativizing sin is that there is no forgiveness and therefore no cleansing; the cost of worshiping self is that this god is so small we never rise higher than self.

I do not want to be too critical. But insofar as psychology and psychiatry have sold out to philosophical materialism, their understanding of human nature, sin, guilt, needs, salvation, hope, despair, purpose, and a host of other things is bound to be profoundly disappointing. Insofar as these things impinge on the treatment of a particular "patient" or "client," so far also is their counseling likely to be skewed. Moreover, it is not reassuring to read some reports showing that, as a group, psychiatrists themselves ask for psychiatric care more than any other professional group and that the "cure" rates of many psychiatrists treating "patients" regularly over many months or years is not statistically very different from the cure rate of similar "patients" who receive no care.

This is not to say that Christian pastors are necessarily better counselors. They may have their theology straight (or they may not!), but be utterly lacking in people skills or in a real grasp of how sinful patterns of behavior may affect the entire personality. They may be woefully short on experience or in supervised training. Nor are trained Christian psychologists and psychiatrists *necessarily* the best bet. Many of them have taken their psychology at secular institutions where they have gained considerable skills without ever having progressed beyond a Sunday-school grasp of theology. Thus their thinking is shaped by a secular agenda, augmented by a few Biblical proof texts.

For instance, in the current passion to build self-esteem, I do not know how many times I have heard Christian counselors cite our Lord's injunction to love our neighbors as ourselves. From this they immediately conclude that you have to love yourself first, or you cannot love your neighbor. I know what they are getting at. They are not entirely wrong. But I would argue that, first, lack of self-esteem is not the only cause of failure to love one's neighbor and that, in any case, low self-esteem is not what Jesus had in mind.

To explain a little—it is certainly true that self-loathing can contribute to all sorts of psychological and psychosomatic and even pathological disorders. But so strong has been the control of the category "self-esteem" that few counselors think through how much of a problem too *much* self-esteem can be. For the overwhelming majority of people, the reason we do not love our neighbors more does not lie in our failure to love ourselves, but in our indolent *self-love*. And even where there is low self-esteem, from a Christian perspective self-centeredness is almost certainly also involved.

For instance, if a woman has been sexually abused by her father in the past, or if a son grew up in a home where his parents never offered any encouragement and praise, the counselee may well suffer from low self-esteem. But from another perspective, one could say that this counselee has learned how to minimize pain in decidedly self-centered ways. The woman may refuse to face her "shame," or she may protect herself by being unloving and uncaring and ungiving. The young man may either rebel in some grandstand display of independence, or he may compensate for the belittling he suffered by belittling others or by excelling in some restricted field in order to win the approval of his peers—even though when among those who know him best he is filled with resentment and rage. These failures are "sinful" failures. That these particular sinful responses have been elicited by the sins of others does not absolve the counselee of his or her sin, but shows the social and personal implications of these sins. Our sins harm others, not least by leading others into sin. We have not adequately come to terms with the reality that the overwhelming majority of emotional or mental "illnesses" not organically based results from faulty relationships—bad relationships both with God and with other human beings.

For many people, very frequently the best solution is not in building self-esteem per se, but in service, in doing something for others, in giving. For as Jesus has taught, it is in dying that we live, it is in giving that we receive, it is in denying ourselves that we find ourselves. In Jesus' exhortation to love our neighbors as ourselves, He is not commanding us to love ourselves; He is assuming that we do.

Where a person has been brought up in cruel circumstances that have always destroyed self-confidence and jeopardized self-acceptance and feelings of self-worth, I doubt that the standard self-esteem message is the best treatment anyway. The best treatment for such individuals is to introduce them to the Savior who *does* love them, to the joy of being forgiven so that they may learn how to forgive others, to the Biblical worldview that says they are important, to the message of Paul that insists there are *different* gifts, to a warm Christian church where love will be meted out at the practical level, to avenues of Christian service where they learn to do things for others and discover that the teaching of Jesus is true.

(Ed. note: We cannot fail to remark that a recent issue of *Time* magazine, published more than eight years after this letter was written, acknowledged finally that while the mathematical skills of elementary school children in this nation have fallen, their self-assessment, even in mathematics, has risen. Conversely, the mathematical skills of school children in Korea and Japan are much higher, and their self-assessment in this area is much lower. The drum-beat of self-esteem for two or three decades has not produced a saner nation; it has produced a more self-deluded nation.)

Again, having said so much that is negative, I must back off and insist that I have known many counselors who have done an enormous amount of good. I have been grateful to God for competent psychiatrists to whom I have occasionally referred especially difficult cases. The best practical advice I can give is that it is important to find out who is competent to counsel in your area. Such people emerge from many different backgrounds, and the best of them, even while they do much good, are the first to admit that their profession is in considerable disarray and that its pretensions are exaggerated. You are certainly in our prayers, Tim.

As ever,
Paul Woodson

19

Prof. Woodson's reply did not entirely satisfy me. But what I liked about it was the effort to think "Christianly" about a complex issue. During this period I had returned to voracious reading. How I found time for it I'm not sure. But it struck me that it would be worth sounding out Dr. Woodson on two or three other books I had recently devoured.

One of the books that impressed me deeply was Ron Sider's work Rich Christians. At the same time even I could see that one of the most startling developments among evangelicals during the previous four or five years was their massive participation in the political arena—mostly from a stance that was rightist both economically and politically. I asked Dr. Woodson what he made of these polarities within evangelicalism. I am not sure if I agree with all of his response. I have learned that I know so little about economics that I am unfit to judge. But that does not lessen the interest and relevance of his letter.

May 13, 1982

Dear Tim,

One of these days I am going to receive a letter from you asking for a simple bit of information that I can pass on in a line or two. Your letters keep asking me to write books!

Do not misunderstand. I am always happy to hear from you and feel privileged to try to answer your questions. But sometimes when I read what I have written, I feel frustrated that I have said so little on subjects so large and wondered if I have gotten the balance about right to meet you where you are.

The resurgence of the evangelical right into the political arena has certainly been an astonishing phenomenon. It is astonishing, not because evangelicals are doing this (in earlier generations evangelicals were frequently politically active), but because the Fundamentalist wing is leading the way—the very wing that has hitherto been known for its self-distancing from the "world." Needless to say, this political activism infuriates the liberal Left, but the fact of the matter is that Fundamentalists are simply doing what the Left has been doing for decades. The only difference is that the Fundamentalists are now doing it more effectively—partly because their numbers have grown while the numbers of the (organized) liberals have declined, and partly because they are superbly organized.

Note that Jerry Falwell has at least tried to distance his political work from his ecclesiastical work. The Moral Majority is not an evangelical organization. It works, for instance, with Catholics, Jews, and Mormons; at least one Mormon is on its board. Whether the population at large can perceive the distinction is another question.

But your letter focuses on a slightly different question—namely, what we are to make of the polarization within the evangelical camp when it comes to these social issues. (For convenience, I shall assume that the self-designated Fundamentalist wing to which I have referred is part of the evangelical movement.)

Both wings (I shall call them "Left" and "Right") seem more hostage to different strands of societal pressures and less Biblical in their orientation than they think they are. This is true even according to a traditional analysis that recognizes that Christians can be divided into those who embrace culture (either because they hold that every good gift is from God, or because they are seeking to infiltrate it with the gospel) and those who stand against it (because they hold it is essentially evil, and responsible Christian living and evangelism require the erection of alternative Christian priorities in the home, the church, and even the community). The right wing is riding on a crest of national concern about declining values, rising crime, unchecked abortion, broken families, and a perception of international dangers. Almost in reaction to the Viet Nam and Watergate years, millions of Americans want to stand tall and feel proud, and the Moral Majority is certainly fitting into this mood. The religious Right is thus part of the larger "New Right" movement whose numbers are rapidly growing and whose leading intellectuals are showing remarkably robust strength, even if they have so far captured few influential university posts.

But the evangelical Left also reflects rising secular concerns for important causes that are not on the national agenda. The poor and the homeless, the exploited and the abused, the condition of many of our inner cities, the crushing needs of the poor in many "Third World" countries (needs that are increasingly brought into sight and sound—though not smell and pain—in our living rooms), ecological rape—all of these concerns extend far beyond the camp of evangelicals. Indeed, they may in time be reinforced as a kind of reaction to the Reagan years.

I am not for a moment suggesting that any social concern shared by Christian and non-Christian is automatically suspect! Far from it. Biblical Christianity is certainly personal, but Biblical Christianity is never merely private. There are societal implications to what we believe, and we should be prepared to articulate them. I am merely hinting that Christians always need to be careful not to allow themselves to be so tied and allied to larger movements that they are not heard as *Christians,* or, worse, that when the swing of that larger movement loses its momentum, the Christians involved in it will correspondingly lose their vitality, their credibility, or both. More important yet, Christians must never confuse the periphery with the center. If they make even valid societal involvement the *center* of their beliefs and preaching and writing, it will not be long before the reformation of society becomes *more important in practice* (if not in theory) than knowing God. From a Biblical perspective, knowing God must take first place, and then the implications of this knowledge of God must be worked out in every sphere of life.

But judging by your letter, you want me to focus more narrowly yet. You want me to say something about "Left" and "Right" economic views as espoused by Christians. I am no expert, but I'll venture a few lines. You must take these for what they are, the rambling reflections of an aging theologian (only three years from retirement—though mercifully the administration here at TEDS allows us to continue beyond retirement age on a year-by-year basis!) struggling to keep abreast of a rapidly changing world while not losing essential Biblical moorings.

On the one hand, then, it is desperately important that Western Christians learn to be less tied to material goods. I suppose that one important dividing line is what we think is essential. I can remember when televisions were first introduced. Today, for most families a color TV is essential, and there may be many TVs in each household, virtually one for every room. VCRs are just coming in—in a few years each member of the family will have his own. I expect microwaves are already on the way to becoming essential; so are tele-phone answering machines.

Some of this is inevitable in any society with a rising standard of living. There is nothing in the gospel that demands we live without, say, telephones, which in their day were as innovative as the microwave, more innovative than the VCR.

The real question is where our heart is. When we receive an increase in wages, is the first thing we think about how much more we shall be able to give to the Lord's work? Is assuming we shall give 10 percent of this increase to the church the best we can do, when we could easily afford much more? I believe it was John Trapp who said, "They are fools that fear to lose their wealth by giving it, but fear not to lose themselves by keeping it."

One of my students at the seminary has come here from a major executive post in an investment firm. He told me (and the students in my "advisee group") of his experiences studying for his MBA at Harvard. As you may know, the business school at Harvard relies exclusively on the case-study method to build business skills. The motive is always the bottom line. It is considered corny or weak to ask if there is an alternative to shutting down the plant and putting hundreds out of work or to question an expensive ad campaign based on snob appeal in order to sell a slow-moving deodorant.

We can live more simply and still not be social misfits. My brother and his wife sharply curtailed the amount of television their children watched as they were growing up; for years at a time they did with-out a TV. But they took the children to a library almost every week and read to them (and later read with them) to stimulate their imag-ination and thought. If the children sometimes felt deprived because they did not have everything their friends had, my brother and sis-ter-in-law tried to expose them to friends working and serving in the "Third World" so that the children would recognize how many things they take for granted. My niece was transformed by the expe-rience of working one summer with a youth group building rudi-mentary housing in Haiti. I am certainly not saying my brother and his wife got the balance right in their family. Doubtless they failed at many levels, and I sometimes think, now that their children are mar-ried and raising children of their own, that my brother and sister-in-law were far too protective and at other times too hard on the children. But I am *quite certain* that principles of generous giving, self-denial, and a certain freedom from preoccupation with material things must not only be taught but *demonstrated* in the home.

But there are some stentorian voices on the left that want to say more than this. They want to make the word of Jesus in, say, Luke 18:22 ("Sell everything you have and give to the poor, and you will have treasure in heaven") as much the definition of who is and who is not a Christian as, say, John 3:5 ("I tell you the truth, unless a man is born of water and the Spirit, he cannot enter the kingdom of God"). Would it be uncharitable of me to observe that some "Third World" evangelicals who expound this thesis at great length seem to live in considerable luxury? But my real problem is a methodological one. How do the bits of Jesus' teaching fit together? Should we assume, for example, that those who have homes or who attend the funerals of their parents instead of preaching the gospel cannot possibly be followers of Jesus (Luke 9:57-60)? Are we really relativizing Jesus' words when we suggest that this seems to be a rather narrow principle of exclusion?

Had I time, I would be prepared to argue that Jesus habitually goes for the jugular. If a would-be disciple's real priority is his family, Jesus insists that those who follow Him must abandon their families; if it is money, they must sell all they have; if it is the security of a home, they must be prepared for an itinerant life. The remarkable flexibility the Lord Jesus displays in His handling of people confirms this approach. The conclusion to be drawn, surely, is this: Whatever functions as a "god" in my life, capturing my thoughts, my imagination, my goals, my priorities, and thus displacing Jesus from His rightful place, should be destroyed.

Incidentally, materialism as a sin is not restricted to those who possess relatively many things. When I have lectured in India, Japan, and parts of Africa, I have always been struck by the driving concern of many people at every tier of the socio-economic ladder to gain more money, to buy things and gain influence, to select jobs and friends and patrons and even (God help us!) forms of Christian service exclusively on a financial basis. It is the love of money that is a root of all kinds of evil, and I have not found that to be an exclusively American sin

One common device many activists use, both Christian and non-Christian, is to encourage poorer people to feel they *ought* to have as much money as some other group or individual. The French have a word for this: *ressentiment*. The "resentment" or "animus" or "envy" that results is surely not a Christian virtue. Where is the Biblical insistence that if we have food and clothing, we ought to learn to be content? Is not covetousness a sin? What right do we have always to compare ourselves with those who have more? Or to encourage others to do the same? Why do we so rarely compare ourselves with those who have less?

Where I have the most difficulty with many of my Christian friends on the Left is in their proposed solutions to problems of poverty, as if all kinds of poverty were caused by the same thing and were amenable to the same treatment. The majority of them, I fear, espouse leftist economic policies—tax more, give the state more power, in particular the power to distribute wealth through a variety of welfare programs. They self-consciously reject both Marxism and capitalism, and they espouse what they judge to be a third way, a Christian way (indeed, *Third Way* is the name of an influential Christian periodical in England; perhaps you came across it while you were there). Often this "third way," where it is not simply *against* things, turns out to be a fairly rigorous form of socialist government. Besides, many of the worst extremes of poverty in the world are tied to war, famine (itself sometimes the result in part of irresponsible government manipulation of agricultural policy), oppression, and graft. Why is it that _____ (Ed. note: a certain West African country, best left unnamed owing to Woodson's ties there) exports an enormous amount of copper, and virtually none of the profit benefits anyone except a handful of embarrassingly rich citizens? And what shall we say for parts of the world where corruption is endemic and where the underlying philosophical substratum militates against self-improvement, crushing it by an astonishing fatalism?

Certainly the simple alternative models of capitalism and communism squeeze us into decisions of doubtful worth. A large and growing quantity of evidence demonstrates that socialist control on the long haul kills incentive, reduces initiative and efficiency, increases a sense of dependence, multiplies bureaucracy, and frequently fosters corruption, thereby making nations unable to compete in the marketplace and driving them into debt; yet the worst problem is philosophical. I agree with those writers who have argued that capitalism and Marxism are not equivalent (though mutually contradictory) ideologies. Marxism is an ideology, indeed, in one sense, a religion. It has its god (Lenin), its eschatology (the perfection of the Communist state with its "new man"), its priesthood (the leaders of the Communist Party), and so forth. It embraces all of life. Theoretically, it excludes other faiths. It is philosophically atheistic, and so eliminates Christians, Muslims, and other people with religious convictions. In practice, some faith may be tolerated within the

Party, but only if it is entirely subservient to Party strictures—this god brooks no rivals. The Communist state must be totalitarian.

By contrast, capitalism is in theory compatible with totalitarianism and with democracy in its various forms. There can be Christian capitalists, Muslim capitalists, Jewish capitalists, etc. Of course, capitalism can embrace all sorts of nasty overtones of greed, brutal exploitation, or enslavement. But at the theoretical level, capitalism is not an ideology, still less a religion. It is nothing more than the observation that at the end of the day a "free" marketplace is where wealth is created.

Taken this way, capitalism does not find its most appropriate analogy in any ideology, but in the law of gravity. You may temporarily defy it if you expend enough energy (as when you fly from New York to London), but sooner or later gravity will triumph. If that is correct, then one should not fight the marketplace, but seek to pass and enforce laws that curb the abuses evil people will introduce into the system (and which ultimately corrupt the "freedom" of the free market). There must be fair competition; antitrust legislation is essential. There must be integrity; kickbacks and bribes must be exposed and punished. There must be fair and honest advertising; deceit is itself wrong, and the shoddy goods cheat the customer. Industry must consider worker safety, ecological security, and fair pay for honest work. It is not hard to think of many more possibilities. But if the legislation becomes so cumbersome as to destroy the freedom and incentives of the market, some other nation or group of workers will take over that sector of the economy—unless equally cumbersome tariffs and trade barriers are erected. But if that is done (not to punish those who abuse freedom by "dumping" but to protect inefficient industries capable of delivering nothing better than votes), the result is still more distortion which, on the long haul, will destroy the economic vitality of the nation.

If this reasoning is correct, then the Christian should be at the forefront of espousing a free market (since the alternative, rising levels of poverty, produces more and more evils). But also the Christian should ask what curbs need to be administered to ensure justice, equity, fairness, and integrity. I do not think that many evangelicals from either the Right or the Left have worked on the problem along these lines. No government can long spend much money to confront social ills if the economy it is managing is shrinking. And if too much of what it spends to repair social ills has the undesirable effect of shrinking the economy, then ultimately it may be the poor and forsaken who get hurt the most. I really do not know where to draw all the lines here.

But even more strongly, I would insist that Christians should convince their fellow citizens (and themselves) that material well-being is not the most important thing in life and should not become an end in itself. For where it becomes the most important thing, it has become a god, an idol. The terrible toll on the family, personal integrity, and use of time becomes simply devastating. I am not sure how long a society that loses a consensus as to moral priorities can maintain the freedom the market needs to operate productively.

Above all, it is essential to maintain Biblical priorities. America's loss of place as a first-rate economic power would not be as great a tragedy as a decline in the numbers of its citizens who know and love God and seek His face in worship and prayer. Given America's cultural heritage, however, the two may be tied more tightly than some think. It is doubtful that we will find our cohesion in anything less than Biblical Christianity (unlike, say, Japan)—which means that America is set either for genuine revival and reformation under the gracious hand of God or for long-term (and perhaps catastrophic?) decline.

Despite this possible link, I would still say it is utterly vital for Christians to remember that their citizenship in the new heaven and new earth has far greater importance and must have far greater priority than their citizenship in the United States of America (or of any other country). Spiritual renewal cannot be sought on the pragmatic grounds that it might bring economic benefit. We are to seek God and His righteousness whether such pursuit issues in a stable and relatively just society, or in penury and persecution. As important as the issues you raise are, they are not of *ultimate* importance.

With eternity's values in view,

Your fellow servant,
Paul Woodson

20

*D*r. Woodson's comments about capitalism and socialism, wealth and materialism, as related to the Christian faith, struck an unfamiliar chord in my own thinking. Until I read Sider's book, followed by Woodson's letter, I had never really thought about these matters in any other than secular terms. A few courses in political theory at Princeton had prompted some reflection on the role of "things," but generally the discussion was pursued in terms of how states competed with each other economically. With my job in New York City, however, I began to be much more concerned about personal ethics. As I mentioned before, I was earning a fair amount of change, still remained single, and found myself purchasing things I had never even contemplated buying during my Spartan days as a student. A few pangs of guilt crowded into my consciousness. As a Christian did I really have to consider whether my income should be spent in one way rather than another? That was a new question.

One day while browsing through a bookstore not too far from the office building in Manhattan where I worked, I stumbled upon a volume by Daniel Yankelovich entitled New Rules: Searching for Self-Fulfillment in a World Turned Upside-Down. The title grabbed me. I bought the book along with a couple of Sherlock Holmes mysteries I had never encountered before.

Yankelovich's study turned out to be a real page-turner. He argued that in the 1950s and 1960s most middle class Americans still followed a "duty-to-others" motif. That is, society told fathers that they were successful if they worked hard and provided a good home for the family. That description fit my own dad to the tee. Society told mothers they were successful if they worked hard to raise well-adjusted children by providing them with a caring home life. That description fit my mom as well. Despite all the clatter and fireworks of the '60s, a competing "duty-to-self" motif had been basically quarantined to the youth culture, the women's liberation movement, and various cause groups.

But then in the early 1970s a sea-change in values for the middle class occurred. According to Yankelovich, 17 percent of the American population opted to make a virtue of following a "self-fulfillment" or "duty-to-self" ethic. They almost felt obliged to "swing." At the other end of the spectrum, 20 percent of the population held on to the duty-to-others motif. In between ranged 63 percent of Americans who moved back and forth in their ethical decisions using the duty-to-self criterion for some decisions and the duty-to-others criterion in other circumstances. The pollster believed that he could explain changing attitudes of Americans towards divorce (the rising divorce rate), the status of the single woman (more societal acceptance for the single woman), a liberalizing tendency in sexual attitudes (less condemnation of premarital sex, for example), a new evaluation of work (if a job does not satisfy me, I will find one that does), and other changes in social patterns by relating it to Americans' search for "self-fulfillment in a world turned upside-down." If Americans did not feel that a job, or family life, or a person brought self-fulfillment, many would abandon the alleged "encumbrance" in the quest for something that would.

I was struck by this analysis. Even though Yankelovich did not couch his appraisal in Christian categories, he made sense of what I had experienced as a child and what I was feeling as a young single in New York. To be sure, I was a committed Christian, but the tug of doing what I wanted to do without reference to the welfare of others was strong. Perhaps I was seeking self-fulfillment more as an overarching end than I had ever admitted to myself, despite Christ's teaching that we should love our neighbors as ourselves.

Should the concept of self-fulfillment play any role in the life of a disciple of Christ? I vaguely remembered something I had memorized as a Presbyterian kid, paraphrased loosely as, "Man's chief end is to love God and to enjoy Him forever." I had no idea how that thought fit with my own yuppie tastes.

In any case, I wrote to Dr. Woodson about the insights I had garnered from Daniel Yankelovich's book. My letter was larded with statistics and my own pop sociological perspectives. I wanted Dr. Woodson to benefit from what seemed to me a landmark assessment of American culture. The book was so new I rather doubted that he had read it. Fortunately, as it turned out, Prof. Woodson was unaware of the book's existence. This gave me a *sense of satisfaction. It was rather nice to be on the giving end of our epistolary conversations.*

June 14, 1982

Dear Tim,

Thank you for your letter. I am responding to it immediately. Why? Quite frankly I was bedazzled by its richness of detail and insight. Yankelovich's study appears to be one of those signally important books that crosses our intellectual horizons on occasion. I have not, however, read it myself. But your enthusiasm for it and your relation of its contents create strong commendations for the book. I will try to pick it up sometime in the near future.

Yankelovich's description of the 1960s and 1970s seems to mesh with what I witnessed during those decades. During the '60s I encountered large numbers of people who did not seem much enamored with the so-called youth culture in which an ethic of doing your own thing seemed to sprout like a wildflower. A movie book I have read for sermon illustrations offers a good example. In the film *Wild Angels* (1966), directed by Roger Corman, Heavenly Blues bemoaned the death of one of his fellow bikers, "Life never let him alone to do what he wanted to do; [everybody] wanted him to be good." Heavenly Blues explained what made the gang of bikers act the way they did: "We don't want nobody telling us what to do. We don't want nobody pushing us around. We want to be free. Free to ride without being hassled by the man; we want to . . . have a good time." Resistance in the name of freedom to a fixed ethic of Judaism and Christianity based on the revealed Word of God marked major segments of the youth culture. A generation gap loomed large between the older and younger generations.

But by the 1970s, more and more middle class Americans were looking out for Number One rather than for the welfare of their spouses or their children. I witnessed this in numerous counseling sessions. A tidal wave of messages in society sold the motif of self-fulfillment. The statistics Yankelovich sets forth appear irrefutable and are amply sustained in my meager experience.

What staggers me personally is the ultimate simplicity of Yankelovich's analysis. I think I mentioned in an earlier letter my perception of the difference between the conservative '50s and the current conservatism. Yankelovich provides much more insight and solid evidence. In hindsight, what he describes seems to be accurate. What I cannot figure out is why I did not sense the scope of this social revolution when it was taking place. Perhaps I was benumbed by reading all the books that fell off the presses about the evangelical resurgence of the '70s: Donald Bloesch's *The Evangelical Renaissance,* the work *The Evangelicals,* edited by my own colleagues at Trinity, David Wells and John Woodbridge. Heady feelings spun through evangelical circles when the media designated 1976 as "The Year of the Evangelical." How intoxicating! But I suspect I have underestimated how badly the general culture and even some of the Christian folks I worked with were being hit by self-fulfillment propaganda. Evangelicalism was prospering in one sense but getting broadsided ethically in another.

What I am saying is that your letter has prompted immediate reactions that I have not had the time to sort out. Yankelovich may be affording us with at least one key for understanding why the evangelical movement with its vast personnel and financial resources seems such a tame pussy cat. It may be that the evangelical community was subverted by the self-fulfillment motif in the same time frame it gained media attention. Now George Gallup, Jr., is discovering that evangelicals often do not live any differently than non-Christians. A common commitment to an unharnessed self-fulfillment motif may explain why. Perhaps *worldliness* (that old Fundamentalist word) has been swamping the evangelical boat, and we who teach at seminaries did not know that the ship was foundering so badly.

I am so pleased that you brought my attention to the book. I fear that at times my own interests in theology keep me from learning about books that could enhance my understanding of the wider world. I am in your debt for opening my old mind a bit wider about what is going on in the lives of my fellow pilgrims.

As to your personal concerns about whether you are becoming materialistic, I think the fact that you even raised the issue is a good sign. The issue has never passed through the minds of many Christians, even for a split second. Is it not interesting that your sensitivities in this area were heightened by reading a secular book?

Please write and tell me what your thinking is concerning your own personal interaction with "things." I am convinced that our attitude towards "things" is one of the better indices of what the nature of our Christianity actually is—over against what we say it is.

Cordially,
Paul Woodson

21

I *had turned at least a minor corner regarding the yuppie lifestyle*
I had been pursuing in New York City. The things I had pur-
chased I did not discard, but at least I was tithing, saving more, and
finding quiet opportunities to give some of that money away. By the
autumn of 1982 I was leading two Bible studies, one of them evan-
gelistic, speaking occasionally at various youth meetings, enjoying
my own reading of Scripture, and learning a little better how to
pray. The pastor of my church asked me if I had ever prayed about
going into the ministry. I had thought about it from time to time,
but had never prayed about it. But now, as I saw the Word of God
genuinely transforming the lives of a few people in my Bible study
groups, I easily believed that the most important work anyone could
do would be to introduce people to Jesus Christ and help them to
know Him better.

Without telling Dr. Woodson that I was now thinking seriously
about entering the ministry (though he must surely have guessed
what lay behind my question), I asked him what, in his view, lay at
the heart of good pastoral ministry, what went into the shaping of a
good pastor.

November 15, 1982

Dear Tim,

I know quite a few pastors who have been in the ministry for
twenty years who would like an answer to your question. The difficulty in answering turns in part on the need to justify the criteria used
to assess "good pastoral ministry" or what it means to be a "good
pastor." I am sure you do not mean to say "successful pastor," at
least as "successful" ministries are often portrayed—rising numbers,

an excellent public face, a building program, and so forth. Yet signs of growth are not intrinsically bad! Even so, in the same breath I want to insist that some "good pastors" may be called to discharge their ministries in small, difficult contexts where they serve with great integrity and spiritual wisdom for years, but without much observable fruit. In some cases, they become the sowers; the harvesters will come along after they have gone.

These brute realities make me want to erect criteria for "good ministry" that are relatively free from outward signs of "success."

Quite apart from success is the challenge of thinking through the relationship between Biblical priorities and current pastoral practices. The modern pastor in America is expected to be a preacher, counselor, administrator, PR guru, fund-raiser and hand-holder. Depending on the size of the church he serves, he may have to be an expert on youth, competent on a Gestetner, something of an accountant, janitor, evangelist, small groups expert, an excellent chair of committees, a team player, and a transparent leader. Of course, his own home must be exemplary, and he should never appear tired or discouraged, since he must always be spiritual, prayerful, warm-hearted, and passionate but unflappable. He should spend no fewer than forty hours a week in sermon preparation, no fewer than thirty or forty hours in counseling, at least twenty hours in regular visitation of his flock, another fifteen in door-to-door evangelism, at least twenty in administration, another ten in hospital calling, a further ten to forty (depending on the area) in ministry to the poor and deprived—leaving about fifty for miscellaneous matters (especially being available if anyone wants to see him at any time of the day or night). And then a neighbor will ask his wife, "Excuse me, I don't mean to be rude, but I'd really like to know: What does your husband do the rest of the week, apart from, you know, his work on Sundays?"

The truth is, no matter how hard a pastor tries to maintain Biblical priorities in the ministry, he will butt up against the expectations of the people he serves—especially when he first goes to a church. But granted these realities, I would still say he must establish certain priorities and work to see himself and his ministry in their light.

So much pastoral energy focuses these days on the relatively peripheral that very little is preserved for the center. We need to *trust* Christ, to *believe* that the gospel is the power of God for salvation for everyone who believes. There is instead an inordinate dependence on means, technique, organization, manuals.

The first thing to observe about the New Testament passages on pastoral ministry is the unexceptional character of most of the qualifications (read 1 Timothy 3:1-7; 5:20-22; 6:11-12; Titus 1:5-9; 1 Peter 5:1-4). Several of the lists are remarkable for being unremarkable—one must not be a drunk, must have a good reputation, and so forth. This suggests that the criteria sometimes raised today—superior intelligence, a charismatic personality, and so forth—receive no emphasis in Scripture.

Indeed, the prime characteristic for the spiritual leader is consistent integrity, both in his grasp of the faith and in the conduct of his own life. That is the burden of, say, 1 Timothy 3:1-11, taken as a whole. Looking at the first seven verses regarding the qualifications of the "overseer" or "bishop," we find such entries as "temperate" (that is, clear-headed, self-possessed, not an extremist), "self-controlled" and "respectable" (perhaps too bourgeois a translation; the idea is "well-behaved," almost "dignified"—though that might sound a trifle pompous). In short, he is to lead an ordered life. Both "hospitable" and "able to teach" are bound up with the task itself—expanding Christian witness and edifying and instructing Christian believers. If he is not to be a lover of money or given to much wine, it is in large part because the slave of Jesus Christ must not be a slave of anything or anyone else. Although he must contend for the faith (Jude 3), he must not be contentious—ready to fight and apt to enjoy it (contrast 2 Timothy 2:23-26).

I need not go through each entry on the list. You get the idea. Elsewhere we learn of the importance of avoiding favoritism (1 Timothy 5:21), of preserving all godly virtues (1 Timothy 6:11-12), of expecting serious difficulties and challenges, and proving consistent and persistent in facing them (2 Timothy 2:3-7, 15; 3:10-15; 4:5). In short, God looks for character and spiritual maturity rather than natural ability. Thus the pastor is not qualitatively different from other Christians. The virtues that are to characterize him are elsewhere mandated of all believers. But because he is to be a leader of the people of God, a shepherd of God's flock under the Chief Shepherd, Jesus Christ, he must set an example and a direction by the quality of his own life (1 Peter 5:1-4).

The one distinctive characteristic of an elder, overseer, pastor (in my view, these three terms refer in the New Testament to one office or role) is that he be able to teach. That includes at least three elements—knowledge of the truth and of God Himself, an ability to articulate that truth in teaching others with wisdom and discernment, and transparent modeling.

This last point deserves a little expansion. There is considerable stress in the pastoral epistles and elsewhere on the importance of observable growth in both doctrine and life (1 Timothy 4:14-16; 1 Peter 5:1-4). Spiritual leadership is a balanced combination of example and oversight. Where leadership depends on insisting on the authority of the office, spiritual credibility and authority soon vanish, except among the cultic followers. Where leadership turns on self-denying, Christ-honoring modeling of the Christian life and way, it is astonishing how much moral authority begins to accrue to the leader. On the other hand, where there is modeling but no verbal instruction, the attachment is to the pastor, but not to the Word of God. The modeling can then become a form of enslavement. In short, the pastor must say with Paul both, "Follow my example, as I follow the example of Christ" (1 Corinthians 11:1) and, "I have not hesitated to proclaim to you the whole will of God" (Acts 20:27).

So far, I have written mostly about character and priorities. But discussion of priorities brings us to the actual *task* of any pastoral work worthy of the name—the ministry of the Word and prayer. That means long hours of study, meditation, reflection on the meaning of the Word and its application, and it requires sustained periods of praise and intercession before God on behalf of the people God calls one to serve.

Everything else ought to flow out of these priorities. For instance, administration is doubtless important, especially in a growing work; but it must never become an end in itself or merely a copy of the latest secular management seminars. Some churches I know of are so smoothly organized that the Spirit could get up and leave and no one would know He had gone—at least, not for a while. I am certainly not advocating *poor* administration. There are of course all kinds of important skills to be learned in this area, especially (as I have said) in a large or growing work. But administration ought to bear in mind the glory of God as the ultimate goal and the edification of God's people, not the manipulation of people for institutional purposes. Administration ought to serve the ministry of the Word and prayer at every level in the congregation—house groups, youth groups, etc., all the way up to large corporate meetings. Similarly, all kinds of "people skills" are necessary, and doubtless some of these can be taught. But, foundationally, these are the outflow of the fruit of the Spirit (Galatians 5:22-26) in the believer's life rather than the result of a Dale Carnegie course.

Above all, if the Biblical priorities are preserved, pastors will constantly monitor their own use of time, lest the important be sacrificed on the altar of the urgent. There are always more people to counsel, more letters to write, more people to visit, more abused people to help. But if these excellent activities become so all-consuming that the pastor is not genuinely giving himself to the ministry of the Word and to prayer, he has forsaken his calling, jeopardized Biblical priorities and, in the long haul, diminished both his obedience and his effectiveness. Whatever place all of these forms of service have in any pastor's life (and the proportion will certainly vary with the circumstances), the fundamental priorities must never be compromised. Similarly in a multi-staff church, whatever "specialization" obtains, the New Testament pastor must be profoundly committed to prayer and to the ministry of the Word (and the latter is not restricted to preaching!).

To put the matter another way, if our aim, with Paul, is by all possible means to win some to Christ (read 1 Corinthians 9:19ff.), if our goal is to build up the Body of Christ, and if the primary means are the ministry of the Word and prayer, then everything we undertake, all of our structures and organizations and copiers and buildings and committees and what have you, must bend toward such ends. The pastoral ministry keeps such ends in view and through the Word and prayer seeks to prepare men and women for eternity.

There is no one style of ministry that is productive and no one type of personality that represents good pastoral ministry. The sheer diversity of personality types among ministers is surely a sign that any particular personality type has little to do with the building of the Church. But the pastors whose ministries I particularly applaud (whether successful in the eyes of the world or not) are those whose love for the Lord Jesus is transparent and growing, whose ability to expound the Scriptures with devotion, clarity, practical application, and real unction is increasing, and whose love for people is not artificial or sentimental but self-denying and perceptive (this is essential to what is often called "pastoral care"), and whose desire to proclaim the gospel and work out its implications dictates the focus and priorities of their lives.

And who is sufficient for these things?

Warmly,
Paul Woodson

P.S. You could with profit read Richard Baxter's *The Reformed Pastor* (at the time it was written the title meant something like "The Renewed Pastor"). In many respects it is now terribly dated. But it has the priorities about right.

22

*D*r. Woodson's next letter so clearly picks up on what I wrote to him around Christmas that the context is self-explanatory.

January 12, 1983

My dear Tim,

How delighted I am to hear of your growing relationship with Ginny (is her real name Virginia?). She sounds like a lovely young woman. Her musical gifts and training must be exceptional if she is working on her Master's degree at Columbia. What a wonderful gift from the Lord to have found a mature and wonderfully stable Christian like Ginny. When will my wife and I have the opportunity to meet this young lady?

I am no less delighted to hear of your reading. Yes, Packer's *Knowing God* is a book to be read and re-read. If the Lord does not return for a hundred years, it will prove to be one of the few from this century still read by Christians in the next. And I'm glad that you have worked your way through Baxter's *The Reformed Pastor*.

Friesen's work on knowing God's will is of course bound up in your mind with your present wrestling over whether you yourself are called to pastoral ministry. The question of determining God's will in such matters is difficult. Friesen represents a needed response to one extreme. Most of the Biblical passages that deal with the will of God focus on holiness, living in harmony with one's family, obeying God and the like. The kind of determining of God's will that utterly depends on voices, internal promptings, "burdens," and the like can indeed prove far too subjective, especially when such experiences are invested with an authority that challenges the criteria of Scripture or the consensus wisdom of mature, spiritually minded Christians.

Equally suspicious is the "bull's-eye" view of the will of God—as if God's will were a series of concentric circles with increasing values as one approaches the center. In this view, one can easily find God's "second best" and "third best," but zealous Christians will strive for the very best, the bull's eye of the will of God. This, too, needs to be debunked and demystified (though I am not sure that Friesen has adequately probed the diversity of ways in which the Bible can speak about the will of God).

So you wonder if you are called to the ministry. Where shall I begin (without writing another book for you!)?

At one level, I must say how pleased I am that you are struggling with these things. A number of years ago I read a book with the title *Give Up Your Small Ambitions*. I sense that you have grown into the maturity that recognizes monetary gain and social advancement as ephemeral advantages at best, and at worst as traps that sidetrack Christians from the prior goal of laying up treasure in heaven. But such growing maturity does not itself constitute a "call." Indeed, in once sense, I think I should now erect a few hurdles and tell you the reasons why you should not enter vocational ministry. I shall explain why in just a moment. (Incidentally, by "vocational" ministry I mean nothing more than financially supported ministry—see 1 Corinthians 9:3ff.; Galatians 6:6; 2 Timothy 2:2-4.)

First, it might be helpful to survey a few passages of Scripture to observe some of the diversity of the evidence. This list is by no means exhaustive; many more things need to be said. But this will at least start you off.

There is the conversion and call of Saul/Paul (Acts 9 and parallels). Here there was no prior sowing of seed (at least, not in an open or friendly environment!). By supernatural and unique self-disclosure, the resurrected and exalted Christ appeared to Paul on the Damascus road while he was engaged in persecuting the church. Paul's conversion and his call to apostleship were part of the same experience—he himself cannot separate them (e.g., 1 Corinthians 9:15-18).

In Acts 13:2-3 the Holy Spirit tells (presumably through one of the prophets) the church in Antioch (or at least its prophets and teachers) to set apart Barnabas and Saul for the initial organized church-planting evangelistic expedition that is reported in Acts 13-14.

In 1 Timothy 3:1ff., Paul writes that if anyone "sets his heart on being an overseer, he desires a noble task." Paul then lists the qualifications that must be met. This list of qualifications, clearly, can exclude someone who "desires" to serve in this way. At the same time, observe that here, on the human plane, the initial impetus comes from within the would-be candidate. I shall return to that in a moment.

Quite different is the emphasis in 2 Timothy 2:2: "And the things you have heard me say in the presence of many witnesses entrust to reliable men who will also be qualified to teach others." The implication, I think, is that Timothy has a responsibility to seek out "reliable men" so that the propagation of the gospel may continue. There is further evidence of initiative "from the top" of a slightly different nature in Titus 1:5: "The reason I left you in Crete was that you might straighten out what was left unfinished and appoint elders in every town, as I directed you." Qualifications are then listed.

In James 3:1 is somber warning, "Not many of you should presume to be teachers, my brothers, because you know that we who teach will be judged more strictly." Thus although all Christians are to be involved in mutual admonition, exhortation, and fellowship, relatively few are to assume the role of recognized teachers in the church, and this with the full recognition that their task has its perils.

Moreover, in any full-orbed discussion of call, we ought to wrestle with Ephesians 4:11 in its context. It is God Himself, Paul insists, who gives certain people as apostles, prophets, evangelists, and pastors and teachers to the church. This no more ensures perfect conformity to God's will among the appointees than the appointment of an individual to the throne of David ensured his godliness and faithful obedience to the God who had appointed him. But it ought to make us wary about so institutionalizing the notion of "call" that it becomes safe, domesticated, merely ecclesiastical.

A certain amount of reductionism characterizes the contemporary debate about the call of God to vocational pastoral ministry. Those of more charismatic or pietistic background may emphasize a certain subjective sense that God has called them to ministry and given them no choice. They see themselves like Jeremiah—even when he wanted to be silent, the Word of God burned in him, and he could not hold his peace. But in some instances people claim just such experiences even though churches and church leaders are unanimous in withholding any attesting approval. Others begin with, say, the great commission and argue that this commission is sufficient call for anyone. "You *ought* to get out there and serve to the best of your ability, and that certainly includes vocational ministry unless the door is positively closed to you." Other patterns are pretty common.

For myself, I do not think there is a single pattern in Scripture. Ideally, the three major threads should combine—a burning desire to serve in this way (1 Timothy 3:1), the approbation (and sometimes the initiative) of well-informed leaders, and the satisfaction of the Biblical criteria.

What has made the discussion difficult, I think, is that on the one hand the adherents of the charismatic traditions and some (other) pietistic groups have greatly stressed the subjective sense of God's call, often to the exclusion of other factors. Almost by way of reaction, many in the noncharismatic traditions have detected in this stance a form of revelation that jeopardizes the authority and finality of Scripture and have therefore espoused a kind of rationalism that leaves spiritual experience entirely out of it. I am personally uncomfortable with both approaches.

If we reflect on the desire to be an overseer, to which Paul alludes in 1 Timothy 3:1, it is hard to imagine that what Paul has in mind is simply a self-confident desire to seek a certain job. He thinks, rather, of Spirit-prompted desires to serve Christ in a certain way—desires that must nevertheless be tested in a variety of ways, in this instance by meeting certain criteria as a first hurdle.

I would go further and say that there is likely to be quite a bit of difference in the sense of call from person to person. We must not too rigidly institutionalize our own particular experience. But if there is *no* sense of burning compulsion to serve Christ in this particular way, one begins to wonder how much of the "desire" is nothing more than a kind of lust for ecclesiastical importance. Indeed, if I had time, I would try to tie this sense of compulsion to larger New Testament themes that deal with spiritual experience.

When denominational leaders complain (as they frequently do nowadays) that too few would-be pastors are coming forth with a sense of call, it is important to understand what they mean. Admittedly, some simply come out of a fairly mystical school, and it is less than clear what they mean. Perhaps in their own spiritual pilgrimage this has been one of the most looming features of their own pursuit of pastoral ministry. But in my experience, what they often mean is something like this: They ask some prospective candidate why he wants to serve the Lord in this way, and the answer comes back with a rather unfocused, "Well, I really enjoy leading Bible studies, and I think I'd like to serve Jesus this way"; or, "Several people have been telling me that I ought to consider pastoral ministry, and because they are respected leaders I think I ought to take their views seriously"; or half a dozen other variations. Where is their own passion? Where is their desire? Where is their sense of compulsion? If candidates introduce early into the conversation retirement benefits, housing allowances, and severe strictures on where they are willing to serve, they should be gently funneled into computer science or sanitary engineering or something. Whatever you call it, whatever the variations in human personality, there must be a servant heart, a single-eyed devotion to Christ that wholeheartedly desires to serve Jesus the Lord and His church in this way.

That is the framework out of which, at this point, I want to discourage you from pursuing this matter any farther! At very least, examine your own heart, your motives, very carefully. Very few ministers serve large, thriving churches. If that is your vision of what is ahead, discount it. God may open up such formidable doors of opportunity; but you cannot count on it, and it must form no part of your decision. The overwhelming majority of pastors serve relatively small and unprepossessing churches. Many of them are called on to do what no amount of money could ever reimburse them for— officiating at the funeral of a town drunk whose intoxicated live-in girlfriend mutters and shrieks throughout the sparsely attended funeral service; burying a child dead of cancer at the age of nine months; presiding over a church broken up by angry and powerful members who show nothing of forbearance or grace (or even good sense). Out of the heat of these and countless other impossibly difficult circumstances, a heart for ministry (in the old sense of that word) is confirmed.

Read through Paul's epistles rather rapidly in three or four sittings and observe that it was his relations with Christians that gave him the greatest pain. Should you end up in vocational ministry, your experience will not be any different. By all means, talk to the leaders of your church and work through the Biblical passages on elders, pastors, and overseers; but above all, seek the Lord's face in prayer. You need not demand a kind of Damascus-road experience—few enjoy so immediate an experience of call. But if you know nothing of Spirit-prompted compulsion and a servant heart that has, as far as you know, counted the cost, I beg of you to relinquish all aspirations to pastoral ministry.

What does Ginny think of all this?

In the love of Christ,
Paul Woodson

23

*O*nce again Dr. Woodson's letter seemed a little overbearing. Nonetheless I was greatly interested in his description of the ministry and his warning about the demands it can place on an individual. But I must confess his last comments were ones that really jolted me. He actually begged me to "relinquish all aspirations to pastoral ministry" if I knew nothing of "Spirit-prompted compulsion and a servant heart." During the month or so after I received his letter, I pondered its contents. Moreover I experienced a few dark nights of the soul in which I tried to examine my own motivations. I was not certain I even knew what Dr. Woodson was talking about in portions of his letter. And the thought that people might feel they owned me body and soul, not least my time, gave me the shudders. With an attitude like this, could I really have a servant heart?

And yet I thought to myself, what harm would it do if I at least explored the matter of pastoral ministry further? Ginny agreed that this was not a bad idea, although she would not comment much on what she knew had been my deep bouts of soul-searching. Not that she was uninterested in my perplexity and dark thoughts. Just the contrary. But in large measure she kept her opinions to herself. I learned later that she had determined that the matter was a deeply personal one—between God and me. I needed to heed what I thought was God's will for my life. As it turned out, she was hoping all the while I would become a minister.

I concluded that I should at least ask Dr. Woodson for advice concerning the enigmatic issue of how to pick a seminary. I had no idea what the differences were between them, if any. I couched my inquiry in rather vague terms so that he would not pick up on the fact that I was really interested in his response. I feared that if I gave him any indication of the depth of my preoccupation with the subject, he might attempt to pressure me, albeit subtly, towards the pastorate.

Pressure in any form was the last thing that I wanted at this vulnerable time.

I finally wrote in a fairly off-hand manner and asked how he would go about selecting a seminary if he had to do it all over again. To divert his attention somewhat, I made passing comments about the perennial capacity of the Chicago Cubs to swoon late in the season—citing the 1969 Cubs as a prime illustration. I recalled the glory of my marvelous Mets' triumph over the faltering Cubbies. I guessed Dr. Woodson had become a devoted Cub fan, given his lengthy stay in Chicago. Any favorable comment about the Mets could keep him going for at least a page of a good-natured rejoinder, if he were the Cub fan I supposed him to be.

March 12, 1983

Dear Tim,

(Ed. note: We have deleted about a page of this letter. It contains a rather awkward explanation of why the Chicago Cubs folded in the summer of 1969, why the Mets were "perversely lucky" to beat out the Cubs, and some playful comments about Tim's inability to make proper ethical decisions given his inordinate loyalty to the Mets.)

Now on to a more pressing issue than the character of the Cubs (although admittedly I fear that many of my fellow Chicagoans would not rank these two concerns in this order in any of their conversations).

As you suggested, there are pros and cons in choosing an evangelical divinity school as over against a nonevangelical one. After this basic choice, you must then choose which evangelical school or which nonevangelical school is best suited to your commitments and temperament.

My own sentiments on this important question were somewhat shaped by my father's counsel. His premise was simple. Go to an evangelical school for your theological training. You want to study where you need not remain always on your theological guard, given the energies you will have to expend in interacting with a basic Masters of Divinity program (Ed. note: Of course, in Woodson's day, the first theological degree after a college degree was more commonly designated Bachelor of Divinity.). Then, should the Lord lead you to further graduate study, select the finest program associated with your specialization, whether the program be evangelical or not. Having studied in an evangelical context, you should have a sturdy theological foundation upon which to build your ministry. Your further specialization should not subtract from that foundation but add new dimensions to it.

Moreover, you might put aside your understandable fears regarding the quality of education at evangelical schools. A number of evangelical schools have become notable for their academic credibility. Indeed, in some ways you now gain a better "liberal" education (in the best sense of that word) in a good confessional school than in a broader one. The reasons are twofold: First, the confessional schools by and large still require basic competence in Greek and Hebrew precisely because they think the ministry of the Word is of paramount importance; and second, the best of them require familiarity with secondary theological literature across the spectrum, while the so-called liberal schools tend to ignore conservative theology generally and evangelicalism in particular.

Even after you have chosen to study at an evangelical seminary, you must consider the theological distinctives of these schools. Certain ones have a dispensational orientation; others are characterized by a commitment to Reformed or Wesleyan or Pentecostal/charismatic distinctives. Still others are broadly evangelical with faculty members who come from a variety of evangelical traditions and yet work well together because they agree on the "evangelical essentials."

I particularly appreciated the fact that I made a few friends for life at the evangelical school I attended. Indeed, many of my student colleagues shared a common vision of ministry and service and encouraged and prayed for me during the rough patches of seminary days.

This leads me to another point. You may presently have a distorted perception of what attending an evangelical divinity school is like. Many folks do. Believing students and professors remain sinners/saints. A divinity school is neither the antechamber to heaven nor a gathering of a perfect church. Jacob Spener rightly insisted that seminaries should be workshops of the Holy Spirit. But real people sometimes hinder the work of the Spirit, and not many seminaries measure up to Spener's standard. Although one can expect to enjoy much of divinity school life, one should not anticipate that all will be spiritually uplifting.

In fact you may find yourself beset by a dryness of soul at seminary. What accounts for this? Why do so many divinity school students become spiritually parched? One possible explanation is that they begin to treat the Bible as a text to be coolly analyzed rather than as the very Word of God written—from which to gain spiritual nourishment. Students who maintain a regular devotional life throughout their seminary days almost inevitably exhibit greater spiritual vitality after three or four years than those who do not. Seminary students and professors should not neglect the counsel of Psalm 1 about meditation.

Another suggestion for keeping faith vibrant in seminary is to engage in an outreach program that keeps you involved in the real world. To see the power of the gospel transform lives is a marvelous impulse for keeping the mind renewed.

A third suggestion is to view theology as the human quest to think God's thoughts after Him. If evangelical practice is to flow from doing good evangelical theology, then theology should become one of the most important disciplines you pursue at a divinity school. As you might suppose (given what I teach), I am utterly convinced of the validity of this premise.

Obviously, I have a definite preference for evangelical schools. But what are some of the advantages of nonevangelical schools? Although they are catching up substantially, evangelical schools as a group have not reached the academic standards of some nonevangelical schools. A number of these better nonevangelical schools have extensive libraries built over a century or two. They often have distinguished teachers who are better known in the wider theological community than evangelical scholars. One cannot gainsay the value of studying under these professors. Moreover, a number of these schools do have evangelical professors on their faculties—i.e., components of evangelical faith are sometimes found at these schools.

But there is a down side to education at a nonevangelical divinity school that is hostile to Biblical faith. Whereas one risks coming out with too narrow a viewpoint in certain evangelical schools, in many nonevangelical schools one risks emerging not having the grounds for believing in anything at all. Did you happen to see last year Clark Pinnock's article in *Christianity Today* (February 5, 1982), entitled, "Liberals Knock the Center Out of Theological Education"? Pinnock, who used to teach here at Trinity, paints a fairly "dismal" (his word) picture of liberal schools, basing his comments on an analysis by Edward Farley (who teaches at Vanderbilt) that appeared in *Theological Education* (Spring 1981, p. 32). Pinnock writes:

> The traditional pattern [based on a belief in the infallible authority of the Bible] has been undermined by the negative impact of criti-

cal historical study. The foundation stone of the edifice has crumbled, and the whole structure is giving way. There is no sure knowledge of divine revelation to study and apply any more. There is no material for normative systematic theology and no need to defend the faith. The authority formerly thought to underlie the whole enterprise has been relativized and dissolved away. We no longer have an infallible divine teacher in the Scriptures, only a cacophony of human voices. The members of the faculties are therefore less like an orchestra playing the same concerto than one tuning up, with each musician playing his own cadenza, at odds with his neighbor.

Now this may be too harsh a judgment, but it should at least give one pause when thinking about choosing a nonevangelical environment in which to prepare for the Christian ministry.

I hesitate to say much more (though you may say that has never stopped me before). You may suspect that I am somehow trying to persuade you to come to a place like Trinity or Gordon-Conwell or Dallas or Westminster and that I have a rank prejudice against nonevangelical schools. What matters to me is that if you ever come to a settled conviction that you should enter the ministry, you pursue training that equips you to declare and live out "the whole will of God" (Acts 20:27).

Whatever you do, Tim, please be assured that I want only the best for you and Ginny. To my mind the best is doing what you believe the Lord's will is—even if that means faithfully serving Him in the rough and tumble of the business world in Manhattan. We need bold witnesses for Christ there as elsewhere in this secular culture.

In any event, I trust that things will go well for you in days ahead. I will pray to that end. Please give my best to Ginny, whom I am really looking forward to meeting someday.

Cordially,
Paul Woodson

24

*In May of 1983, I finally came to the conviction that God was call-
ing me into the Christian ministry. I had read the story of how
Billy Graham had surrendered his life to be a preacher while trudg-
ing alone one moonlit evening over a golf course bounded by moss-
laden trees in Tampa, Florida. Symbolically enough, Graham made
his commitment to the Lord at the edge of the green of the eighteenth
hole.*

*My own specific moment of conviction was much less dramatic.
I was taking another one of my "thought walks" in a neighboring
park. My mind was racing, but my feet were only ambling along.
Almost without realizing what was happening, I found myself saying, "OK, God, I will go into the ministry, but You know full well
what You are getting. My weaknesses dwarf my strengths; I am not
certain I can preach. Moreover, I often feel hypocritical, and I am
more selfish than I care to admit to myself. But I am willing to do
what You want me to do. Lord, please have mercy on me, weak sinner that I am and give me Your strength." Without exaggerating, I
did feel a sense of peace coming over me as I made my way back to
my apartment by way of side streets.*

*I saw Ginny the next evening. She took one look at me and
smiled. Then she said, "Tim, you have decided to go into the ministry, haven't you?"*

*I was thunderstruck. I asked her, "How did you know?" Now this
may seem a touch mystical, but she said something to the effect that
I looked more relaxed and my face was less drawn. To this day, I do
not really understand how she knew. But she was delighted. She
finally confided to me that she had hoped all along I would enter the
Christian ministry and that she had been praying about this for
months. I had become so impressed by Ginny's faith in and love for*

the Lord. She was, and is, a far better Christian than I am. About this, I have no doubt.

A few days later, after talking it over with my pastor (he, too, told me he had been praying I would move in this direction), I was suddenly overwhelmed by the implications of my decision. Spring had sprung. If I were going to attend seminary, it was already late, and I had better apply to a divinity school right away. Without thinking about it much at all, I decided to apply to Trinity because I knew at least one person there—Dr. Woodson. I had not even read a Trinity catalog. So much for all my careful musing and research on how to choose a seminary.

But Trinity was in Illinois, a long way from New York City where Ginny had secured a good job. Throwing caution to the wind again, I decided that the next evening I would ask Ginny to marry me. After all, how could I concentrate on my studies at Trinity if I were always thinking of Ginny back in New York City? Of course, for some months I had been thinking about asking that question. But now I would wait no longer.

The next afternoon at work, the hour hand on the clock in my office seemed frozen in place. I found myself quite irritable and sometimes just a little short of breath. Finally, six o'clock came. I raced home to my apartment and then drove over to Ginny's apartment by 7:15 P.M. Her roommate Cheryl told me that Ginny would be ready in a few minutes. Another wait. Only fifteen minutes, but it seemed an eternity. Ginny and I finally set off for one of our favorite restaurants.

I do not recall tasting what I ate that evening. I cannot for the life of me even remember what the main course was. We finished our meal after recounting a few of the day's war stories from office politics. While we were sipping our cappuccinos (one of our special shared treats), I summoned my courage and asked the momentous question.

Ginny paused for a moment, and then a broad smile broke over her beautiful face. I will never forget what she said, but what it was will remain our secret. At least, I can acknowledge that her comments encompassed the pivotal word yes. I was overjoyed. But I was also in a sense awed, for I was asking her to give up a job she really enjoyed in New York City and to move away from some special friends. Both of us shed a few tears that evening. Emotions are funny things. Joy and sadness are more intertwined with each other than we sometimes think.

Brimming with news, I wrote Dr. Woodson a letter that must have *resembled a verbal geyser, spouting words in every direction. I rapped off the fact that I had decided to prepare for the Christian ministry, that I was applying to Trinity, that Ginny and I were engaged and were planning to get married during the summer, and that we would be in Deerfield, Illinois, by September. As an after-thought, I indicated that if Dr. Woodson had any advice about mar-riage, now was the time to unload it on a fellow who knew next to nothing about the topic. And of course I invited him and his wife to our wedding, tentatively scheduled for the middle of August.*

Even as I wrote, my painful experience in Paris clouded my mind once again. I hoped Dr. Woodson wouldn't remember it.

To my delight Dr. Woodson replied to my letter in the return mail. To my dismay he had not forgotten my moral lapse in Paris.

May 11, 1983

Dear Tim,

How shall I begin to respond to your wonderful letter! All I can say is that after I received it, I got down on my knees and thanked the Lord for both you and Ginny. Then I called Mrs. Woodson and passed on the splendid news. She was as happy as I was. She mar-veled that not only are you going into pastoral ministry, not only are you coming to Trinity, but you will also have a warm-hearted life partner. What a joy all this news is for her. We are still praising the Lord for His goodness to you.

You want whatever advice I can give regarding engagement and marriage? A veritable cottage industry in literature on this topic is churning out book after book. In fact, you might want to read a crit-ical review article of a number of these books in *Newsweek* (February 1, 1982). The article is provocatively entitled, "The Bible in the Bedroom" (p. 71). The authors of the piece, Kenneth Woodward and Eloise Salholz, scoff at the contents of evangelical books by Charlie and Martha Shedd, Ed and Gaye Wheat, among others. But the reviewers' critical remarks might mean that the books are actually Biblically responsible. Your pastor may be able to provide you with a list of good titles.

May I suggest that you and Ginny take the time to receive pre-marital counseling either from your pastor or someone he might rec-ommend. I know you are busy, but that is no excuse in a matter of this importance. The counseling sessions could make your adjustment to married life go all the more smoothly.

Perhaps you will forgive me if I offer a few comments from my own experience. One piece of advice was given to me by a seminary professor before Mrs. Woodson and I were married. I have always treasured it, and I would like to share it with you. He indicated that as much as I loved Elizabeth, I would probably find 5 to 10 percent about her that I really did not care for. He then indicated that in marriage it is important to keep one's focus on the 90 to 95 percent that you love about your wife and not let the 5 to 10 percent replace it. In other words, think about the 90 to 95 percent when the other 5 to 10 percent is bothering you. Then my seminary prof said, "And remember, Paul, Elizabeth probably finds 5 to 10 percent about you she really doesn't like either." As I thought about the professor's last point, I could easily imagine that the percentage surpassed the one he gave. Indeed, Mrs. Woodson has been longsuffering, I assure you, with the 5 percent to ? percent about me she does not like.

I am not certain how to raise a second issue. Do you remember what we discussed when you wrote to me from Paris? I never asked you specifically what was troubling you. But unless I am mistaken, the moral lapse of which you spoke involved a relationship with a woman. My problem in understanding your situation is that I was raised in a different environment than you. In our church sexual immorality was so frowned upon that some of us may have been "moral" out of downright fear. We were too scared to stray from the straight and narrow, and we assumed that when we married a Christian spouse, both of us would be virgins. To many this concept seems quaint today, but it was a wonderful "given" in most evangelical and Fundamentalist circles a few decades back.

My own recent counseling experience has taught me that today's era of "freedom" has paradoxically spawned much addiction and guilt in matters having to do with sexuality. Even Christians are now entering marriage feeling guilty about their former lifestyles and deeds (read "sins"!).

Undoubtedly one of the great consolations of Christianity is the forgiveness of sins we find in Christ. Even David, an adulterer, was forgiven. But there are consequences to sin. And feelings of guilt can rush back and overwhelm us—even guilt associated with sins for which we have asked forgiveness. If you are troubled by guilt over past sins, may I encourage you to find an older brother in the Lord whom you trust and talk this issue through with him? The only reason I am so bold as to suggest this is that I have encountered people

145

in ministry who have not dealt with aspects of their past and who later find that they cannot shake these memories and feelings of guilt. Far better it is to work on these matters now. Should you want to talk further, why don't you just call. That might be an easier way to discuss these sensitive issues rather than trying to unpack them in letters.

In a totally different vein, I am so pleased that you are coming to Trinity. I hope you do not feel that I either pressured you to prepare for the pastoral ministry or to choose Trinity. I do not really know, for example, if Trinity is the right school for you.

But I must tell you one thing that I just learned. During the forthcoming school year, 1983-1984, I will be away on sabbatical. I had applied for a study grant and just learned that it has been awarded. Moreover, the school has graciously supported this venture as well. In consequence, Mrs. Woodson and I will return to our beloved Strasbourg during the academic year. There I will try to finish a manuscript on John Calvin's perspectives on the relationship between special revelation and natural revelation.

Please be assured, Tim, that Trinity functions very well without me! You should enjoy your time at the school very much. I do, however, regret that I will not be in Deerfield to provide a warm welcome to you and Ginny. In fact, if your wedding is set for August, with profound regret we will have to miss that as well.

Mrs. Woodson and I have already marked it down in our minds that one of the first things we will do after we return from Europe (D.V.) is to invite you folks over to our home for dinner. My guess is that you will have made many friends in the Trinity community during our absence.

Again, Tim, thank you for your wonderful letter. How pleased I was to receive it. Should Ginny wish to write Mrs. Woodson about any matters, please encourage her to do so. Elizabeth would be very happy to correspond with her.

> With prayers for your life,
> home, and service,
> *Paul Woodson*

25

*O*n August 10, 1983, Virginia Anne Swanson of Flushing, Long Island, and Timothy Mark Journeyman of Flemington, New Jersey, were joined in holy wedlock at the First Presbyterian Church of Flushing, Long Island. The bride . . . " So began a rather clipped description of our wedding in a local Long Island newspaper. Truth is, even a gifted wordsmith would have been pressed to capture the range of emotions Ginny and I felt on that special day. During the wedding and reception, Ginny looked so stunning and self-assured. As for me, I felt that I was having something akin to an out-of-body experience. Perhaps you have had the feeling. You are there, but you are not there. There is no there, there—to quote a famous line. At least I didn't faint.

All the members of my immediate family came to the wedding. My mother shed a few joyful tears. My brother Jack gallantly wished Ginny and me well; my sisters Rose and Pat seemed to hit it off very well with Ginny. Strange as it may seem, they were meeting her for the first time.

Ginny's parents and siblings also attended the service held at her home church. Two of her sisters were bridesmaids. All of the members of the Swanson family are Christians—an amazing phenomenon for a former worldling like myself to consider.

A number of my college friends from Princeton days and several close business associates from my office also attended. They seemed to enjoy themselves enormously (even without the aid of liquid mood boosters). A few of them whispered in my ear at the reception that they could not believe old Tim would give up being a single and that he would forsake a fast-track business career to become a preacher.

I doubt if the pastor's well-chosen words of Christian admonition during the service made much of a spiritual dent on my friends. But who knows? At least my mother and other family members heard the gospel at the wedding.

Ginny and I took our honeymoon at a resort located near Lake George in the Adirondack Mountains. As a youngster I had spent marvelous hot summer days at a camp in this region of New York State. Scenic as it is, Lake George is admittedly no Zermatt, Switzerland. But Ginny and I did not have the leisure time to go too far afield. Nor did we have money to burn; we would soon face school bills. Moreover, we knew that in the next few weeks we would have to throw ourselves into a mad quest to tie up loose ends in New York City before heading out to Deerfield.

I must confess that Dr. Woodson's news that he would not be at Trinity during the school year disappointed both Ginny and me. Dr. Woodson was the principal reason we were going to Trinity. Of course, I did not tell him this in the two (otherwise frank) long-distance phone conversations we had in May and June. There was no reason to burden him.

In any case, the move to Trinity went more smoothly than we could have hoped. We decided that the first year I would try to find a part-time job in banking in the North Shore area. As it turned out, we happened upon a remarkable live-in situation in Lake Bluff which took care of our housing needs. Then in God's grace I was hired in a part-time position in a bank in Highland Park. What a relief! Ginny could relax somewhat, being responsible only for certain duties associated with our live-in situation. She decided that she wanted to take a few classes at Trinity and work on a MAR degree (Ed. note: Master of Arts in Religion). That prospect delighted me no end.

Orientation sessions came and went, and classes were suddenly upon both of us. Among required M.Div. courses, I took European Church History 1 from Dr. Woodbridge. On occasion, he spoke so extravagantly about the glories of France that I suspected he and Dr. Woodson talked the same language when they swapped Francophile stories in the faculty lounge.

I was particularly taken by a class in apologetics. Before enrolling in the class, I had no idea that apologetics actually represented a discipline of study. I knew that at Princeton I had been "accosted" a few times by my friends who wanted to know why I had "suddenly" become a Christian. I had responded with my best arguments concerning the evidence for the resurrection of Christ. But now at Trinity I was asked to probe "theistic proofs," Thomism, the relationship between faith and reason, to ask if there is evidence that

148

demands a verdict, to assess the alleged collapse of foundational-
ism—a whole bevy of questions and items I never knew existed.

About my fourth week of class I wrote a letter to Dr. Woodson.
I related my first impressions of Trinity, and then I informed him that
I was particularly intrigued by what I was learning in the class on
apologetics.

A month or so later I received in the mail a letter postmarked
Strasbourg, France. I eagerly opened the envelope.

November 5, 1983

Dear Tim,

Warm greetings from Strasbourg, France, one of my favorite
haunts in Europe. You may not recall, but I was here during the student revolt that brought the city of Strasbourg to her knees in May
and June 1968 (Ed. note: Woodson describes his adventures in
Strasbourg to Tim in Letter 12). The city is much more placid now.
Walking by its tree-lined canals, I do on occasion catch myself
rewinding the film of my mind to those tumultuous days of 1968
marked by revolutionary excesses and excitement. I well remember
sitting on a park bench near one of the student restaurants and wondering how in the world de Gaulle could bring France out of this
state of chaos. It seemed as if there were no rabbits left in his political hat. If I recall correctly, so cornered was de Gaulle that he trav-
eled to West Germany to see if his generals were still loyal to him.
They were.

This city with its resplendent cathedral really is spectacular. I
almost feel guilty sometimes because I love wandering down side
streets so much. Mrs. Woodson and I especially enjoy going out for
lunch at a little restaurant where you can get a great omelette and
french fries for a reasonable price. The combination may seem
strange to you, but it is really quite tasty, especially if you dip the
french fries in mayonnaise!

Thank you for your letter describing your transition from the
rough and tumble world of Manhattan to "tranquil" student life at
Trinity. I trust that you and Ginny will find a suitable church in the
area, make many new friends, and benefit from the education offered
at the school.

Your comments about your apologetics class stimulated a number of thoughts. The project I have been working on for more than

a decade is related to your questions. I have been trying to sort out what John Calvin thought about "natural theology." Many years ago I had the opportunity of taking a course from noted Swiss theologian Karl Barth. So fascinated was I by Barth's thought that I subsequently devoted much time to the reading of "neo-orthodox" literature. I became convinced that Barth's negative assessment of natural theology did not correspond squarely with John Calvin's view on the same topic. This perception spawned my present project—to try to determine the similarities and differences between their perspectives on this issue.

What role does Calvin assign to rational arguments in sustaining a person's belief in the divinity of Christ or in the authority of Bible? Issues like these are dominating my research. As you can well imagine, they directly impinge on the study of and even the possibility of apologetics.

I hesitate to get into a lengthy theological assessment of the relative merits of various schools of apologetics. There are many people at Trinity and neighboring Wheaton College with whom you can discuss this intriguing topic. Moreover you are obviously reading extensively in the field. Whatever I might say would probably be repetitive for you.

I should alert you, however, to the presence of a powerful anti-apologetics tide sweeping through certain quarters of evangelicalism right now. Often this tide is pushed forward by scholars who claim that Augustine, Calvin, and Luther, among others, denied the value of presenting "historical evidences" or "theistic proofs" to defend the Christian faith. For some of these modern anti-apologetics apologists, there is no evidence that demands a verdict. They believe that only the work of the Holy Spirit can bring about the conversion of a sinner and create the conviction that the Bible is the Word of God. As a Calvinist, I entirely agree with this claim if it is carefully explicated.

But some of these aggressive apologists go a step further. They say that the apologetic enterprise (including the use of the theistic proofs and historical evidence for the resurrection) is clearly wrong-headed. So darkened is the mind of a sinner that he or she can never understand any argument in a way that leads to justifying faith.

At one level this is surely correct. We are by nature "dead in transgressions" (Ephesians 2:5). But anti-apologetics apologists draw out a misleading inference from it. Unlike Paul, they conclude that Christians therefore have no responsibility to present reasonable evidence for belief in the resurrection (to take one example). Whatever their intentions, they leave the distinct impression that "true faith" cannot be tied in any way to an argument or evidence in the public arena. True faith is free-standing so that it may remain "faith."

Here I demur. The Apostle Paul tells us that if Christ were not risen from the dead, "preaching is useless and so is your faith" (1 Corinthians 15:14). Then he refers to the value of eyewitness reports in confirming the truth claims of the resurrection (1 Corinthians 15:3-7, 15). In other words the Apostle Paul seems to provide us with Biblical warrant for some form of evidentiary apologetics. According to Luke, Paul entered the synagogue at Thessalonica and *"reasoned* with them from the Scriptures, *explaining* and *proving* that the Christ had to suffer and rise from the dead" (Acts 17:2, 3).

According to the apostle, persuasive evidence *does* exist to sustain a belief in the resurrection and in God's existence. The problem is that the unregenerate mind rejects the persuasive evidence (Romans 1 and 2). It will not believe, or else it will transmute belief in the true God, for example, into heinous idolatry. Only the Holy Spirit can open the spiritual eyes of a blinded person. Indeed the Apostle Paul himself cites the evidence from Creation confirming God's existence to explain why unbelievers remain culpable—they reject the existing evidence.

John Calvin followed closely in the Apostle Paul's footsteps. He believed that the resurrection of Christ was attested by eyewitnesses. In other words, there are good evidentiary grounds for believing that the resurrection of Jesus Christ actually took place. At the same time, Calvin understood very well that a sinner will not confess Christ as Savior and repent of his or her sins unless the Holy Spirit regenerates the individual.

Now why would such talented Reformed theologians, historians, and philosophers argue the way they do? I can only surmise the reasons: 1) Several seem to have been quite charmed by Barth's arguments against natural theology; 2) Perhaps even more to the point, some seem to think that the philosophical stance known as classical foundationalism has collapsed so disastrously that its own resurrection would be nothing short of a miracle.

In a seminal article titled "Reason and Belief in God" (in *Faith and Rationality: Reason and Belief in God* [1983, p. 18] edited by Alvin Plantinga and Nicholas Wolterstorff), Professor Plantinga, a brilliant philosopher, describes what foundationalism is.

According to the foundationalist, some propositions are properly basic and some are not; those that are not are rationally accepted only on the basis of *evidence*, where the evidence must trace back, ultimately, to what *is* properly basic. The existence of God, furthermore, is not among the propositions that are properly basic; hence a person is rational in accepting theistic belief only if he has evidence for it.

In a sense Plantinga welcomes the alleged collapse of classical foundationalism. A good number of atheistic foundationalists had exploited its premises to countermand any arguments for God's existence. For these atheists belief in God is impossible because there is "insufficient evidence." Nor is the belief in God "properly basic," for it is neither self-evident, nor open to the senses, nor incorrigible.

Plantinga then has his sights primarily set on atheistic evidentialists. If he can demonstrate that a belief in God is in fact "properly basic" and does not need to measure up to any "evidentiary standard," then he thinks he has rescued theism from its atheistic foundationalist detractors.

To clear the way for this rescue operation, Plantinga launches a hard-hitting critique of classical foundationalism. He authenticates, at least to his own satisfaction, that it has collapsed. Pushing aside the debris of this fallen epistemology, he then tries to build a case for his own crowning "apologetic" gambit—the demonstration that belief in God is properly basic.

If Plantinga's readers have accepted his arguments up to this point, then he can take his next giant step. He can postulate that belief in God does not need evidence to sustain it, as both Christian and atheistic foundationalists had assumed.

But in ambushing atheistic classical foundationalists, Plantinga also brings all forms of Christian evidentialism under sustained fire. He believes that given the collapse of classical foundationalism, the approach of *all* Christian evidentialists to defending the truth claims of the Christian religion is also irremediably flawed. To fend off their expected counterattack, Plantinga takes it upon himself to answer their most powerful objections in advance.

Thus Professor Plantinga understands very well that he is breaking ranks with a long tradition of Christian apologists. But he takes comfort in the fact that another group of believers had earlier recognized the wisdom of the position he is now advocating. Indeed, he attempts to give legitimacy to his cause by citing the names of an impressive company—the Biblical writers, the Reformers (especially John Calvin), and Karl Barth, among others. Thus for Plantinga the

"Reformed epistemology" he is espousing has sterling Biblical and evangelical credentials.

You probably sensed from my earlier remarks, Tim, that I am not especially enamored with Professor Plantinga's arguments. Let me try to explain a few of my reservations. If belief in God is "properly basic" and you assume that God exists, then why should you be a Christian rather than, let's say, a Buddhist or a Hindu or nothing at all? It is indeed comforting to know you are within your own epistemic rights to be a theist, but why should you not be an atheist?

Although Plantinga tries to answer this objection in a section called "The Great Pumpkin Objection," (p. 77), he cannot really do so persuasively. He writes:

> The Christian will of course suppose that belief in God is entirely proper and rational; if he does not accept this belief on the basis of other propositions, he will conclude that it is basic for him and quite properly so. Followers of Bertrand Russell and Madelyn Murray O'Hare may disagree, but how is that relevant? Must my criteria, or those of the Christian community, conform to their examples? Surely not. The Christian community is responsible to *its* set of examples, not to theirs.

It appears that Plantinga has no way to reach out to Russell and Murray or the "Great Pumpkin" missionary but to say, "You are wrong and we Christians are right." Or to put it another way, apparently he does not believe there is any evidence which could help the atheist or the Buddhist or the high priestess of the "Great Pumpkin" sect to say, "Now I see. There are powerful arguments why I should at least consider the truth claims of Christianity." Thus a radical anti-apologetics stinger resides in the tail of Plantinga's proposal.

In fact, I would go so far as to argue that the apologetic enterprise—in which Christians like the Apostle Paul, the "early Christian apologists," Tertullian, Clement of Alexandria, and others engaged—dead-ends in Barth and in his stepchild, the new "Reformed epistemology." This is confirmed by another article from the book Plantinga edited. Written by D. Holwerda, the piece is entitled, "Faith, Reason and the Resurrection in the Theology of Wolfhart Pannenberg." Flying his fideistic colors high, Holwerda marches swiftly and boldly beyond the pale of Calvin's thinking into a position that some might suggest recreates the *cul-de-sac* of "Postmodernism." He writes, "Reason is not autonomous, nor does it establish autonomously its own criteria for rationality in matters of either faith or science. Beliefs of various kinds are inevitably involved in establishing the definition of rationality. Such is the thesis of the various essays in this book."

One of the best *brief* critiques of Professor Plantinga's position appeared a few years ago in *Christianity Today*. It was written by a philosopher/theologian with a Dutch name that now escapes me. You might want to see if you can track down the essay in copies of *CT*. I do not have access to a full set here in Strasbourg. Otherwise I would have tried to find the reference for you.

The author raises at least by implication the apologetic "dead-ending" of "the Reformed epistemology." Does Plantinga have anything to say to a nonbeliever who does not share his "properly basic" belief that God exists? The writer thinks not.

On another front, I do not think that Professor Plantinga's proposal meshes as cleanly with the thought of John Calvin as he claims. For example, Plantinga cites Calvin to this effect: "Even the common folk and the most untutored, who have been taught only by the aid of the eyes, cannot be unaware of the excellence of divine art, for it reveals itself in this innumerable and yet distinct and well-ordered variety of the heavenly host."

Upon a first reading one might easily suppose that Calvin is suggesting that common people by *observing* (empiricism?) the heavens recognize the work of a divine artist due to "the well-ordered variety of the heavenly host." According to this reading, the common people infer God's existence—a divine artist—from the order of His artistic creation. Does this not smack of the old-fashioned teleological argument?

Obviously, Professor Plantinga cannot allow Calvin to be interpreted in that way. This would imply that Calvin retained room in his thinking for "classical foundationalist apologetics." Consequently, in what I think is a huge reach (or a genuine misreading), Plantinga tries to explain what the passage really means. He writes:

It is not that such a person is justified or rational in so believing by virtue of having an implicit argument—some version of the teleological argument, say. No; he does not need any argument for justification or rationality. His belief need not be based on any other propositions at all; under these conditions he is perfectly rational in accepting belief in God in the utter absence of any argument, deductive or inductive. Indeed, a person in these conditions, says Calvin, *knows* that God exists. (p. 67)

Tim, for Professor Plantinga to persuade us that the "Reformed epistemology" meshes cleanly with John Calvin's thought, he must furnish more careful readings of Calvin's writings than this. His proof-texting is selective and his exegesis not very convincing. From my own research in this area it seems to me that Calvin holds a very sophisticated and complex stance, dare I say *tertium quid* position (Ed. note: "a third position"). This may explain why both rationalistic evidentialists and fideistic-leaning "Reformed epistemologists" can find passages that seem to confirm their own stance. To put it another way, Calvin's thought does not perfectly align itself either with Plantinga's "Reformed epistemology" nor with the hard evidentialism characterized by the claim that there is "evidence that necessarily demands a verdict." Once I have finished my research on this topic, I will share my findings with you, for what they are worth.

You should know that I have great admiration for Professor Plantinga and those of his distinguished colleagues who are trying to give warrant to "the Reformed epistemology." Professor Plantinga has helped make discussion of theism a more legitimate enterprise among professional philosophers. But my own studies in the history of the Reformed tradition lead me to believe that there have been multiple ways "Reformed" Christians have viewed these complex issues.

Nor is Plantinga's view well informed regarding the history of "evidentialism." Plantinga and his colleagues do not seem to understand that in the history of Christian thought there have been various forms of "evidentialism." On the contrary, they have apparently adopted the Barthian complaint against natural theology to the effect that any presentation of arguments to an unbeliever as to why Christianity is true somehow represents a horrible sell-out to the dictates of "autonomous reason"; it inevitably leads to nefarious consequences.

If I had to guess, a very strong "fideistic" reaction to the alleged collapse of "classical foundationalism" has played a decisive and yet lightly advertised role in shaping the contours of this new "Reformed epistemology." To put it more simply, the rather simplistic evidentialism of some Christian apologists, who seem to imply that the evidence is so overwhelming that if people do not become Christians they must be rebels or twits, has been so systematically destroyed in philosophical circles that this new "Reformed epistemology," in a classic overreaction, wants to build theology on an epistemology *divorced* from evidence, witness, argument. I think I want to say both sides overreach.

From one perspective, God has supplied such ample evidence that men and women are without excuse; from another, the evidence is never such that *in itself* it overcomes our innate self-centeredness, our profound lostness, our deep rebellion. We sinners can always find reasons for dismissing or domesticating God. God has ordained that through the preaching of the gospel—which certainly includes the report of witnesses as to what took place in history—lost men and women will come to saving faith. But the ultimate factor in bringing about this transformation is not the witness per se or the preaching itself, but the Spirit of God (see 1 Corinthians 2:6-16). It seems to me that this new "Reformed epistemology" has not adequately grappled with the entailments of our fallen nature or of the nature of the Spirit's work of illumination. In any case, Plantinga categorically denies that his approach is in any sense a reaction, but his response does not seem compelling. His approach is surprisingly ahistorical.

Despite advertisements aplenty to the contrary, I simply do not find in the writings of the proponents of the "Reformed epistemology" a careful exegesis of Scripture, a sustained study of Calvin's writings, or an openness to re-examine the neo-orthodox historiography of Ernst Bizer, which allegedly justifies Barth's complaint against natural theology. The recent studies of Professors Jill Raitt, Olivier Fatio, and Richard Muller help us understand that the Barthian historiography is not as sturdy as the proponents of the "Reformed epistemology" assume. In the near future Bizer's historiography may itself collapse.

I do hope Professor Plantinga will devise a way to meld "apologetics" more successfully into his program. My guess is that he will. There is a very practical reason for hoping this will happen soon. On university campuses and in the broader culture many individuals are perplexed by the question of how to sort out the "truth claims" of the various world religions. When I spoke to a student group at a university last year, a student who was apparently an unbeliever asked me explicitly during the Q. and A. time why I thought Christ is the way, the truth, and the life rather than Mohammed or Confucius. Even many evangelical students are perplexed by this question. Regrettably, it does not appear that proponents of the "Reformed epistemology" have much of anything to say to these students. Indeed I wonder how a proponent of the "Reformed epistemology" would respond to a seeker who asks, "Why Jesus and not Mohammed?" And are we not as believers to try to answer such questions even if it means risking the use of "evidence?"

I am writing this letter late in the evening. When I am tired, I often say things in too unguarded a fashion. I may have done so in this letter. You may have noticed me doing this before. If I have, I regret that very much.

Trust that all is well. Give our best regards to Ginny.

Warmly yours in
Christ Jesus,
Paul Woodson

26

I hesitated to write Dr. Woodson frequently during the academic year, 1983-1984. During my first week at Trinity I had observed firsthand the diversified tugs on the time of faculty members. I began to appreciate how generous Dr. Woodson had been in carrying on such an extended correspondence, probably owing to the personal affection he bore for my father. Certainly he needed a respite from any queries I might have during his sabbatical. In any case, there were a number of professors at Trinity against whom I could bounce off the questions jockeying for attention in my mind.

Rookie as I was at the divinity school, I discovered many things too alluring. A professor would bring up one intriguing thought, only to glide effortlessly to another subject, leaving me thrashing in his or her wake. My mind was quickly overloaded with information. Titles of books that I was told I "must read" were scribbled down, hastily creating an ever-expanding list. Was I really supposed to read all the assignments in my course syllabi? Would the material be covered on exams? And what about this "must" list of books that was not assigned reading? Moreover when I walked into the bookstore, I wanted to buy everything. My mind was boggled by it all. I was a victim of "the-first-quarter-at-seminary syndrome," and I didn't even know it.

In the early weeks of the quarter Ginny and I would almost compulsively gobble down our supper, wash the dishes, and then figuratively disappear into our private reading worlds. When we did resurface and actually talk to each other, we tried to make sense of our frustrating new predicament. We were being sideswiped by a vocabulary we had never heard before (the words praxis, ontological, reprobation, concursive, third declension *had not been used by my co-workers in the office in Manhattan*); and yet our fellow students seemed to understood this arcane language. We were also *being engulfed by waves of ideas we had neither the time to reflect on nor the skills to sift.*

Our only hope was "eschatological"—a term I picked up from one of my friends while relaxing over a coke in the White Horse Inn. (Ed. note: The White Horse Inn is the name of the student snack shop at Trinity. The shop was christened after an inn in Cambridge, England, where some of Martin Luther's earliest student followers gathered to discuss the reformer's ideas; the students were quickly nicknamed the "Germans.") By eschatological I mean that Ginny and I had come to hope in a coming day called graduation. It was rumored about that people had actually completed their work and graduated from this school. Some had even come from backgrounds such as our own.

One issue did come to the fore that first quarter. Two of my new student friends, Vincent Parker and Richard Strawbridge, both from Jacksonville, Florida, filled my ears with accounts of evangelical debates over the meaning of Biblical inerrancy. Both were theologically aware because this was their second year at Trinity, and they rehearsed for me their "informed" versions of what had happened at the Christmas 1982 meeting of the Evangelical Theological Society where Professor Robert Gundry of Westmont College became the epicenter of a storm for his particular use of redaction criticism. I pretended to listen attentively, but I had no idea what Vince and Richard were talking about. Also they mentioned that Professor Ramsey Michaels had been asked to step down from his teaching post at Gordon-Conwell. This was reported in Christianity Today *(July 15, 1983). According to the article, a significant number of Michaels's colleagues and the trustees at Gordon-Conwell did not believe he upheld a proper viewpoint on inerrancy.*

I had not encountered the word inerrancy *extensively before I applied to Trinity. Nor did I have any sense of what all the brouhaha was about. I believed that the Bible was the inspired Word of God and truthful in what it affirmed. If that is what inerrancy meant, then I guess I was an inerrantist. But I had not thought about the issue much.*

Early in the fall quarter in 1983, I did read Dr. Kenneth Kantzer's insightful editorial in Christianity Today *(October 7, 1983), entitled "Biblical Authority: Where Both Fundamentalists and Neoevangelicals Are Right." To the question, "Is authority limited to faith and practice?" Dr. Kantzer responded:*

On the practical side, moreover, the evangelical points out that faith and history are closely related, and so are faith and the facts of science. If the Bible is not entirely trustworthy, it loses its authority for us unless we are able to distinguish what in it we have a right to trust and what not to trust. Unfortunately, there does not seem to be any clear line we can draw between important history and unimportant history, or between important fact and unimportant. The end result, if we do this, is that we build a theology not on the whole teaching of the Bible but rather on our own very selective use of what we choose to take from the Bible. We then stand in judgment of the Bible. The Bible does not stand in judgment over us.

Dr. Kantzer's editorial seemed a sane, calm, and reasonable analysis. It teased out for me a little further the significance of the various debates.

I began to wonder what Dr. Woodson thought about the inerrancy fire storm that nobody seemed capable of putting out. He had never discussed the matter with me. This seemed strange given what I was now learning about its scope. I decided to risk breaking into his sabbatical reveries and wrote him another letter. I described my recent "baptism" into the inerrancy debate. I also expressed my concern that the controversy might hinder evangelicals from working together in common causes such as evangelistic outreach and social action. I suggested that, given his research interests, Dr. Woodson might find Dr. Kantzer's editorial instructive because it included sections with these subtitles: "Karl Barth on Biblical Authority"; "Karl Barth on the Humanity of Scripture"; "What Evangelicals Can Learn from Barth"; "Where Barth Went Awry." Dr. Woodson had said that he did not have a run of CT available to him at Strasbourg. I thought he might have missed this editorial.

December 22, 1983

Dear Tim,

Elizabeth and I want to extend to you and Ginny warm Christmas greetings from Strasbourg. Our good wishes will reach you after the day we celebrate our Savior's birth. Nonetheless, our sentiments of love and thankfulness for you remain no less genuine.

Tim, you need not be so apologetic (here I use the term in another sense!) about disturbing me on my sabbatical. Receiving a letter from you was a treat. In one sense you represent home even if it is a new "home" for you. I was delighted to be brought up to speed on your studies at Trinity.

Undoubtedly the debate over Biblical inerrancy has been a painful one for evangelicals. You are right that the controversy has been an intense and unhappy one. People from both sides have indulged themselves in self-serving rhetoric and said things that they probably regretted later. I am afraid that I am guilty myself somewhat on those two counts.

I am pleased you have read Dr. Kantzer's editorial. Thank you for bringing it to my attention. I had not read it as I have not had access to recent copies of *CT* and missed this particular editorial. Dr. Kantzer, whom I respect both for his wisdom and for his humble walk with the Lord, has briefly spelled out an admirable case for Biblical inerrancy. I would only like to add a few other points that may help you understand why many of us have found the doctrine to be so important.

First, I would bring your attention to the Bible's high view of its own authority. One of my colleagues, Dr. Wayne Grudem, has written a recent article you might find illuminating—"Scripture's Self-Attestation and the Problem of Formulating a Doctrine of Scripture," which appears in *Scripture and Truth,* edited by Professors Carson and Woodbridge. I do not have the volume here, but I believe it was published by Zondervan this year. Dr. Grudem reviews numerous passages in Scripture which have to do with the witness of canonical Scripture about its own truthfulness. He makes a good case for the premise that "the Bible is 'truthful'" is the self-attestation of Scripture itself.

Obviously it is important to define what "truthful" means in Biblical categories. Professor Roger Nicole addresses that topic in the same volume.

In his editorial Dr. Kantzer also speaks about the nature of Biblical "truth."

> It should be added that when evangelicals describe the Biblical statements as true, they are using the word "true" in its epistemological sense as describing a statement that conforms to reality in a meaningful way. "True" is contrasted with "false." The Biblical statements are always true and never false. Some writers today are unwilling to admit that in their view the Bible is false or untrue in this sense. They continue to describe the Bible as true, but shift the meaning of "true" to its ethical sense.

Over the years I have noticed that those who believe that the Bible does have errors in it seldom attempt to build a case using the Scripture's own doctrinal statements to buttress their argument. The reason for this may be fairly obviously—it is difficult to do.

Nor is the doctrine of the Bible's infallibility (a term I personally prefer) a recent Fundamentalist innovation. Rather it was the "central teaching" of the Christian churches in Europe until at least the last decades of the seventeenth century on the Continent and much later in the United Kingdom.

In the United States the doctrine of the Bible's infallibility was espoused by most Americans until the 1890s. For example, Washington Gladden argued in 1893 that the vast majority of American Protestants believed that the Bible was "free from all error, whether of doctrine, or fact, or of precept." He observed, "Such is the doctrine now held by the great majority of Christians. Intelligent pastors do not hold it, but the body of the laity have no other conception" (from *Who Wrote the Bible? A Book for the People,* p. 357).

Moreover, Randall Balmer has provided in his Trinity M.A. thesis overwhelming evidence that the teaching of the infallibility of the original autographs of Scripture was a commonplace throughout the nineteenth century in the United States. Balmer's thesis countermands the interpretation of Professor Ernest Sandeen, who contended that in the article, "Inspiration," (1881) the Presbyterians B. B. Warfield and A. A. Hodge had proposed the doctrine of the inerrancy in the original autographs for the first time. Unfortunately, a number of notable scholars have followed Sandeen unquestioningly. Interestingly enough, the two Presbyterians never mentioned the word *inerrancy* in this famous piece; they used the traditional word *infallibility.*

How unfortunate that many in the scholarly community still believe that the 1881 article was the birthplace of the doctrine of Biblical inerrancy. In fact, I would contend that a belief in the inerrancy of Scripture has been the central tradition of the Christian churches since the patristic era.

One of the most telling witnesses to this tradition was a learned Roman Catholic, Johann Maier Von Eck. In 1518 Eck entered into a significant epistolary exchange with Erasmus over the question of the Bible's infallibility. Erasmus had raised among other hypotheses the possibility that due to a slip in memory the evangelist Matthew had made a mistake in Matthew 2:6. Listen to Eck's rejoinder to Erasmus's avowal:

First of all then to begin at this point, many people are offended at your having written in your notes on the second chapter of Matthew the words "or because the evangelists themselves did not draw evidence of this kind from books, but trusted as men will to memory and made a mistake." For in these words you seem to suggest that the evangelists wrote like ordinary men, in that they wrote this in reliance on their memories and failed to inspect the written sources, and so for this reason made a mistake. *Listen, dear Erasmus: do you suppose any Christian will patiently endure to be told that the evangelists in their Gospels made mistakes? If the authority of Holy Scripture at this point is shaky, can any other passage be free from the suspicion of error? A conclusion drawn by St. Augustine from an elegant chain of reasoning.* (my emphasis)

Now please note, Tim, Eck could not imagine that *any Christian* would allow Erasmus to affirm that an error, even of the small variety, existed in Scripture. Moreover, Eck believed that his own stance mirrored a tradition that stretched back to Augustine. According to this perspective, the truthfulness of the Christian religion was related to the infallibility of Scripture. (Parenthetically, Erasmus did reverse himself on his comments about Matthew 2:6, but for reasons that are difficult to discern.)

Luther, who debated Eck at Leipzig in 1519, at least shared with his disputant one point of agreement—a belief in the infallibility of the Bible. Wrote Luther, "But everyone, indeed, knows that at times they [the fathers] have erred as men will; therefore I am ready to trust them only when they prove their opinions from Scripture, which has never erred."

Both Luther and Eck looked back to Saint Augustine as an authority on this issue. The Bishop of Hippo had written:

For it seems to me that the most disastrous consequences must follow upon our believing that anything false is found in the sacred books. . . . For if you once admit into such a high sanctuary of authority one false statement, as made in the way of duty, there will not be left a single sentence of these books which, if appearing to anyone difficult in practice or hard to believe, may not by the same fatal rule be explained away, as a statement in which, intentionally, and under a sense of duty, the author declared what was not true.

Or again, Augustine had declared:

I have learned to yield this respect and honor only to the canonical books of Scripture: of these alone do I most firmly believe that the authors were completely free from error.

Augustine had observed that non-Christians were attacking the harmony of the Gospels with a view to overthrowing the Christian religion itself. He decided to write a work to show that the accounts of the evangelists are harmonious. In the preface to this book *The Harmony of the Gospels,* Augustine explained his goal:

And in order to carry out this design to a successful conclusion, we must prove that the writers in question do not stand in any antagonism to each other. For those adversaries are in the habit of adducing this as the palmary allegation in all their vain objections, namely that the evangelists are not in harmony with each other.

But returning to Luther, I think you should know that neo-orthodox theologians have tried to argue that the great German thinker made a distinction between the Word of God and the Bible. (Ed. note: Woodson's argument here, though of historical interest, may be theologically confusing. There is a sense in which the Bible and "Word of God" *cannot* be simply identified, if we base our judgment on Biblical use. For instance, when "the word of the LORD" comes to this or that prophet in the Old Testament, the text does not mean that the Bible somehow came to him. But within the Bible, "the Word of God" or similar expressions *can* refer to antecedent written Scripture—i.e., to the Scriptures, to what we now call the Bible. Those contemporary scholars who want to make an *absolute* disjunction between "Bible" and "the Word of God" are usually interested in weakening the authority of the Scriptures per se. In this case, they would be right to say that "the Word of God" cannot simply be *equated* with "the Bible"; it is quite mistaken to think that "the Word of God" cannot refer to the Bible or is an inappropriate category to be used with reference to the Bible. Woodson's opponents are real people.) Their arguments really are not persuasive, but it would take too lengthy a digression to explain why. I am encouraged that scholars like Professors Jill Raitt, Olivier Fatio, and Richard Muller are examining afresh key assumptions upholding the neo-orthodox historiography. This historiography, largely created by Ernst Bizer (for the Reformed tradition), who was a disciple of Karl Barth, may not be able to survive their withering revisionist criticisms.
The first person I have been able to find who clearly makes the dis-

tinction between the Bible and the Word of God is Baruch Spinoza. In his *Tractatus Theologico Politicus* (1670), Spinoza (d. 1677) acknowledged openly that Christians of his day upheld the doctrine of the Bible's infallibility. With more than a touch of disdain for theologians among his contemporaries, Spinoza wrote:

> . . . not content to rave with the Greeks themselves, they want to make the prophets rave also; showing conclusively that never even in sleep have they caught a glimpse of Scripture's Divine nature. The very vehemence of their admiration for the mysteries plainly attests that their belief in the Bible is a formal assent rather than a living faith; and the fact is made still more apparent by their laying down beforehand, as a foundation for the study and true interpretation of Scripture, the principle that it is in every passage true and divine.

Spinoza took it upon himself to overthrow the widely held belief in the Bible's infallibility.

Jean Le Clerc, a Remonstrant church historian and man of letters, also assumed that Christians of his day upheld the doctrine of Biblical infallibility. In the mid-1680s he attacked this belief in a straightforward fashion in his significant debates with the French Biblical critic, Richard Simon.

Tim, I am afraid that I am getting carried away again. Hopefully, even from these meager examples, you can see why I proposed that the doctrine of the Bible's infallibility is not a late seventeenth-century innovation as Professors Jack Rogers and Donald McKim have proposed, or a late nineteenth-century innovation of the Princetonians as Professors Ernest Sandeen and George Marsden have suggested. Rather the doctrine dominated the thinking of Christians on the Continent until the last decades of the seventeenth century.

In fact, so confident were some Christians in the truthfulness and accuracy of the historical accounts of Scripture that they believed they could calculate the very dates certain events recorded in the Bible took place. For example, Melanchthon, the brilliant colleague of Luther, signed off a letter of 1546 to John Calvin with these astonishing words: "Farewell. On the day upon which, 3846 years ago, Noah entered into the ark, by which God gave testimony of his purpose never to forsake his Church even when she quivers under the shock of the great sea billows." Apparently, Melanchthon believed the Biblical accounts were so precise he could make this calculation.

But this anecdote leads me to reflect on Professor Marsden's recent influential interpretation that the doctrine of Biblical inerrancy in its late "precisionistic" form was shaped by the influence of Baconianism and Common Sense Realism upon the thinking of nineteenth-century American evangelicals. I dare not begin to assess that interpretation. If I do, this letter may never end. Suffice it to say for the moment, I have never been convinced by Professor Marsden's winsomely presented interpretation. Christians living centuries before the nineteenth believed in the Bible's infallibility and had credited its historical accuracy with a level of precision which could match, if not surpass, the "precisionist" inerrancy Marsden attributes to the Princetonians (see the chapter, "Presbyterians and the Truth" in his 1980 book on Fundamentalism). Perhaps on another occasion I might interact with Professor Marsden's historical reconstruction in a more responsible fashion.

Please give our best to Ginny. We do miss Trinity and our friends there. On the other hand I would not be candid if I didn't say we are enjoying ourselves immensely here in Strasbourg. This sabbatical appears to be evaporating before our very eyes. What a scary thought.

Cordially,
Paul Woodson

27

They say at TEDS that the most discouraging time of the year for most students is the month of February. That was certainly my experience. The winter is long, the academic pressure considerable, and students are still far enough away from the end of the year that no relief is in sight.

By this time, too, I was experiencing what most seminary students face at some point in their studies—the difficulty of integrating devotion and scholarship, piety and academic rigor. In a confessional school like Trinity, it was not as if the courses were formally destroying faith; indeed, at a certain intellectual level, I was being force-fed vast quantities of information that was in its own way interesting, relevant, helpful. But somehow the joy of the Lord was being snuffed out. I had once read my Bible with delight; now it was becoming a textbook. It was a textbook I enjoyed, but rather more as a field for my intellectual plow to furrow than as the primary means of knowing and worshiping God.

A couple of weeks before the exams at the end of term, I wrote Prof. Woodson frankly describing my bleak mood and observing that I was not the only one on campus who felt this way. I did not really take into account the array of circumstances that contributed to my gloom. I cast the question almost entirely as the challenge seminary students face of studying the Bible academically while drifting toward a burned-out feeling. I wanted to know what could be done to prevent this drift.

In retrospect, the answer I received from Dr. Woodson three weeks later was at one level not very shrewd, pastorally speaking. He might have been wiser to sidestep my question and point out how many factors—even mundane ones such as stress and amount of sleep—contribute to spiritual well-being. But at another level, Prof. Woodson's answer was superb. Because he answered the question I posed, he did not really address the deep questions behind my ques-

tion; but for the same reason, he provided a clear description of what it means to love God with one's mind and to live an integrated Christian life that combines both thought and devotion.

March 19, 1984

Dear Tim,

The subject you raise is of extraordinary importance. I shall reply with some observations on a passage of Scripture and then with some practical conclusions I have come to after years both as a pastor and as a teacher of theology in the academic environment of the seminary.

It will help you to follow what I say if you sit down and read Mark 12:28-34 and hold that passage open before you.

Focus especially on verse 30: "Love the Lord your God with all your heart and with all your soul and with all your mind and with all your strength." The heart of this saying is that love for God is far more foundational than a religion of mere rules. The rabbis eventually codified the law into 613 commandments. The scribe who approaches Jesus asks which commandment is greatest. Jesus replies with the one that gets behind all of them. It is utterly vital to return to such basics again and again.

The love Jesus demands that we exercise toward God, as He cites Deuteronomy 6, springs from the whole person—heart (which, as you know, signals not mere emotion but the entire personality) and soul and mind and strength. That mind is explicitly mentioned is of no small importance. We often think of loving God with our "heart" in the *modern* sense, that is, with our emotions; we merely *serve* God with our minds. This text suggests our understanding is distorted. We are to *love* God with our minds, as well as with heart and soul and strength. These are not mutually exclusive categories, and I need not probe them all here. My point is that at least some of the tension you feel may be because you think of devotion toward God in categories that are too narrow. Unless you *feel* on a "high," you wonder if your love has slipped.

The implication of the text, surely, is that if we love God with our mind, we will find out more about Him; we will think more about Him; we will feed our minds with right material about Him. John Wesley's advice to a young preacher is still pertinent even though his letter was first published in *The Arminian Magazine* in 1780:

What has exceedingly hurt you in time past, nay, and I fear, to this day, is want of reading. I scarce ever knew a preacher who read so little. And perhaps, by neglecting it, you have lost the taste for it. Hence your talent in preaching does not increase. It is just the same as it was seven years ago. It is lively, but not deep; there is little variety; there is no compass of thought. Reading only can supply this, with meditation and daily prayer. You wrong yourself greatly by omitting this. You can never be a deep preacher without it, any more than a through [Ed. note: thorough] Christian. Oh begin! Fix some part of every day for private exercises. You may acquire the taste which you have not; what is tedious at first will afterwards be pleasant. Whether you like it or no, read and pray daily. It is for your life; there is no other way; else you will be a trifler all your days, and a pretty, superficial preacher. Do justice to your own soul; give it time and means to grow. Do not starve yourself any longer. Take up your cross and be a Christian altogether. Then will all the children of God rejoice (not grieve) over you; and in particular yours.

Perhaps it is worth remarking that this "most important" commandment begins with the words, "Hear, O Israel, the Lord our God, the Lord is one." Of course, in the first instance that tells us how we are to think of God—He brooks no rivals, for He stands alone—He is One. But with the commandment itself following on immediately, it is hard not to see a connection between the oneness of God and this command to love God. As the Lord our God is one, so we are to love Him wholly—that is, the whole of each of us, the whole person. *All* of life must contribute to our love for God, for there is but one God, and He is the God of all of our life. We learn to love Him in chapel when with hundreds of other students we sing "Majesty" or "And Can It Be," and the pipe organ swells in anticipation of the praise of heaven; we love Him diligently when, seated in the Rolfing Library, we are studying for the next Greek test, assured that this is the service we are rendering to Him and that the training of our minds has a contribution to make to the nurture of God's people through the ministry of the Word in years to come.

The "first" commandment, properly understood, *entails* the second—to love our neighbors as ourselves—for it overcomes that selective piety that enables too many believers to overlook the second. I think it was David C. K. Watson who slyly wrote:

> *Like a mighty army moves the church of God;*
> *Brothers, we are treading, where we've always trod.*

We are all divided, many bodies we,
Very strong on doctrine, weak on charity.

Now I would be the last one in the world to want to *weaken* doctrine. But I would like to see doctrine taught *and assimilated* in such a way that it contributes to our knowledge of God and our love for God. If that is the case, then God's own mandates to us, not least His insistence that we love the church and that we love our neighbors, will be part of our thinking and part of our mandate.

So let me venture some practical words of advice.

First, part of what you are going through stems not from the academic study of theology (despite what you may think!), but from the sheer pace of life in an academically respectable grad school. There is always more to do; that means there is always pressure on you, on your use of time; and that in turn means you need to erect some priorities and stick with them. If you sacrifice a regular time for prayer, thanksgiving, and meditative reading of the Word, then the problems you are facing will multiply. You may kid yourself into thinking that you can abandon your quiet time because you are studying the Bible all day. The truth is, you need it all the more. But the payoff is also great. If you set yourself to seek God's face at the beginning of each day, then you will be far more likely to turn the more academic parts of your day into devotion.

There is always more to do. Quality education exposes you to the vistas, the distance between you and the horizons of knowledge out there. Indeed, as you study more, the horizon will seem farther away! You arrive at seminary secretly thinking there cannot be all *that* much to Bible study. After all, it is only one book. But the farther you progress, the more you discover the vast fields of learning that open up before the diligent student of Scripture and of cognate disciplines. Part of the purpose of your education is to achieve precisely this— to make you realize a little of what is out there. But these extensive vistas must never be permitted to sidetrack you from what is important. Precisely because you can never exhaust all there is to know about the Bible and theology, you may just as well get your priorities right and self-consciously slow the pace down a little.

Second, grades aren't everything. They are important; they are not all-important. What shall it profit a man if he gain a 3.8 GPA and lose his own soul? If grades mean *that* much to you, extend your study over an extra quarter or two; but set a watch on your priorities.

Third, do not think that what you are facing as a student is unique. Not only is it the challenge of most students, it is also the challenge of most people in any form of vocational ministry. There are *always* more things to do than we can possibly accomplish. And it has always been that way. I love this passage from Luther, written to his friend Lang in 1516:

> I could almost say that I need two secretaries; I do hardly anything else all day long than write letters. I am the monastery preacher; I am delegated to read at table; I am expected to preach daily in the parish church; I am head of the monastery school; I am vicar of the monastery Order which means a prior eleven times over [Ed. note: because there were eleven cloisters in the district]; I am the officer responsible for the fish-pond; I act as substitute; I lecture on Paul and am studying the Psalms; and then all this correspondence which takes up the greater part of my time; I have scarcely any left for my private prayers, never to mention the special temptations of the flesh, the world, and the devil.

But precisely because he was so busy, Luther set aside time to pray. The habits you form now will bless you or haunt you for the rest of your life and ministry.

Fourth, recognize that the seminary cannot make you into a man of God. The seminary is a peculiar, somewhat distorting institution. We require that you spend a disproportionate percentage of this part of your life in study. But we are not a local church, with its diversity, many kinds of ministry, different ages and interests, and so forth. There are some experienced people here who will teach you out of the fruit of their own study and out of the years of their own considerable experience of ministry and mission. What the seminary does, it does reasonably well. But it cannot guarantee spiritual maturity; and it operates best when its students are well-grounded in local churches and actively engaged in some form of Christian ministry. The ratio of hours spent in such ministry, to hours spent in study, will vary enormously from student to student; a host of factors intrudes. But no thoughtful student can afford to let his entire life revolve around the seminary.

Fifth, even in a confessional school, capable students will go through periods of self-examination and doubt as they learn to wrestle with difficult questions. Do not be frightened by doubt; learn to handle it properly. In the last century, F. J. A. Hort wrote, "Beliefs worth calling beliefs must be purchased by the sweat of the brow. The easy conclusions which are accepted on borrowed grounds in evasion of the labour and responsibility of thought may or may not be coincident with truth; in either case they have little or no share in its power."

Sixth, avoid the arrogance of many young academics who become intoxicated by their newly discovered intellectual draughts; equally, avoid the arrogance of some zealous souls who are intoxicated by the assurance of their own spiritual prowess, and who in consequence feel they need not work diligently at their studies. None of us is what we ought to be; all of us should be much farther down the Christian way.

Finally, pursue Biblical balance—especially in those aspects of the Christian life to which you feel least drawn. You are a competent student. In time, your danger will be that you are so confident on the intellectual side of things that you will be tempted to ignore relational development and the discipline of personal prayer and meditation. Others are gifted with people skills but find it difficult to rub two theological thoughts together. Still others are inward and pietistic. In part we should simply rejoice at the diversity of people God calls into His church, at the diversity of gracious gifts He dispenses. But that diversity must never be used as an excuse to impede our pursuit of Biblical balance, Biblical wholeness, Biblical maturity—loving God with heart and soul and mind and strength, and our neighbors as ourselves.

Your fellow pilgrim,
Paul Woodson

28

*A*lthough I appreciated the basic sanity and balance of Dr. Woodson's last letter, rightly or wrongly I felt it did not do justice to the diversity of gifts in the Body of Christ. In any case, I had always been drawn to the academic side of things, so I justified my increasing focus on that side of life by assuring myself that I was simply nurturing my God-given gifts. By the end of the third term, I had decided that I would transfer to Yale Divinity School for at least the next academic year. But I decided I would tell no one until the current academic year was over. I certainly did not want to engage Dr. Woodson on the subject.

So Ginny and I moved to New Haven, and then as a matter of courtesy I wrote to Dr. Woodson about my decision. I told him that this decision was prompted not least by my growing conviction that evangelicals must be academically respectable to win a hearing for the gospel in the academic marketplace. Of course I was sorry to leave Deerfield just a week or two before his own return from Strasbourg, but I felt my priorities were right. This was his reply, written within days of his return to Deerfield and TEDS.

August 1, 1984

Dear Tim,

Thank you for letting me know of your decision. I'm sure you have thought about this matter carefully and prayerfully. It was about a year or so ago that I wrote you of my own views about the pros and cons of studying Scripture and theology in a confessional environment, or otherwise. There is no point in repeating myself, and I have no doubt you took what I said into account when you made your decision.

(Ed. note: Woodson goes on to express regret that he and his wife were not around to send Tim and Ginny on their way, perhaps help with packing and the like. The paragraphs are reserved and slightly awkward, as if Woodson feels slightly guilty that he did not keep a closer, encouraging hand on Tim's shoulder, or perhaps slightly disappointed that Tim did not feel able to talk these matters out before he left the Chicago area. Then there is an amusing paragraph that draws attention to the fact that his personal letters are no longer being written out with a fountain pen. For the first time, they are being produced on a computer—though it is Woodson's wife who is doing the inputting. This makes it possible, Woodson observes with a scholar's eye for detail, to abandon underlining and take up italics.)

At the risk of sounding pedantic (though realizing I sometimes come across that way), I doubt very much that evangelicals are wise to pursue academic respectability. What we need is academic responsibility. There is a world of difference.

Elevating academic respectability to the level of controlling *desideratum* is an invitation to theological and spiritual compromise. I do not find Jesus angling to become a member of the Sanhedrin in order to gain a more public voice; I do not find Paul pursuing academic respectability in the categories of his day, for then he could not have written the kinds of things he did about rhetoric (e.g., 1 Corinthians 2:1ff.). Academic *responsibility* is something else. This means that we pursue integrity in debate, that we eschew harangues, that we seek to give an answer to everyone for the hope that is in us, that we persuade people with the truth. Academic respectability, in my vocabulary, has too much self-interest in it for me to trust it; academic responsibility, on the other hand, calls me to discipline and work.

Not long ago, a colleague of mine applied for an important chair in Biblical studies at a major university. He wrote to his *Doktorvater*, the scholar who had supervised his doctoral dissertation, to ask him if he could use his name as a reference. The *Doktorvater* assured him of his personal encouragement and support, but regretfully declined. He would, he said, have to mention my colleague's views on the authority of Scripture, and that could hurt him.

Now this raises a host of interesting questions. In a confessional school, it is a matter of integrity that faculty members should stick with the confession or leave the institution without dissembling. In a modern secular university, however, I would argue that only competence in the field is important—nothing else. Thus in one history department, it is possible to find, say, a Marxist historian (Ed. note:

How strange that today "Marxist historian" already sounds passé.) and a historian of the "Annales" school (someone doing the kind of work that has made Emmanuel Le Roy Ladurie popular, especially owing to his much-acclaimed book *Montaillou*), and others. Similarly, in a Biblical studies department, it might be possible to find, say, an atheist (Michael Goulder), a post-Bultmannian existentialist (John A. T. Robinson), a classic liberal (Geoffrey Lampe), a conservative Catholic (Ignace de la Potterie), a liberal Catholic (Raymond Brown), and an evangelical (Howard Marshall)—not to mention any number of other brands.

In practice, however, if the Marxist historian is in the chair, he or she might be able to block the appointment of a junior member to the department if that junior member opposes Marxist historiography. Similarly in a department of Biblical studies, if the existing members are united in opposing an evangelical's view of Scripture, questions of competence may prove to be of marginal importance. In that sense, I suppose I am more liberal than some of my liberal friends. I would argue that in the university *any* view may be permitted, provided there is competence and rational, critical discourse. By "rational" I mean that one's position must be maintained with vigorous reason and not by merely emotional appeals; and by "critical" I mean that any opinion must be justified and not merely pronounced.

But the problem goes deeper. For many people, the university is the place where the autonomy of human reason must prevail. Those of us who hold that what Scripture says is authoritative threaten the autonomy of reason; indeed, we hold that reason itself is tarnished with the Fall. That does *not* mean we should appeal to the irrational; it means that what is called rational cannot always be trusted. More important, the notion that human reason is autonomous is itself an ideological position that must be assessed. When this is done, it turns out that it is quite reasonable (!) to doubt the autonomy of reason. Certainly there ought to be place for a rigorous presentation of an alternative view.

But if you try to make your way in a society of scholars where the autonomy of human reason is a "given," or where any notion of revelation must finally be non-propositional, the price of "respectability" may prove unacceptably high. Either your views capsize, or you decide to hold your peace and not let anyone know what you really think. That price, for a Christian witness, is too high.

On the other hand, academic responsibility is another matter. We have to say, with considerable embarrassment, that for much of the last fifty or sixty years, the majority of evangelical scholarship has been largely intramural and has not engaged the intellectual challenges of the day, except at the popular level. When it has attempted to do so, it has often been so incompetent that its weaknesses have been glaring to those able to see them. Of course, there have been wonderful exceptions, but the stereotype is close enough to the truth that we have nothing to be proud about.

But now a new generation of young evangelical scholars is arising. The challenges and the opportunities are alike daunting. But there is an equally daunting temptation—gain academic respectability, for that is the path of jobs and influence. The temptation is as great for, say, evangelical church historians as for evangelical Biblical scholars.

I think this is tragic. I do not believe that God honors such timidity and fearfulness. Talk to believers behind the iron curtain and discover what they have to put up with by way of opprobrium and closed doors to academic advancement, simply because they confess Jesus as Lord. Our temptations are subtler, but no less dangerous for that.

If God were to call you to a life of scholarship, then pursue academic responsibility with your whole heart—not as a new god, but as an offering to God. It may well then be that your work will influence your times and make a difference in the intellectual climate. At very least you will then serve the interests of some younger scholars coming along behind, who will model themselves after you and learn the way of discipleship as scholars. Pursue academic responsibility, and trust God to work out the details of who hears you and what influence you have. Responsible scholarship has far more potential for discovering and buttressing truth and for winning people's minds than mere respectability anyway. If instead you take the lower road and pursue mere academic respectability, you may gain more plaudits from the world, but it is far more doubtful that you will have the approbation of Heaven. Once in a while there have been scholars who have gained both; it is doubtful if they have ever done so by pursuing respectability.

Now that you have decided to attend Yale, would I be presuming too much to offer some advice? I would say something similar to you if you went to Yale (or some other renowned theological institution) for a second theological degree. The advice becomes more urgent when your formal theological training is still only one year old.

First, do not hide your doubts and struggles. Dishonesty is *never* the best policy, whether in scholarship or in the faith. Work them through. And in your context that means you will need to keep in touch with people who can provide you with additional reading lists, people who can serve as sounding boards, people who have passed through these struggles themselves.

Second, be at least as critical of criticisms (your own and others') as of the things criticized.

Third, be prepared to suspend judgment. You are not going to find all the "answers" to difficult questions in your first couple of years. I was speaking to a colleague in the New Testament department a few weeks ago, and he mentioned that when he was pursuing doctoral studies twelve years ago in Europe, he did not have a clue how to relate John 1 (where Jesus, very early in His ministry, is regarded as Son of God, Messiah, King of Israel, Son of Man, etc.) to Matthew 16 and parallels (where, perhaps halfway through His public ministry, Jesus is confessed as Messiah and Son of God, as if this confession were an entirely new thing). Of course, my colleague knew the standard theories and especially the dominant view that John's Gospel at this point stands so loose to history that it is in fact a reflection of what was going on in John's church, not what was happening in Jesus' day. John's Christology begins (it is argued) where the Christology of the other evangelists leaves off. Only three years ago did my friend find an answer that entirely satisfied him.

The point is that in any theological education, you will be exposed to many things you cannot resolve. That is as true at Trinity as at Yale; it is simply that the areas of debate are different; we operate within a simple but firm confessional commitment. But in principle the best way to handle unresolved issues is clear. You must set yourself to resolve *some* of the issues to the best of your ability and be prepared to suspend judgment on some others.

Fourth, do not neglect what used to be called the regular means of grace—prayer, meditative reading of the Word, fellowship and worship, and instruction with God's people, and so forth. And get involved in some ministry. If you fail in these areas, the chances are very good that you will capsize. The stability of one's faith turns on far more than mere intellectual debate. And do not become a "one-issue" person. Remember, for instance, that according to the Bible, salvation turns on trusting Jesus Christ as He has disclosed Himself, not on articulating a certain view of the doctrine of Scripture—as important as such articulation is to the broader doctrine of revelation, of which it forms a part.

Fifth, do not become defensive or passive, grimly hanging on. If God wants you at Yale, get involved. Discuss, debate, talk, read, think. It could be a wonderful experience for you. If I may be permitted a word of testimony, it took me quite a while to recognize a truth so elementary I am ashamed I did not see it earlier. My more liberal colleagues always seemed to me to be setting the agenda. We were left in defensive trenches. They asked exciting new questions, even if those questions sometimes emerged from worldviews I could not accept; we were left asking either the same questions that were asked in the last century or wondering how we could respond to *their* questions.

But I no longer see things that way. I think that, just as they raise questions out of their matrix of thought, so I may, indeed I must, raise questions out of mine. In other words, although I want to engage with some contemporary thought, I refuse to allow my entire agenda to be set by others. I have my own agenda. I am capable of asking some questions that they could not possibly ask or answer, precisely because their matrix is so alien to mine. But, I would argue, at least at some points, my matrix is closer to the presuppositions of the thought of Scripture, and therefore my answers are more likely to endure into the future. Some of my writing is now far freer, perhaps a little more creative, hopefully more interesting, than it was twenty years ago. I only wish I had learned this lesson earlier.

Enjoy your year! Keep in touch.

Much love in Christ Jesus,
Paul Woodson

29

*M*y first weeks and months at Yale were immensely stimulating. Most of my courses were enjoyable, and, despite my fearful expectations, I found few objections to my stance as an evangelical. Only toward the end of November, when Ginny and I went to her parents' home on Long Island for Thanksgiving, was I able to articulate the nature of the openness that I found at Yale Divinity School.

It dawned on me that evangelicalism was warmly welcomed, along with every other brand of theology, provided it made no absolute claims. Any opinion could be tolerated, even respected, except those that said some other opinion was wrong—especially if the opinion being condemned belonged to the avant garde. Above all, it was impossible to say that you were against, say, the ordination of practicing homosexuals, let alone the ordination of women, without inviting a furious rejoinder. The net effect was that evangelicals, simply grateful to be there and enjoy the fabulous library, rich heritage (names like Jonathan Edwards and Timothy Dwight were on every building), and generally high-quality teaching, learned to hold their tongues. In time, they became toothless evangelicals, domesticated evangelicals. Many still retained, at least in basic structure, the convictions with which they entered, but their tolerance levels soon became so smoothly adjusted that they could accept far, far more than Paul (that most flexible of apostles) could—indeed far, far more than Jesus Himself could.

I wrote asking Dr. Woodson if he thought I was sizing things up rightly.

November 30, 1984

Dear Tim,

Thanks so much for your remarkably astute letter. It astonishes and delights me how quickly you have been able to put your finger on the pulse of things.

There was a time when ecumenism was the watchword for a large segment of world Christendom. If I am not mistaken, ecumenism has now largely been eclipsed. Of course, enormous amounts of money and effort still go into it, but in many circles it seems faintly quaint and irrelevant. It has been overtaken, on the inside track as it were, by a more powerful vehicle—the juggernaut of pluralism. Historic ecumenism sought to accommodate differences by seeking out the lowest common denominator of faith and churchmanship in order to gain agreement and a show of unity. By contrast pluralism rejoices in the diversity—and insists that the diversity does not matter because no view is better than any other view. The only view that is utterly unquestioned, absolutely unbending in its regal demands, is the doctrine of pluralism itself.

Pluralism may not have reached so far at Yale. Yale's focus is still *Christian* theology. But last year one of my colleagues, Dr. Carson in the New Testament department lectured at one Ivy League seminary (though of course not at the invitation of the seminary in question, but only of a miniscule evangelical caucus of students there) where an American Indian on one recent occasion led the student body in animist worship.

A Christian Indian scholar (from India, this time!), Dr. Sunand Sumithra, successfully defended his doctoral dissertation at Tübingen a few years ago, in which he showed, on the basis of his research into WCC documents in Geneva, that at least some senior personnel in the World Council of Churches saw it as their long-range mission not only to bring about the union of Christian churches but the union of world religions. The published form of his work is *Revolution as Revelation: A Study of M. M. Thomas's Theology* (Tübingen: International Christian Network/New Delhi: Theological Research and Communication Institute, 1984).

Yet the hard fact of the matter is that when all values are equal, no value is worth anything. It is far wiser to argue that in a democracy all values may be firmly and vigorously debated, rather than to argue that all values should be treated as if they were the same (when transparently they are not). Theism and atheism are not the same; theism and deism are not the same; theism and monism are not the same; trinitarian monotheism and unitarian monotheism are not the same. It takes an extraordinary leap of faith to conclude that the profound differences among these worldviews are of little consequence, either because those who uphold this or that view are sincere (which makes being sincere more important than truth), or because all of these views belong in some elusive way to a larger "truth" (which is palpable nonsense).

The first sacrifice of pluralism is rationality; the second is intellectual integrity; the third is genuine tolerance, for in my experience no group is more *in*tolerant than the committed pluralists. Genuine toleration in a society exists where groups with mutually exclusive values try to convince others they are right at certain points and others are wrong and undertake this exercise openly, frankly, courteously. Phony toleration exists where every effort to win another to your view is denounced as "proselytism" and where genuine debate and rigorous discussion are sharply curtailed under the ill-focused assumption that we are all saying the same thing anyway or that it does not matter what we believe since we are all entitled to our opinions. We may well be entitled to differing opinions, but that is a long step from concluding that they are all of equal worth.

At the intellectual level, pluralism is linked with the so-called new hermeneutic. How much reading you have done so far in this area I have no idea. I risk simplification in describing the "new hermeneutic" as the view that there is so much subjectivity tied to our own attempts to understand that one cannot properly speak of the meaning of texts but only of the meaning we *find in* or even *bring to* texts. The focus is not on the text's meaning (it is commonly argued that texts have no univocal meaning), but on whatever meaning I find there, granted who I am.

There is a considerable literature on the subject, important literature that gleans a great deal of worth in the new hermeneutic (for instance, all kinds of warnings about our subjectivity, our cultural arrogance, our blind spots), or that warns us of the theoretical limitations of the new hermeneutic and points out the dangers of any position that drifts toward solipsism. But my concern is theological. In the Christian view of things, indeed in any responsible theistic view of the world, what ensures that we do not slide into a morass of utter relativism is God Himself. He knows what is true and what is not. It may not be easy to discern His thoughts, and of course we can never grasp the thinking of an infinite God in all its complexity; but at least we have a structure that enables us to be self-consistent when we insist there is such a thing as truth—truth as God perceives it, truth that is objectively true regardless of what we think of it.

In other words, pluralism makes a certain sense (though it is, intellectually speaking, one of the sloppiest worldviews, in my opinion, the history of intellectual thought has ever seen) *only* if one has already denied the existence of a personal/transcendent, thinking, speaking, omniscient God. Otherwise it doesn't. And the cost is unbearably high anyway. It demands an unquestioning allegiance while insisting that all allegiances must be questioned; it insists that no interpretation can have coercive force over other interpretations, except for the interpretation that insists that no interpretation can have coercive force over other interpretations.

Of course, most people do not take pluralism on board at so self-conscious and philosophical a level. But that is precisely the problem, isn't it? For pluralism has become the dominant "background noise" in much of the Western world. It is thought to be wise, broad-minded, gentle, forbearing, patient, intelligent. It is none of these things, and it cannot even preserve the safeguards that it rightly seeks. But because it is associated in the public mind with a catena of virtues, it is hard even for mature Christians to escape the tentacles of its influence. The result is a form of belief that is not robust or confident enough to evangelize anyone or to feel sympathetic to any of the frankly *exclusivist* claims of the New Testament (e.g., read John 5:19ff.; 14:6; Acts 4:12; Galatians 1:8, 9; etc.).

In short, the emperor has no clothes, and the world will be a better place when he wakes up and realizes it. Meanwhile, anyone who approaches this emperor's throne with an announcement about the emperor's nakedness cannot count on having the scepter handed to him.

Unless you understand that this lies at the heart of the dominant strands of American (indeed, Western) culture at the end of the twentieth century, the effectiveness of your ministry will be sharply curtailed. I am quite sure the spiritual instincts you have shown on this matter will serve you well. I look forward to hearing from you again. Elizabeth and I are rooting for you, Tim.

Yours in Christ's service,
Paul Woodson

30

*D*r. Woodson's *warnings about pluralism's allure sounded strangely familiar. Then I remembered why. During my days as a student at Cambridge, he had penned a letter that really upset me. In his closely reasoned epistle he challenged the premises of the "universalism" espoused by my agnostic friend Laura. At the time, Laura was quite suspicious of anyone who claimed to know "the way." I liked her so much that I really did not want to hear anything critical of her. Infatuation does strange things to a person.*

Dr. Woodson's new letter echoed themes of the earlier one. It evoked memories of those emotionally charged conversations with Laura. It also brought back uncomfortable memories of my own petulant reaction to the letter. I had stormed out of my residence and rushed into a cool Cambridge evening, so exercised was I by Dr. Woodson's "insensitivity."

Now, perhaps a little more mature in the faith, I did not brush off these warnings that a pervasive pluralistic environment might taper one's belief in the uniqueness of Christ as Savior. Even though I believed my feet to be more firmly planted theologically, I had to concede that I was not totally immune from pluralism's charms. I was concerned that it was affecting my own way of thinking, especially regarding the lost condition of persons who knew nothing of Christ.

I do not want to give the wrong impression. I was not dissatisfied with the education I was receiving at Yale. It was generally of a high academic quality. Moreover, I loved to study in the Beineke Library. What a treasure trove of books and manuscripts!

On occasion, however, I found the teaching in a few classes frankly illiberal. A responsible evangelical literature addressing theological, Biblical, and critical issues was simply ignored or appraised as intellectually retrograde. It was often excluded as even a foil in classroom discourse. For all practical purposes, it represented a "nonliterature." I could not reconcile the close-minded attitude of several of my professors towards evangelical scholarship with the way they vaunted their pluralistic credentials. With them, religious pluralism seemed to stop at the door of evangelical faith, or what a few opprobriously styled "Fundamentalism." Happily, a good number of the professors were not so narrow-minded and ideologically blinded. I especially enjoyed talking with Professors Hans Frei, Paul Holmer, and Abraham Malherbe.

I did not want to admit to Dr. Woodson my mixed feelings about Yale. He might think that I was a terribly flighty person because I had studied at Trinity, only to drag Ginny off to Yale, only to be troubled in turn by the theological environment there. In consequence, I wrote to him about a secondary issue only tangentially related to the problem of pluralism. I discovered that my book-buying habits were directed more by impulse than considered design. At Trinity, I had purchased a sizable number of books written from an evangelical point of view; now at Yale I was purchasing a fair share of books written from a more liberal optic. Self-confessed bibliophile that I was, I knew I would continue to purchase books. But might there be some way to indulge this delightful mania in a manner less whimsical, more cost-effective, and ultimately more satisfying?

I wrote to Dr. Woodson and asked his counsel on how to put together a library. A self-confessed bibliophile himself, he had undoubtedly wrestled with the same issues. To deflect his attention even further from my own experiences at Yale, I also devoted a fairly lengthy discussion to Ginny's activities at our church in New Haven. She was teaching a women's Bible class. She said that she got more out of the class than anyone else because she had to prepare the lessons. Sometimes she asked me questions that forced me to dig into commentaries as well. It was fun working together, we often said to each other.

December 19, 1984

Dear Tim,

Mrs. Woodson and I trust that this Christmas season will be one of your happiest. Are you and Ginny staying in the New Haven area, or are you going to visit Ginny's family on Long Island or your Mom in Flemington?

We are planning to stay in Deerfield and visit with friends, and Elizabeth's sister Margaret will spend a few days with us. Particularly at Christmastime Elizabeth and I wish so much that the Lord in His providence had allowed us to have children. We still sometimes imagine what it would have been like to have had our own kids gathered around a beautifully lit tree. A roaring fire would warm the room on a crisp Christmas Eve. Elizabeth would have read to the children Christmas stories until they dozed off into the wonderful world of dreams where only children venture freely and adults cannot follow.

Despite our musings about children, we cannot doubt God's wisdom in our lives. He has been so faithful. I have on my desk at school an embossed copy of the poignant response of Polycarp to an interrogator who was asking him to deny Christ. Said Polycarp, who knew that his statement would hasten his own martyrdom, "Eighty and six years have I served him and he hath done me no wrong. How then can I blaspheme my King who saved me?" Tim, as you know, I am no paragon of virtue. I have not suffered much for Christ. And I have not served Christ for eighty-six years. But I concur wholeheartedly with Polycarp's sentiments: He hath done me no wrong and I trust Him with my life.

Elizabeth and I have determined that one of these days we are simply going to pop in the car and drive directly to New Haven to visit you. Does this not sound presumptuous for us old folks to talk so irresponsibly, inviting ourselves to your home? We would really love to see you sometime. It staggers my mind that we have spent so little time together.

I have pondered your question regarding how to build a library. I will try to give you a few suggestions based on my own experience. You should recognize these for what they are. They are simply reflections of a lover of books who has muddled through putting too many books on the shelves in his office at school, his office at home, and in a storeroom reserved for even more books in our basement. These comments do not come from a professional librarian. Moreover, you may want to read Walter Elwell's intriguing article in CT (May 4, 1980), "Bibliomania: Eight Ways to Avoid It," to rectify any false information I give you.

My own first principle is this—there are books, and there are books. The first category of books are simply the ones you want for your library; the second volumes are all others that do not mesh with your criteria for inclusion in that library. Books vary in value according to the worth people place upon them. Most books have value for someone. Most books will have little lasting value for you. You want to build a library that accords with your personal assessment of what books will be valuable for you in your ministry.

One of the pivotal temptations that theological students face is that they want to buy everything. This of course is impossible and unnecessary. Their desire exceeds their pocketbook. Moreover, frustration sets in because most books bought on impulse quickly lose their luster. A student's interests change, and then he or she finds that a library of unread and unhelpful books has to be lugged around from place to place. Take my word for it—once you have books on a shelf, it is difficult to throw them away.

This leads us to a second principle—it is not important to buy many books; rather it is important to buy good books. A librarian at the national library in Paris (the Bibliothèque Nationale) once told me that approximately 50,000 volumes out of a collection of between thirteen and seventeen million are used over and over again. The huge remainder (whatever the exact figure is today) are seldom, if ever, consulted. This datum implies that if we select "good" books, we will have at our disposal the books we will actually use. A number of university libraries have set aside study rooms for core collections—that is, their most frequently used books. You and I can go to specialized collections to consult volumes we do not have in our own libraries.

Most of us have relatively little disposable income to spend on books. Thus it makes sense to invest our money in what are "core" books for us.

The third principle is this—what constitutes a core library for one person may not be a core library for another person. If you are going into the pastorate, then your core of books will differ substantially from the core books of a church historian, for example.

What might make up a good core collection for a pastor? You can well imagine the categories for which you will want the best books available—the "best" commentaries, devotional works, language tool volumes, theology texts, church history studies, homiletical works, biographies, and books devoted to ethics, Christian counseling, Christian education, and management. I may have left out a few categories. Once again, you do not need many books in these areas, but you want at least a few of the "best" books in the respective fields. The Lord may call you to minister in a town where a good library is not present. Then the importance of having built a good core library will be patent.

But how do you determine which are the "best" works? By assigning books to students, professors vote concerning their estimation of the relative merits of various books in their discipline. In consequence, you may already have in your library many "good" books. But the professors' "good" books also need to be "good" volumes from your point of view. If the books assigned for class do not meet your personal standards, you may want to sell them. Then again, professors vary among themselves in their assessments of books. I would ask other profs for the list of the "best" books in a discipline you are attempting to strengthen in your collection. Through a careful sifting process, you will be able to establish a very useful and personalized core library. You may not end up with many books, but they will be good books from your point of view.

A fourth principle is more a suggestion than anything else—you may want to choose one or more specialized areas of book collecting in addition to setting up your core library. In my twenties, I decided that one of my specialization areas would be theology textbooks. And now, forty years later, I do have a fairly decent collection of theology texts. Reading them over the years has given much joy. But should you ever care to see a great theology text collection and you are in the neighborhood of Gordon-Conwell, drop by the office of my dear friend Professor Roger Nicole who teaches there. (Ed. note: Dr. Nicole is presently teaching at Reformed Seminary in Orlando, Florida.) Professor Nicole has one of the finest private collections of theology texts I have seen in the United States. One afternoon he very graciously recounted for me marvelous tales of how he put together his fabulous library. I was utterly bedazzled by his ingenuity and skill in figuring out how this should be done.

Here are a few additional thoughts which come to mind.

1) You might join several academic societies so that you can receive their journals. If certain journals have a particular interest for you, it is good to begin your collection of their fascicles even while you are in grad school. I wish someone had told me that when I was a student.

2) You might share books with other students or pastor friends; a cooperative venture in book collecting could be very beneficial.

3) May I propose that you take advantage of any interlibrary service near you. This way you might be able to consult a book that is not in your library before you decide whether or not you really want to buy it.

4) Try to have your name put on the address lists of discount book distributors. Probably the vast majority of the books I have purchased have been on sale through discount book catalogs.

5) Plan ahead. For example, if you intend to begin in six months

to preach a series of expository sermons on Isaiah, start devoting your book-buying budget to good commentaries and studies on Isaiah.

Tim, I could write about this subject forever. I really do love books, and some of my own have become almost like genuine friends to me. This may sound strange, but it is true.

Elizabeth just called me to the dinner table. Thus you are spared from more of my rambling about "how to build a library."

For honesty's sake, I should quickly add a final word. I presently have hundreds of books gathered from hither and yon that do not belong to my own core library or fall under the purview of any conceivable research interest. Will I sell them or give them away? I doubt it. I have a hard time parting with any books, especially those I have sheltered for twenty or thirty years. I mention this fact so that you will realize that there is more than a touch of hypocrisy in the principles I have proposed to you. Perhaps you should understand this letter in terms of suggestions of what I would do if I could do it over again, rather than as guidelines I have actually followed.

Please give our love to Ginny. Trust all is well and that the New Year will be a great one.

Cordially,
Paul Woodson

31

I did not know how to react to Dr. Woodson's last letter. Despite his self-deprecating remarks, his tips for building a library were quite instructive. To create a core library would be a prudent measure for anyone going into the pastorate. And I immediately pinpointed an area where I wanted to create my own specialized collection—Puritan devotional literature. I had become a genuine devotee of the writings of Sibbes and Baxter. Moreover, I had benefitted enormously from reading J. I. Packer's book, Knowing God— a work reflecting many Puritan themes. (Ed. note: Since then Packer has come out with A Quest for Godliness: The Puritan Vision of the Christian Life [1990].)

But in candor, I was discomforted by Dr. Woodson's almost too restrained account of how he and Mrs. Woodson had imagined together what it would be like to have had children. He had not intended to make us feel sorry for them. And we did not feel "sorry" in a secular sense. We, too, understood, at least in theory, that God's perfect will was being worked out in the Woodsons' lives. By this time Ginny and I knew that the Christian way is Christ's way; it is not a journey in which God's children inevitably get exactly what they want.

But how could I write back anything genuinely consoling to the Woodsons? Ginny and I did not have any children. But we certainly hoped to be parents some day. Our situation was not like the Woodsons'. Thus we felt that we were in no position to claim that we empathetically understood what they were experiencing. We were quite certain that we did not.

And yet had not Dr. Woodson counseled me in so many areas? Shouldn't I at least try to come up with the right words of comfort for him and his wife? But I felt completely bereft of wisdom regarding what those words were.

Then again, one of my friends from church, whom I shall call

"Bob," knocked on our apartment door in late December. He was disconsolate. Earlier in the day his wife had walked out of the house and said she was not coming back—ever. Ginny and I couldn't believe it. "Bob" and "Sally" seemed an ideal Christian couple with three lovely children. "Bob" taught the men's Bible class, and "Sally" was very active at church. When "Bob" poured out his heart to me and Ginny, I was staggered by the realization that behind the public facade, their marriage had been a disaster.

"Bob" had come to me because he knew I was training for the ministry and we were real friends. But I soon discovered that I had nothing profoundly helpful to say. I did not have the understanding to deal with these people's problems. I felt as if my counsel to "Bob" consisted of mere platitudes.

Drubbed by these experiences, I began to wonder about the value of my preparation for ministry. Here I was studying Greek and Hebrew, ecclesiastical history, theology, and a whole host of other subjects. To my mind I was receiving an excellent formal "education." But I did not seem to know how to provide an encouraging word to Dr. Woodson when he had confided his pained sense of loss; I had no idea how to counsel "Bob" save to say that he should seek immediate help from our pastor. Was my divinity school education with its specialized subject matter and vocabulary actually relevant to the hurting people I would encounter in ministry? For me, the Woodsons and "Bob" and "Sally" began to represent the hundreds of other people trapped in troubling situations whom I would be called to counsel in the future. And I had little to say.

Serious self-doubt crept into my heart. At that point I could not share my feelings with Ginny. After all, I had persuaded her, somewhat against her will, that we should take the opportunity of enrolling at Yale. Nor could I tell Dr. Woodson that his Christmas comments were partially responsible for prompting me to ask if I were capable of ministering to hurting people. I felt alone. With whom could I share my anxieties and self-doubt?

I wrote to Dr. Woodson and completely sidestepped his Christmas letter. Rather I obliquely referred to my passing concern that a formal seminary education, while certainly useful, may not be the best preparation for ministering to people. My allusion was so oblique (partly, I think, because if I said more, I would have felt like a failure) I wondered if Dr. Woodson would pick up on it. He did.

January 15, 1985

Dear Tim,

(Ed. note: The date of this letter largely explains Woodson's opening gambit.)

I hope that while you were in the Chicago area last year, you gained at least a little appreciation for the Chicago Bears. Doubtless the New York Giants remain your favorite team. Some of us here in Chicago have a premonition that next season the Bears might be quite ferocious. Wouldn't that be something if you and I had to root against each other next season in a Giants-Bears play-off game?

In my last letter I failed to ask you about an article that appeared in the November 9, 1984, issue of *Christianity Today*. The article is entitled "Evangelical Students Gain Visibility at Yale." I would be grateful if you would share your perspective on the article, given your earlier comments about your studies at Yale.

I do not know if I am reading more into your most recent letter than is there, but I sense that you are having serious second thoughts about the training you have been receiving for pastoral ministry. Should that be the case, you would not be the first divinity school student to feel this way. In fact, many individuals training for "professional" jobs (I use quotes because quite frankly I do not like to apply that word to pastoral ministry, which must be characterized rather more by servanthood than by professionalism) find themselves learning a vocabulary absolutely foreign to those outside their discipline. Moreover, as a specialist, one is obliged to study long and hard to become reasonably competent in a field. Are you not more at ease to learn that a physician who is going to operate on you has attended a fine school and has studied diligently?

So, too, a pastor has specific tools that are important to master. If you do not know Hebrew and Greek, you are more dependent on inferior commentaries than you should be when you prepare your sermons. If you do not know church history reasonably well, you may have a difficult time answering the misinformation distributed by Jehovah's Witnesses. As you know, they go door to door indicating that the doctrine of the Trinity did not exist until the Council of Nicea (A.D. 325). What will you say to your parishioners who ask you about the claims of the Jehovah's Witnesses? If you have never studied theology seriously, you will be less capable of teaching your people the great truths of the gospel. These are only a few illustrations of the very practical value of seminary education. They provide an ample justification for pursuing it.

Let me guess what your response to this opening salvo might be: "Your rationale sounds a touch defensive. You know that I already accept the points you are making. Why then do you review them? Can you not discern that my disquiet runs far deeper than this? I feel that I am gaining an education but losing my own heart for ministry, my capacity to minister. My education seems to be taking me away from the very people I want to reach with the good news of Christ. Both my vocabulary and my technical knowledge of theology are creating barriers between me and many of my brothers and sisters in Christ, let alone the unchurched."

If this is your complaint, it is well taken. Some of us who have been teaching in seminaries for years fail to understand that preparation for ministry is far more than passing exams in the "right" subjects. Some of us have assumed that students would be good in ministry if they had jumped high enough over the proper academic hurdles we set up for them. But in truth, a prospective minister's heart will mean more to his people than his head knowledge. I have known some godly pastors who can't preach well, but their churches grow nonetheless. The people love them. I have seldom encountered a spiritually alive church where the pastor has prodigious head knowledge but no heart for the Lord. A pastor must be able to relate to people, feel for people, and pray for people. A pastor must be able to bring the Word of God to bear on the difficult problems of life.

Above all, a prospective pastor needs to know the Lord well. This means that preparation for ministry also includes spiritual formation—developing the disciplines of prayer and Scripture reading.

It is difficult to know what kind of "program" could offer all of these elements. I suspect that you have taken a preponderance of "theoretical" courses in the M.Div. program and have not yet had much pastoral theology. But in addition you might take specific measures to balance an overemphasis upon academics in your preparation. You might consider doing an extended internship with a competent senior pastor so that you can obtain more firsthand experience. When you take a course in church history, you might attempt to learn what characterized those men and women who were especially used of God. When you exegete passages for a New Testament class, you might think through how you would preach the passage. When you study theology, you might determine how to apply Biblically derived doctrine to area after area of life and thought. In this matter the Puritan literature is among the most helpful you will find. Make every allowance for the datedness of its language and of some of its perspectives, but study how in their sermons and writings the Puritan pastors and theologians were determined to articulate the "uses" to which any doctrine must be put.

But as I said before, the indispensable element of preparing for ministry is to know the living Christ, who as Luther says, reveals to us the loving heart of our Heavenly Father. Some pastors are as orthodox as can be regarding Christology, but they do not know Christ well. Other pastors may not be seminary trained, but when they sing "What a friend we have in Jesus," you know they are singing from the heart. They know the Master. You can sense that. They seem to know the "right" word of comfort to give to the troubled soul. I am praying that you will be a pastor who both knows Christ well and can teach others well about Him. To my mind, that is the ideal pastor. You might want to read Baxter's *The Reformed Pastor* once again.

Please give our warmest greetings to Ginny.

Your fellow servant,
Paul Woodson

32

*I*n January I had started auditing an elective course on liberation theology. I read through two books by G. Gutiérrez and some essays and books by a host of other writers, many of them scholars from Latin America. Some of it I found dense and tortuous; some of it was intensely interesting and made me think of the theological reasoning that accompanied the American War of Independence. At the same time, I was uneasy about how the Bible was being handled in some of these discussions, even though I couldn't put my finger on the source of my discomfort. My letter to Dr. Woodson brought a reply framed by broader considerations than the hermeneutical ones I had brought up.

February 1, 1985

Dear Tim,

Your exposure to liberation theology is a good thing. Yet I wonder sometimes if anyone can appreciate the powerful appeal of liberation theology who has not lived for awhile among the abysmally poor, in countries where there is also an oligarchic minority that is notoriously wealthy.

Your reference to the American Revolutionary War is pertinent, though the parallels should not be pressed too far. Some scholars have examined many hundreds of sermons preached in America in the second half of the eighteenth century and observed the implicit and sometimes explicit linking of America and American destiny with Old Testament Israel. The sense of being under God's hand, of furthering God's redemptive purposes, of being surrounded by a sea of dangerous foes whom God Himself opposes, is very strong. When war broke out with England, many of those who could not share this theology and who remained loyal to George III migrated north to what became Canada and were eventually dubbed "United Empire Loyalists."

On any showing, however, most scholars today would not try to defend the use of Scripture that ties America (or any other nation) to Old Testament Israel. The antitype of ancient Israel is the new covenant people of God—the church; or among traditional dispensationalists, even if the church is considered a relatively independent body, ancient Israel is tied to modern Israel by organic and covenantal connections and should not be confused with America. That does not mean the Revolutionary War was wrong; it means that some of the Biblical reasoning that went into justifying it was wrong.

Of course, a pacifist might argue that it was wrong to take up arms at the time of independence and that it is wrong to do so today. But most of us, I suspect, think that the fathers of our nation were right to bear arms in defense of freedom—and that means that in principle at least we must allow that it may be justifiable for a revolutionary movement to do so in defense of freedom today. That does not mean we should justify every revolution; it does mean we are ill-placed to condemn *all* revolutions without further reflection.

Among Christians, much of the debate has turned on the interpretation of Romans 13:1ff. Those who argue that revolution is always wrong frequently cite these verses. In that case, of course, consistency demands that they should also condemn the war that brought our own country to birth. Alternatively, some argue that the explicit assumption of Romans 13 is that the "governing authorities" are basically *just*. They are God's servants to do good, to punish the wicked. But suppose the governing authorities are thoroughly corrupt, the locus of most of the evil they themselves are supposed to be suppressing. What then? Doesn't the time ever arrive when oppression by formally constituted authorities becomes so intolerable that the only responsible course is to revolt and throw off their shackles? Certainly our fathers thought so; certain it is, too, that in several Latin American countries today, the amount of injustice perpetrated by the state is far more appalling and brutal than anything our fathers had to face at the hands of the British.

That still does not necessarily mean that the alternative the revolutionaries want to introduce is superior. It is disconcerting to recognize how frequently a revolution against oppression issues in a regime still more oppressive. But at least one can understand that, in principle, comfortable middle class American Christians whose nation was born in revolution, based in part (if only in part) on arguments from Scripture now judged indefensible, should not be too quick to write off liberation theology without listening closely to what is being said and why.

Indeed, not a few Latin theologians argue that what they are doing is theology in their own context—contextualized theology. (This is one of the spin-offs of the "new hermeneutic" I briefly mentioned in an earlier letter.) Therefore people (like us) who have never lived in their culture are ill-placed to judge it. It is not enough, they insist, to export U.S. home-grown theology to Latin America; the Latins must produce their own.

Once again, they are saying something important. To take an entirely different example for a moment, a responsible systematic theology constructed in sub-Saharan Black Africa by Africans would doubtless give far more place to family and family connections than one written by Europeans or Americans. The numerous family metaphors for the church, the sense of corporateness that permeates the New Testament (something we ignore or find strange) would be for them important grist for their theological mill. They would doubtless devote far more space to demons and to casting out demons. Salvation would be portrayed more strongly in terms of a power encounter and perhaps less strongly in terms of forensic categories. If our hypothetical African theologian is wise and well-read, he or she will not *discount* the Biblical categories that stress the individual and the forensic (any more than a wise and well-read Western systematician would fail to deal with the corporate nature of the church and the gospel as power encounter between God and Satan), but the *balance* and *proportion* of the two works are likely to be significantly different. But—and this is very important—provided the African and the Westerner were agreed that the Scripture they interpret is itself authoritative, they would also agree that they should learn from each other and be corrected by each other. Both may insist, rightly, that the shaping of their work for their respective cultures should properly be done by someone from their respective cultures. But they are not saying that *anything* they say about the Bible is immune to criticism from those of another culture. At least in theory, they ought to be humble enough to admit that they may have notorious blind spots, that their own cultures may have tripped them up and caused them to make major interpretive errors. That is why we need one another; that is why we can learn so much from Christians from other cultures.

But where the Bible is not reverenced as the agreed authority, the influence of the new hermeneutic is likely to be far more pernicious.

Now both sides will argue that the other does not have the *right* to criticize. My interpretation, springing from my own cultural experience, becomes unassailable. And suddenly, unwittingly, the Bible becomes domesticated. I use it and brandish about its vaguely perceived authority, but what it says is what I find in it, simply because of the singularity of my cultural experience. At that point the Bible no longer stands over culture; it has been domesticated by culture.

So when I turn to, say, Gutiérrez, I need to be careful lest I criticize out of my own cultural blindness and inexperience; but I also need to insist that *no one* has the right to domesticate the Word of God.

The thought of Gutiérrez is complex, and I do not have the time to write a lengthy review of his work. But let me raise a couple of questions about his handling of Scripture—the focal concern in your letter. Gutiérrez chooses to make the Exodus the controlling pattern for his theological reflection. Here God brings the enslaved people out of bondage and into the promised land. This, he says, should be the controlling paradigm for people living in oppression today, and to this he links the notion of *praxis*—the actual *doing* of God's work as the framework out of which any genuine theological reflection must take place.

My first question is this: What reasons control the choice of this particular paradigm? Why not choose, say, Jeremiah at the time of the exile, telling the people to submit to the foreign power? Or after the revolution succeeds, what stops these theologians from choosing, say, the command to wipe out the peoples of Canaan as the paradigm to authorize revolutionary genocide? (I'm not of course suggesting they *would* so choose; I'm merely asking, on methodological grounds, what there is to stop them.) What gives Gutiérrez the right to choose the exodus? Pacifists would argue that he should choose the Sermon on the Mount. Where is the *warrant* for his choice?

I would argue that any such choice must be constrained by (among other things) canonical connections. What place does the exodus have in the history of redemption? What is the antitype of the exodus in the New Testament? It is not the overthrow of the Roman government!

And if one is going to choose the exodus, what gives one the right to choose only one part of the narrative? Is not the Biblical account of the exodus steeped in *God's* initiative, rather than in mass revolutionary fervor? Is it not linked to God's gracious self-disclosure in miracles and plagues? Is it not linked to the salvation-historical giving of the law at Sinai? I believe I can tie the exodus to all of these events and then link the exodus to the salvation brought to fulfillment under the new covenant, and thus make sense of the whole and of the parts within a canonically constrained system. I do not see how Gutiérrez can do the same.

In short, so far as I can see, the warrant for the choice of the exodus is not in any profound sense Biblically or canonically constrained. The warrant is extra-Biblical—the situation of poverty and oppression in many Latin countries. That makes me exceedingly nervous; it is, in my view, another way of domesticating the Bible to get it to say what I think needs saying. There is no profound, principled submission to God's Word.

I hasten to add that I am most definitely not suggesting there are no insights in the work of Gutiérrez, nor even that, if I am right, no case can be made for revolution in this or that particular case. At this point, it is solely the use of Scripture that concerns me.

What also concerns me, though far less, is that most of the liberation theologians I have read espouse an essentially Marxist analysis of history and economics and thus a Marxist prescription for righting the evils in their societies. Perhaps I would see things differently if I had lived for years in Latin America; my quick trips do not qualify me to write with any authority, and I frankly acknowledge I am no economist. But then again, neither are most of the liberation theologians! It seems to me that preconditions for healthy economies and widespread distribution of wealth include healthy competition, adequate respect for a free market, rising commitment to education, a worldview that does not think of work as an evil but as a virtue, enough government controls to reduce the number of monopolistic bullies and ensure a safe working and living environment (but not too many more beyond that!), a free press (to distribute the power and ensure the possibility of criticism so that the human drift to corruption is partially checked), a societal moral consensus that thoroughly opposes corruption, and, the final condition, a fair bit of time. I'm sure a little reflection would happily add a couple more entries. But in any case, only a few Latin countries enjoy more than two or three elements from this list.

I do not want to end with so critical a tone. It is all too easy to sit back and take potshots at those who are doing something—just because we do not like what they are doing. On the other hand, just because *something* needs to be done does not mean that what is actually being done is wise. What has encouraged me on my occasional trips to Latin America has been the number of churches where personal godliness and practical caring, devotion to Christ and self-sacrificing service, living faith and compassion for the poor and needy, go hand in hand. Whatever structural changes are needed, they will not long survive unless more and more of the populace is transformed and suffused with such faith, values, and conduct.

With all good wishes,
Paul Woodson

33

*M*y year at Yale was providing me with an uncommon vantage point to assess the strengths and weaknesses of "mainstream liberal" theology. In addition, I was enjoying cordial friendships with a number of students at the divinity school. One, an African-American named Frank Crawford, would join me on my "thought walks." A dyed-in-the-wool theological liberal, he could not figure out why his "Fundamentalist friend," Timothy Journeyman, believed what he did. He forced me to think about subtle forms of racism that I as a white had never realized blacks and other minorities faced. When Frank was striding beside me, my thought walks became "talk walks."

Frank was outgoing and generous, fun to be around. He, Ginny, and I would sometimes have supper together at our apartment and then go out to a small restaurant to indulge our passion for cappuccinos and pastries. I wondered what Frank would be like if he ever confessed Christ as Lord and Savior. His potential seemed unlimited, his heart for the inner cities of the country much more sensitive than my own.

Slowly, I came to the conclusion that it would be better for me to finish the M.Div. degree at an evangelical seminary. When I asked Ginny what she thought, she agreed. I could tell she was quite pleased; once again that inimitable smile swept across her face. I wrote to Trinity and requested permission to be readmitted in the fall quarter, 1985-1986.

The rationale for this change of plans was something like this. As much as I relished the specialized courses I had been taking at Yale (the Liberation Theology course was an eye-opener regarding racism and economic repression), I was not progressing well in my knowledge of the Biblical languages. Moreover, I had learned much about Biblical criticism, but less about the actual contents of the books of the Bible. As a future pastor, I wanted to preach Biblical content, not

Biblical critical theories, as important as some of them are. I really did not know what a few of my more "radical" student friends would preach.

If I did have another disappointment connected with my year at Yale, it is one I have already mentioned. I couldn't understand then, nor can I understand now, why responsible evangelical articles and books were not on occasion referenced at least as a foil for refutation by several of the professors. Isn't this rank prejudice? Certainly a segment of evangelical scholarship does lack luster, but other segments are commendable and cannot be dismissed as intellectually obscurantist.

When evangelicals were cited in classes, it was generally those scholars who had themselves challenged conservative evangelical doctrines in one way or another. For example, Professor Marsden's explanation (1980) of the alleged recent origins of Biblical inerrancy was warmly greeted by several professors. His thesis helped them justify in their own minds why the doctrine of Biblical inerrancy could be dismissed as a Fundamentalist innovation and why it was certainly not a central Christian tradition. Students in class never heard about the potentially fatal weaknesses in Professor Marsden's historical reconstruction.

I wrote to Dr. Woodson that Ginny and I were planning to return to Trinity for the school year, 1985-1986. I tried to set forth as coolly as possible the reasoning behind our decision—the pros and cons of staying at Yale; the pros and cons of returning to Trinity. I did everything possible to put in bold relief the genuine pluses of my study in New Haven. By no means did I want Dr. Woodson to think that I had "sour grapes" about my experience there. Such would have been a misreading of my true sentiments.

After posting this letter, I had lingering misgivings. Would Dr. Woodson think that I was simply so flighty I couldn't make up my mind about much of anything? His return letter put me somewhat at ease.

April 10, 1985

Dear Tim,

What good news! The Journeymans are at last going to be our neighbors. We are so pleased that you folks are returning to Trinity.

Your mixed emotions about the move are very understandable. Your year at Yale has been a special one.

I have reflected a little further on your perception that certain scholars at Yale apparently have not paid sufficient attention to evangelical literature in class. One plausible explanation may be less obvious but more pertinent than simply assuming it stems from "rank prejudice." May I try to explain?

Nearly everyone functions with significant presuppositions. Even scholars who pride themselves on their objectivity (implying freedom from bias) in their research do not escape from positing hypotheses based on their own pre-understandings.

Now presuppositions are not necessarily ruinous to even-handed research. If a scholar is forthright and announces his or her presuppositions in a preface to a work or in the first sessions of a class, other scholars and students may factor them into any assessment of the person's work.

My guess is that those professors at Yale who do not refer to evangelical literature are not as self-consciously malicious in their "silence" as you suppose. Rather they may be working on the basis of an unannounced presupposition. It flows from their own personal experience. What is this presupposition? It is the simple premise that no responsible evangelical scholarship (by their standards) exists. They did not encounter any such literature in their graduate school education.

Tim, you need to recall that a strain of anti-intellectualism did run deeply within Fundamentalism during the early decades of this century. Brilliant young conservative Christians were warned about the dangers of losing their faith if they studied at a secular university. To reverse this tendency, a group of young evangelicals like E. J. Carnell, Kenneth Kantzer, Samuel Schultz, Carl F. H. Henry, and others decided to go to Boston in the late 1940s and early 1950s to gain a first-rate education at schools like Harvard and Boston Universities. But even then, for several decades evangelicals produced relatively few works judged to be noteworthy by proponents of the reigning theological paradigms of neo-orthodoxy and Bultmannianism of the 1950s or the radical theologies of the 1960s. Evangelical scholars were outsiders looking in on the religious establishment.

But it was during the same decades of the 50s and 60s that many of today's professors who have tenure at mainline divinity schools received their graduate education. And their own professors gave little heed to what evangelicals and Fundamentalists from Westminster, Dallas, Wheaton, Westmont, or Fuller were writing.

You should talk with Dr. Harold O. J. Brown about his training at Harvard Divinity School in the 1950s. Few there were among the students who claimed to be Fundamentalists or evangelicals and fewer still among the professors. As Dr. Brown tells it, Professor George Florovsky, the distinguished historian of Orthodoxy, was considered an exception at Harvard Divinity School because he acknowledged he was Orthodox and evangelical. Professor Florovsky would frequently remark, "Around here [at Harvard] they call me a Fundamentalist because I actually believe in God."

Nurtured in the ambiance of this mainstream theological education, a number of today's professors have a difficult time imagining that a responsible evangelical scholarship exists. It was not a part of their own experience. Or if they at one time bolted out of an evangelical or Fundamentalist home, they may have wanted to distance themselves from anything that reminded them of conservative Christianity, including its literature.

Complicating matters even further, for some of these professors the expression "evangelical scholarship" has the ring of an oxymoron. Evangelicals cannot be true scholars because they lack "objectivity" in their research. Why is this so? Evangelicals are hobbled by the presupposition that the Bible is the Word of God. They will inevitably back away from the findings of their research if these findings contradict the teachings of Scripture. More "liberal" scholars pride themselves on letting the evidence take them where it will.

Now if you view the world of scholarship through these lenses, you will understand better why those professors who pay scant attention to evangelical literature feel justified in their attitude.

What may be less obvious to these same professors is the fact that they themselves often work with sets of presuppositions that make their own research less objective than they claim. What are these presuppositions? A dominant presupposition is the belief that each person has the duty to judge his or her own beliefs, institutions, and traditions using reason as the standard. The goal of this exercise in criticism is to shed ignorance, prejudice, or whatever hinders the human spirit. A premium is placed on Kant's dictum (often misinterpreted), "Have courage to use your own reason."

On the face of it, this presupposition is attractive. We should seek to discriminate between good and bad and between truth and error. But in the name of what? For many modern thinkers the only proper response is, "In the name of my own reason."

But if my critical spirit melts down all authority in the name of the authority of my own reason to judge all things, then I will believe whatever appears rational to my own mind. If other people follow the same course, then they will believe whatever is "right" in their own eyes. When apparently irreconcilable opinions emerge among them, a belief that "reason" is the authority with which to sort out truth may itself become suspect. Intellectual anarchy seems inevitable. And affirmations that absolute truth exists are hooted down by the "dogmatic" relativists. Proposals are then made to the effect that "truth" is community-dependent (so, for instance, Thomas Kuhn).

Now if there is no such thing as "truth" and "right and wrong," the passions, always lingering in the wings and ready to pounce on "reason," have even greater license to pounce. People will do what feels good to them, and no one has the high moral ground from which to tell them that what they are doing is "wrong."

Even now the winds of cultural nihilism are blowing quite strongly within academia. The teachings of the Scriptures and Christian traditions no longer serve as benchmarks for establishing ethics or a worldview or "truth." At some divinity schools scholars have converted the study of theology into the study of epistemology. Postmodernists are not certain that there are any criteria that can help us recognize "the truth"—if in fact "truth" exists. They engage in "culture wars" with Professor Plantinga's remaining classical foundationalists who still believe these criteria exist.

It is difficult to understand in what sense scholars who have assumed a radically skeptical stance believe themselves more objective than evangelical scholars. Have they not confessed that their own personal presuppositions and agendas shape their research programs in a decisive fashion?

Of course, you know, Tim, many academics do admit that they are affected by their own presuppositions. Nevertheless, they do not drop their complaint against evangelicals. Whereas they are affected by their own presuppositions, from their point of view they have at least picked the indubitably correct presuppositions. To their mind evangelicals have undoubtedly chosen the wrong ones.

What then are the "right" presuppositions of modernity? One prominent premise is historicism. In a recent essay, "Historical Consciousness in Nineteenth-Century America," published in *American Historical Review* 89 (October 1984): 910, Dorothy Ross gives a perceptive definition of this ideology: " . . . the doctrine that all historical phenomena can be understood historically, that all events in historical time can be explained by prior events in historical time."

In the second half of the nineteenth century, historicism over-whelmed providentialism in the academic community. It outlaws scholars from positing God's intervention through providence or the incarnation or miracles or the revelation of a divine word. It creates a closed system in which everything is relative because everything is historically conditioned. The Bible becomes a piece of literature like any other piece of literature; the Christian faith has no more special credentials than any of the other world religions, and ethics flow from the cultural "rules" of the particular community to which one belongs rather than from the revealed Word of God.

Some scholars are forthright enough to announce their adherence to the basic premises of historicism. But they are often much less candid in explaining the presuppositions that prompted them to become historicists in the first place. Some, for example, accepted on faith the teachings of their high school teachers thirty years earlier that "naturalistic evolution" was an established fact. Belief in "naturalistic evolution" has remained a cherished dogma for them; it is to be affirmed, not reexamined. They do not seem to know that theories of evolution have themselves *evolved* enormously. Stephen Gould, a leading naturalistic evolutionist, has acknowledged that much of what he believed about evolution in the '60s, he had to discard by the late '70s.

What an irony! The very same people who highlight the importance of a critical spirit to help a person break the shackles of superstition, ignorance, and prejudice will often be very closed-minded if challenged to reexamine the evidentiary claims of naturalistic evolution. How then can one tout an openness to objective scholarship if one is dogmatically committed to upholding a belief and unwilling to subject it to fresh scrutiny? And would these scholars be willing to abandon their commitment to historicism if they discovered that one of its principal pillars, naturalistic evolution, is wobbly?

Indeed so imbedded is a commitment to the "truths" of naturalistic evolution and historicism in the reigning intellectual paradigm of academia that anyone who dares to challenge the doctrines becomes the equivalent of a heretic. Community pressures will build quickly to silence the individual. He or she will often be portrayed as a religious Fundamentalist. The person will be excluded from positions of authority and the meaningful perks of the community (tenure at leading universities, publications at prestigious presses). So effective is the campaign against the dissenter that soon the person will become a "nonperson" or nonplayer in academia.

This may explain why there are so few evangelicals who are full professors, especially in the social sciences and humanities, at major universities in the United States. Often evangelical scholars confront rather stark alternatives. Either they will have to privatize their faith, and thus be silent about it, or make some form of accommodation with the reigning paradigm. Only rarely does one encounter evangelical professors in the social sciences and humanities who have been strong enough to feel immune from these pressures. Interestingly enough, evangelicals seem to populate departments in the natural sciences in greater numbers. Why this is so, I do not know.

What I am suggesting is this, Tim: A number of your professors may be working with a set of presuppositions of which they themselves are unaware. These include the "everyone knows" variety that dominate academia. You just assume without thinking about it that naturalistic evolution is an established fact, that Freud and Marx had penetrating, irrefutable insights. In this light, it becomes clear why much of evangelical literature which eschews these presuppositions seems totally irrelevant.

Those evangelical scholars who are appreciated in the wider academic world have often demonstrated a willingness to make some form of accommodation with the paradigm. For example, they will try to make their "God talk" so inoffensive that it does not really challenge the historicist and evolutionary premises of the reigning paradigm.

By the way, the courage of Professor Alvin Plantinga becomes all the more praiseworthy in this context. As an evangelical scholar, he has challenged directly the set of presuppositions sustaining the closed-world paradigm of much of the academy. What could be a more strategic offensive than his affirmation that a belief in God is properly basic? My reservations about his proposals do not imply for a moment that I do not appreciate his boldness or brilliance.

My guess is that the reigning paradigm will not be really shaken until evangelical scholars, joined by nonevangelical colleagues, provide convincing evidence that naturalistic evolution is not a persuasive ideology and that Marxist canons of analysis are less than convincing. Admittedly, adherents to dogma often have a will to believe that sometimes hinders them from taking seriously evidence that challenges their position.

But this circumstance does not deliver us from our responsibility to try to force them to reconsider their "everyone knows" presuppositions. If enough anomalies appear that cannot be explained by the reigning paradigm, then scholars may suddenly see things in a different way. I am not a great fan of Thomas Kuhn, but some of his insights about the mechanisms of "paradigm shifts" are intriguing. Establishment paradigms (naturalistic evolution, historicism, Freudianism, Marxism) may crack more rapidly than we can imagine.

Tim, again I have fallen prey to my tendency to be prolix. In "brief," what I am trying to say is this. Some of your professors at Yale may appear to you to have slighted evangelical literature by design. I am proposing here another thesis. Some may have never intended to do so. In fact they would be shocked, if not a little offended, to hear your complaint. They believe that they have been open-minded in class discussion. So imbedded are certain presuppositions in their thinking about the academic enterprise that they are unaware that evangelical literature has something to contribute to their own agendas.

If you understand the mind-set of some of these professors, you may be less prone to convert these comments about evangelicals into slights. They may simply be oblivious to the fact that their rhetoric is offensive to evangelical students.

Here is a practical suggestion. You might invite one of your professors out for coffee and discuss with him or her your concerns. You may be surprised by the cordial reception the professor gives to this gesture. Establishing friendships with these people is very important.

Personally speaking, I have developed deep friendships with a number of professors in Europe who are Marxists and who give no quarter to the Christian faith. Obviously they know what my beliefs are, but they also know that I genuinely care about my friends as people. In consequence we are able to discuss some of these questions as friends. I have noticed that a few are not as dismissive of evangelical faith as they once were.

Please give my best regards to Ginny once again. Mrs. Woodson will write her in the near future. If we can do anything in the way of finding housing for you, let us know.

Warmly,
Paul Woodson

34

*I*n June of 1985, after painstakingly packing our trailer, we drove from New Haven to my mother's home in Flemington, New Jersey. We enjoyed her home cooking and visited with friends and relatives, including my sister Rose and one of my elderly aunts. My brother Jack and sister Pat, who were working that summer in Kansas City, Missouri, and Washington, DC, respectively, could not get away from their responsibilities to join us. This was a disappointment, especially for my mother.

During the week of our stay my mother and Ginny got to know each other much better. Once when I saw them sitting on the living room couch together engrossed in conversation, I thought to myself, these are two special people. I wondered if Ginny might be able to present the gospel more effectively to my mother than I had. Perhaps it was because I was her son, but my mother seemed to turn a deaf ear when I broached the topic of "religion" (her term). I could talk much more easily to a stranger about the Lord than I could to my own mother.

After a week Ginny and I drove our 1984 Buick Le Sabre (sans trailer) up to our favorite playground, the Adirondacks, in northern New York State. We had booked a cabin at Camp of the Woods, Speculator, New York. For another week we lazed around and enjoyed the fine Bible teaching in the auditorium. We especially liked to watch the sun begin to set over Lake Pleasant and then disappear behind the gray-green forested mountains. Our cabin was right on the beach so that the lake lapped to within eighty or ninety feet of our cabin door. With an actual vacation I felt as if I were becoming more of a human being. Both of us spent hours reading—I, devouring more Sherlock Holmes mysteries, and she, reading more works by Anne Morrow Lindbergh.

By mid-July we had made an uneventful return trip south from Speculator to Flemington and then west to Deerfield (avec trailer). I was fortunate enough to reassume my job at the bank in Highland Park. This time we moved into a small, lovely apartment the Woodsons had spotted in Highwood. We rented the place sight unseen on their recommendation.

A few days after we arrived, the phone rang. It was Dr. Woodson. He had just returned from teaching the Bible at a summer camp. He asked if we liked the apartment. We did. Then he extended an invitation to come for an informal supper at his home in neighboring Highland Park the next Saturday evening.

Late Saturday afternoon, we arrived at the Woodsons' home, a two-storied Dutch colonial, set back from the road and well shaded by several oak trees. As we climbed out of the car, I could see Dr. Woodson walking spryly to meet us. He greeted us and accompanied us to the front door where Mrs. Woodson was waiting for us. When I referred to him as Dr. Woodson, he immediately interjected, "You folks should call us Paul and Elizabeth." Neither Ginny nor I felt comfortable doing this; there was an old-world dignity in Prof. Woodson which, however much it invited intimacy, gently repelled familiarity.

What a wonderful evening! The dinner was tasty, but I cannot remember what was served. What I particularly enjoyed was the discussion. Another seminary couple, Gene and Mary Petticord, had been invited so that Ginny and I did not feel obliged to keep the conversation going by ourselves. We quickly felt at ease.

After dinner the six of us moved to the living room to talk more and to sip specially blended coffee—a little luxury that the Woodsons apparently indulged in as well. There he was, Dr. Paul Woodson in the flesh—this man with whom I had corresponded for seven years and to whom I could now talk face to face. He was not as tall as I had remembered him. Moreover, he looked older than his voice sounded. His face reflected a certain candor, earnestness, and humility. What particularly impressed me was that he actually listened to what each of us said as if it were important. He did not appear anxious to have the last word on every topic.

After an hour or so, I suddenly realized that the Woodsons viewed Ginny and me almost as part of their family. I gathered this from the way they treated us. Could it be that Dr. Woodson had devoted so much time to trying to keep me on the straight and narrow because they had had no children of their own and I was the son of his best friend from Princeton days? And what was his relationship with the Petticords? Was it the same as with us? Until this day I really do not know, but I suspect that, consciously or unconsciously, the

Woodsons gave themselves to certain of their students with almost parental care. In any case, that evening Ginny and I sensed that the Woodsons were offering to us their friendship in person as much as they had done so through letters.

Gene and I plied Dr. Woodson with perhaps too many questions. He was good natured enough to appear interested and to interact with them. By 11:00 P.M. or so, I could tell he was becoming a little tired. Nonetheless, with a flair for insensitivity, I plunged on. I asked him what he thought about the rising tide of secular humanism. By his flashing eyes I could tell that Dr. Woodson had more than a few thoughts about this topic. He began by saying something to the effect that evangelicals and Fundamentalists should be much more circumspect in making blanket condemnations of humanism. Gene bristled just a bit.

Ginny noticed this and sensed that Dr. Woodson was tiring. She gave me the high sign that it was time for us to excuse ourselves. It really was late. From the corner of my eye I could see that Mary Petticord gave the same kind of sign to Gene. All four of us thanked the Woodsons most sincerely for their hospitality and graciousness and said our respective good-byes. Ginny and I drove back to our apartment in Highwood, happy that now we really were neighbors of the Woodsons.

I didn't see Dr. Woodson the next month. I was working full time at the bank trying to make extra money before school began. Dr. Woodson was apparently on a speaking trip somewhere along the east coast. Then towards mid-September I received a letter from him postmarked Boston.

September 10, 1985

Dear Tim,

Elizabeth and I enjoyed so much spending Saturday evening with you and Ginny and the Petticords a few weeks back. We could hardly believe that the Journeymans were actually in our home after so many years. We couldn't stop talking about the evening and still do on occasion.

For the last month or so Elizabeth and I have been traveling on the east coast. I had a number of preaching opportunities clustered in New England. Moreover I wanted to do at least a little research at Harvard. Next Sunday is free, however, and we hope to worship at Park Street Church here in Boston. The following Tuesday we will visit our good friends the Roger Nicoles. I think I mentioned to you that Professor Nicole has been a distinguished teacher at Gordon-Conwell for decades. He is also "librarian" of his own fabulous library. When we are together, Roger and I will alternate speaking English and French, or at least he puts up with my efforts at French. We love to talk about seventeenth-century theology. But enough of my activities.

Can you believe that you are entering your third and final year of seminary? I hope this year will be your very best one yet. Is Ginny going to finish her MAR degree as well?

Have you ever wished you could add or subtract words from a previous conversation? You replay the conversation in your mind and wonder whether or not you might have been misunderstood.

After our wonderful evening together a few weeks ago, I did have one small regret. If you recall, you asked me what I thought about the advancing tide of secularism. In retrospect, I responded a little too curtly by saying that I wished that some evangelicals and Fundamentalists would be more judicious and not condemn "humanism" in an unqualified manner.

Gene Petticord noticed this and seemed to wince just a bit. Before I could explain what I meant, our evening together concluded. This has been weighing on my mind. Today I decided I would simply jot a note to you to try and clear up the issue. Please pardon the hotel stationary and my scrawl. I do not have a typewriter or computer at hand. I am also writing to Gene. Incidentally, I hope you get to know him well. He is a fine young man. Gene came to the Lord through a former student who works on the staff of InterVarsity at the University of Illinois.

What I was attempting to say is this. We need to be careful to distinguish between the "secular humanism" of the twentieth century and the "Christian humanism" of the fifteenth and sixteenth centuries. Secular humanism draws out implications from the central premise of atheism (in line with Jean Paul Sartre's essay, "Existentialism Is a Humanism"). These include such devastating principles as the following: Because God does not exist, any values that we humans choose in freedom to accept are created by ourselves. No value has divine sanction.

On the contrary, the humanism of the fifteenth and sixteenth centuries was not intrinsically incompatible with theism. In his magisterial works Professor Oskar Kristeller has persuasively argued that this humanism was related to an educational curriculum, the *studia humanitatis*—grammar, history, poetry, rhetoric, and moral philosophy. This humanism neither promoted nor challenged theology directly. If you are interested in an insightful analysis of "Renaissance humanism," you might consult Professor Kristeller's wonderful book, *Renaissance Thought: The Classic, Scholastic and Humanist Strains.*

A good number of humanists were in fact outstanding Christians. Among Roman Catholics, the more notable "Christian humanists" were Erasmus and Martinus Dorp, and among Protestants—Zwingli, Calvin, Bucer, Bullinger, and Melanchthon. These scholars had been trained in the humanist curriculum and used the knowledge gained thereby as a background for their Biblical and theological investigations. As humanists they were often passionately interested in establishing the best possible editions of the literature of antiquity. Many became excellent Latinists and Greek scholars. Their linguistic skills honed in classical studies served them well when they turned to study Holy Scripture.

With a knowledge of Greek, Luther, like Erasmus, came to understand that the Latin Vulgate of Jerome encompassed faulty translations of the original Greek texts. (Ed. note: The Latin Vulgate used by the Reformers had of course undergone significant revision since the time of Jerome. Jerome was the fountainhead of that tradition; the Vulgate of the sixteenth century was substantially removed from what Jerome himself produced.) Some of these faulty translations actually buttressed doctrines of the Roman Church. For example, Luther was struck by the fact that a pivotal passage in Matthew should not be rendered, "Do penance" (as the Vulgate had it), but as, "Be penitent," or "Repent." His understanding of Greek allowed him to see that one of the principal sacraments of the Roman Church had a shaky Biblical foundation.

In a word, the humanist training of some of the Reformers was a significant factor in helping them to understand Holy Scripture better. The Protestant Reformation was in part nurtured by the movement of Christian humanism. Many of Martin Luther's first followers were Christian humanists.

Given this background, I become quite chary when evangelical and Fundamentalist spokespersons condemn humanism without specifying what form of it they have in mind. If they are not careful, they can mislead the evangelical public.

A year or two ago I was watching a program on public television. A conservative Christian spokesperson was lacerating humanism up one side and down the other. A nonevangelical historian on the panel simply waited until the gentleman had finished his unpleasant tirade and then quietly asked, "But was not John Calvin a Christian humanist?" The Christian sputtered but to no avail. The damage had been done.

It was embarrassing. I turned off the television in genuine sorrow for my Christian brother who had seemed so dogmatic and self-assured until he encountered someone well informed and for the audience which had witnessed a nonbelieving scholar masterfully call the bluff of a Christian spokesperson. This could only confirm in the minds of some that Christians are long on dogmatism and short on knowledge and humility.

Tim, I realize that much of what I have scribbled in this letter is familiar to you. You were a history major at Princeton, and you have already studied these issues in your courses at Trinity and Yale. But I simply wanted to explain why I spoke perhaps too bluntly when you asked me that one question. The vivid memory of the television show had flashed into my mind.

Be that as it may, I should be more moderate in my own speech. Little is gained by being overbearing and condescending in criticism. People will ultimately tune you out.

Please give our best to Ginny. We are really looking forward to seeing you folks again after we return to the Deerfield area. Trust all is well.

Yours in the bonds of Christ,
Paul

35

*E*arly in the fall quarter, 1985-1986, Ginny and I had at least a
few occasions to talk with Dr. Woodson. We found it best to
invite him to go off campus with us to Baker's Square where we
could order slices of pie and cups of coffee and then chat at leisure.
Dr. Woodson was in such demand on campus it was difficult to get
ten minutes alone with him without an interruption.

Ginny and I were quite intrigued by a low-intensity debate on
campus over women's ordination. A few of the faculty were conspicuously in favor of women's ordination; a few were conspicuously
opposed. The vast majority did not discuss their views in class.
Returning from Yale where a strong feminist agenda generally set the
guidelines for what was "proper" discourse (and where the issue was
not so much the ordination of women, but the extent to which liturgical and even Biblical language should be changed to avoid "patri-
archal" terms such as Father, Son, and Holy Spirit), we found the
atmosphere at Trinity refreshing. Students could hold a position for
or against woman's ordination without being turned into social pari-
ahs. Ginny and I had a number of straightforward discussions with
our friends about the question. Neither she nor I had taken a firm
stance on the matter.

During one of our off-campus chats at Baker's Square with Dr.
Woodson, I asked him directly what his view was. He began to outline his position but then diverted the flow of his remarks towards a
tributary issue—in what ways did the contemporary cultures of the
Biblical authors shape the content of their writings? Although I had
really wanted to know Dr. Woodson's perspective on women's ordination, I sensed that his detour might not be totally beside the point.

We had begun to sip our second cups of coffee when suddenly Dr.
Woodson looked at his watch and jumped up. He appeared a little
frantic. He said that he had completely forgotten about a faculty
committee meeting that had begun fifteen minutes earlier. Picking up

the check with one swoop of the hand, he thanked us for a delight-
ful time and began rushing precipitously to the cashier's booth.
Ginny and I were barely able to say anything more than a hurried
good-bye. We sat there a touch bewildered. Finally, we put on our
coats and headed to the car. It was a clear but chilly autumn after-
noon.

I did not see Dr. Woodson during the next ten days or so. After
Thanksgiving vacation, however, to my delight I found a letter from
him in my student mailbox. I opened it eagerly.

November 25, 1985

Dear Tim,

I trust that you and Ginny will forgive me for having cut off so
impolitely our *Kaffee Pause*, as the Germans call it. It really was
important for me to get back to the committee meeting. You know
I have passed retirement age and am now on a year-by-year contract.
I do want to fulfill my responsibilities in an appropriate fashion.

Perhaps we will have the opportunity to talk through the question
of women's ordination at a later date. I am especially interested in
Ginny's thoughts on this topic. Have both of you reflected on your
respective roles in the ministry? Pastoral search committees are often
quite interested in the thinking of a couple about this issue.

Unfortunately, I will not be able to enjoy any more of those won-
derful coffee breaks with you folks for the rest of the quarter. Until
Christmas vacation my schedule is *surchargé*, as the French say.
However, Elizabeth and I would very much like to have you both
come to our home for dinner some evening during Christmas break.
Would you be so kind as to suggest to Ginny that she call Elizabeth?
The two ladies could then choose a free evening.

That evening we might even talk a little football. The N.F.L. play-
offs should be on. I can't believe how well the Bears are doing this
season. Jim McMahon, Richard Dent, and the "Fridge" are having
outstanding seasons. But perhaps, rabid fan of the New York Giants
that you are, you might find my glowing comments about this
remarkable Chicago team a bit overBEARing.

I did want to develop further a few lines of thought from our conversation at Baker's Square. As I was saying, there are clusters of
positions regarding culture's impact on the human authors of
Scripture. Three principal clusters come to mind:

(1) Some Christians have argued that God the Holy Spirit dictated Scripture in such a way that the Biblical authors simply put down what they were told to say. According to this theory, the impact of the cultures in which the Biblical authors lived upon the authors' writing was minimal. John Eck, whom I cited in another letter, seems to hold this position. Because God, the Holy Spirit, the Source of truth, is the primary author, the writings of Scripture are infallible. This is sometimes called the "mantic" theory of inspiration. Advocates of this approach will often emphasize a very "literalistic" approach to interpreting Scripture.

(2) Taking note of Luke's prologue (1:1-4) and a number of comments by Moses, other Christians have argued that the Biblical authors on occasion wrote down what God the Holy Spirit *directly* inspired them to say, but on other occasions they used written sources and also wrote out of their own research and knowledge and passion (e.g., 2 Corinthians 10-13; many Psalms). But even here the Holy Spirit superintended their writing so that they made no errors. In this view, the influence of the contemporary cultures upon the way the Biblical authors wrote is manifested in their grammar, choice of verbal expressions, literary genres, historical connections, and much else besides, but their writings remain infallible. As you know, this is sometimes called the "concursive" theory of inspiration. Benjamin Warfield was a defender of this perspective.

(3) Other scholars have proposed that the Biblical authors indiscriminately imported into the Scriptures the cultural beliefs of the societies in which they lived. Because these societies were primitive and superstitious, the writings of the Biblical authors became an admixture of the "infallible word of God" and culturally induced error. The task of the Biblical critic is to winnow from the text what is permanent, the authentic "word of God," from what is transient or ephemeral in value. Johann Salamo Semler, the well-known German "higher" critic of the eighteenth century, represents this position.

Let us turn once again to the debate over women's ordination. Representatives who champion the first way of looking at the Bible will often speak out strongly against women's ordination. They tend to defend a "literal" reading of Scripture without much reflection on what that might mean—and the result is a fairly arbitrary set of readings. Most of them would not argue that "Kiss one another with a holy kiss" should be *literally* obeyed in our culture today; most of them would not argue that washing one another's feet is an activity to be carried out *literally*, like taking the Lord's Supper. But few of them have paused to ask why they take more flexible stances in these passages and not in others. And the strictest defenders of this first position cannot explain the fact that parts of Scripture penned by different human authors betray enormous differences of vocabulary and style. A dictation theory of inspiration cannot easily be squared with the actual phenomena of the Bible.

Representative scholars of the second stance cannot be so easily pigeonholed. They present a mixed response to the question of women's ordination. Some, such as Drs. Osborne, Kaiser, and Kantzer—all at Trinity—favor women's ordination, though not all on the same grounds. At the risk of caricature, Dr. Kaiser insists that fair exegesis of the texts, even passages like 1 Timothy 2:11-15, supports his views and that his opponents are simply mistaken. Dr. Osborne recognizes that there is a restriction in the text, but thinks that it springs from cultural factors in the first-century church that no longer operate. Dr. Kantzer holds that the New Testament makes a distinction between the roles of men and women *in the home* but not in the church—and he argues that 1 Timothy 2 has to do with the home.

On the other hand, some other scholars at Trinity very much oppose the ordination of women, and when they cite 1 Timothy 2, they read it a different way. But their responses to the three just mentioned must be different in each case. To respond to Dr. Kaiser, they must produce a more convincing exegesis of the passage—studying the words, expressions, flow of thought, and so forth to make their case. To respond to Dr. Osborne, they must convince us that when the prohibition, whatever it means, is tied to Creation and the Fall, the justification of the prohibition becomes about as independent of a temporary cultural phenomenon as one can imagine. And in response to Dr. Kantzer, they must convince us that 1 Timothy 2 focuses on the church, not the home.

Neither side of the debate wants to duck what Scripture, rightly interpreted, says, but the interpretative options open out a little more for this second group of scholars than it does for the first group.

Contemporary scholars in group three will generally favor woman's ordination. Like some of their colleagues in group two, they will argue that those who oppose women's ordination have not engaged in proper exegesis. But they will often take a step further by proposing that the passages that appear to forbid a woman to teach in the churches are reflective of the cultural norms of Biblical times and should be ignored in the name of other themes more firmly taught in Scripture—freedom, love, equality, and justice. In other words, many in this group think that the Bible really does make some distinctions in roles between men and women, but because they think the Bible is a mixture of wheat and chaff, they can safely dismiss the parts they think of as chaff.

Historically speaking, position one, which adopts some form of dictation theory of inspiration and tends to emphasize a sturdy literalism in its approach to understanding Scripture, has existed from the earliest days to the present. Position two has an equally long and venerable history. Somewhat less literalistic in orientation and more sensitive to genres, this approach has had many defenders. Augustine and Calvin, among others, argued that God the Holy Spirit accommodated Scripture to our understanding. In other words, Scripture is sometimes written in "phenomenological" language, the language of appearance. We can make sense of it. Nonetheless, Scripture remains infallible.

From a historical perspective, however, position three proposes a rather novel doctrine of accommodation. In this view, God the Holy Spirit accommodated the language of Scripture to the errant cultural belief systems of the Biblical writers. Thus the cosmological statements of Scripture, for example, are deficient; they reflect beliefs of primitive peoples. Behind position three often lurks an unarticulated syllogism:

1) Human authors played an essential role in the writing of Scripture.
2) To err is human.
3) In consequence the Bible as a human production must be errant.

Of course, the weak point in the syllogism is the second member. It is not of the essence of being human that we err, as if error must attach itself to every single thought and word and activity of every human at all times. All human beings say and do some things at some times without error—and they are not less human for that! Thus there is no intrinsic reason why Scripture could not have been mediated without error through humans.

In any case, as far as I can determine, this third way of viewing Scripture appears for the first time in the teaching of Socinus in the sixteenth century. It does not figure in the thinking of the Church Fathers or of the Reformers. You might look at the excellent M.A. thesis by Glenn Sunshine on this topic. Glenn compared Calvin's view of accommodation with that of Socinus. The views of the two men diverged widely. Unsurprisingly, Socinus placed a high premium on the role of reason. He had to find some authority by which he could sort out more authentic Scripture from its transient context. Despite the claims of some defenders of this view that it represents a central evangelical tradition, I do not think a responsible reading of history will justify this conclusion.

Off the Christian spectrum is found a fourth, purely secular, cluster—that of the historicists. They affirm quite bluntly that Scripture should be interpreted solely in the terms of the cultures of the Biblical writers. There is no word of God to find within Scripture because God does not exist.

Admittedly, the above outline of positions is simplistic in the extreme. But I find it useful when I am trying to assess how individuals arrive at a particular interpretation of Scripture. Scholars debating the meaning of a text of Scripture may come up with remarkably differing perspectives, owing to the fact that they are operating out of divergent clusters of presuppositions.

If we disagree over women's ordination (or many other issues), we may discover that our disagreements stem in part from these differing presuppositions. To ensure a genuine meeting of minds then requires cool speech and a fair bit of interpretative sophistication to find out why people disagree so greatly over the meaning of the same texts.

You know me well enough to recognize that I feel most comfortable with position two. It seems to correspond with the teachings of Scripture about itself. I believe it represents the Augustinian position in the history of the church. Moreover, I think it is the only position capable of giving a convincing response to the problems of hermeneutics (Ed. note: the theory and practice of interpretation).

Tim, I know you did not take my elective on hermeneutics, and it would be unfair of me to dump my class notes on you. Nevertheless, let me try to convince you of at least one thing. *All* of Scripture is in several respects culturally conditioned, but this fact by itself does not reduce Scripture's authority. Scripture came to us in human languages—a cultural phenomenon. It deploys literary genres, depicts customs, presupposes courtesies, presents vistas of human history— all cultural phenomena. But unless you hold that human beings are intrinsically incapable of understanding one another, this does not mean that the interpreter of Scripture can afford to relativize Scripture because both Scripture and the interpreter are tied to culture, indeed to different cultures. Our understanding of another's words may not be exhaustive, but there is no reason why it cannot be true. It takes a lot of work to "fuse the horizon of one's own understanding with the horizon of understanding of another" (to use the contemporary jargon) in order to ensure that a responsible transfer of information has taken place, but that doesn't mean it can't be done. In fact, I have always thought it amusing that some of the most skeptical of modern interpreters, the "deconstructionists," write long essays and books trying to convince the rest us that they are right. Some of them become very irritated if they are misinterpreted. Why can't they extend the same courtesy to Paul?

Let me give you a simple example of the kind of cultural problems involved in trying to communicate the content of the Bible to others. This example is not original with me, but it is quite suggestive. Suppose you went to Thailand and tried to explain to a Buddhist monk (we'll assume you know how to speak Thai—a major cultural hurdle in itself!) that Jesus is Lord. If you simply say (in Thai) that Jesus is Lord, the Buddhist will assume that you agree with him that Jesus is inferior to Gautama the Buddha. The reason for this misinterpretation of your intent, of course, is that in Buddhist thought the highest state of exaltation is achieved when *nothing* can be predicated of the person. The Buddha is neither hot nor cold, good nor bad, up nor down, and so forth. Insofar as you are trying to predicate something of Jesus, you are conceding His inferiority.

Of course, I am not saying that it is impossible to affirm in Thai that Jesus is Lord. But for the Thai to hear what the New Testament means by this expression, he or she must understand, so far as it is possible, what that expression meant in New Testament culture and language. The barriers to the Thai understanding of the expression are cultural. They include the whole worldview erected by the Buddhist faith. The missionary in Thailand must not simply parrot expressions, but must convert entire worldviews.

This illustration is "safe," since it deals with people far away. But it is easy to find parallels closer to home. What does "God is love" mean to someone in, say, L.A. with no knowledge whatsoever of the Bible, but who has drunk deeply from the wells of the New Age movement? Unless you explain what sort of God you are talking about and what love is like in the Bible, you will certainly be misunderstood.

My point in these illustrations is that the truth that God discloses of Himself in the Bible is disclosed in a language-culture system, and *all* modern readers live in another language-culture system. All of us must make efforts to spiral in on what the text meant when it was first given. Thus the fact that the Bible is culturally bound, in the way I've just illustrated, does not diminish its authority. It simply means that there are interpretative hurdles to cross if we are to understand it aright.

But this cultural clothing is not always easy to cope with. What is at stake, very frequently, is whether the particular bit of Scripture we are looking at is binding on us *in its given cultural form*. When the Bible says, "Greet one another with a holy kiss," is it offering a theology of kissing? Is kissing part of the mandate or merely part of the cultural form of warmhearted and expansive greeting that signals close fellowship—the kind of fellowship that the church ought to display? Justify your answer!

But this is getting too long. Even though I have barely skimmed the surface of the pool of things I deal with in my course on hermeneutics, I had better leave you in peace. There are other questions I have not even begun to broach here—for instance, the way various Scriptures are tied together, the impact of literary genre on meaning (for example, Bill Gothard has the worrying habit of treating Proverbs as if they were case law), the importance of textual context, and much more. But if I haven't answered all your questions about what the Bible says about women's ordination, perhaps I have said enough for you to probe the question with greater rigor. Perhaps we can talk this out in greater detail when you visit us in a few weeks.

Warmly yours,
Paul

36

*N*ot only did we talk *about hermeneutics at the meal with the Woodsons in December (Mrs. Woodson and Ginny soon steered the conversation in other directions), but I was stimulated to enroll in Dr. Woodson's elective course on the subject, offered in the winter quarter. It turned out to be one of the most enlightening courses I have ever taken.*

I cannot pursue that subject here, however, for my correspondence with Prof. Woodson turned in another direction. While at Trinity, Ginny and I attended a Presbyterian church. One of its ministers was converted at the Princeton Evangelical Fellowship a few years before I was, and we had a great deal in common. He urged me to pursue ordination in the PCA (Ed. note: Presbyterian Church of America). To shorten a long story, that is the course I began to follow.

Without his saying so, I could tell that Dr. Woodson, with his Baptistic convictions, would have liked to straighten me out on that one, but he never confronted me on the subject of church government and sacraments (he would have preferred the word ordinances), and strangely enough we never talked at any length about the matter.

As I approached graduation in the late spring of 1986, I was deeply involved with my own church. Rather surprisingly, I was called to a small PCA church in Florida just outside Orlando. Surprisingly, I say, because I knew no one there. The connections had all been made through ecclesiastical circles. Ginny loved the prospect. She had some cousins in Orlando and had vacationed down there several times. More importantly, both of us felt this was the door the Lord was opening for us.

Our occasional coffees with Dr. Woodson continued, but as I approached pastoral ministry, I found that I was wanting more and more input on the sheer practical realities of ministry. To be frank, I contemplated my first pastoral charge with some trepidation. I became more and more aware of just how little I knew. To bear the burden of the spiritual well-being of some of God's people, to preach and teach the whole counsel of God in responsible and compelling ways—the prospect, though exhilarating, was more than a little daunting.

As I tried to think my way in advance through prospective pastoral problems, some of the ones that seemed most frightening to me then had to do with the popularity of "quick-fix" religion that permeated the popular evangelical television shows, the "miracle-a-day" language of some of them, the rising influence of John Wimber and the Vineyard ministries. Even the bid of Pat Robertson for the Republican nomination exerted a kind of magnetic influence in the religious sphere. How does a pastor compete with these kinds of whirling attractions?

My grades were good enough that, as a prospective graduate, my final exams would be waived, but I was still knee-deep in final term papers. I scribbled a note to Dr. Woodson in early May, indicating that although it would be good to get together and talk this one out, I wasn't sure how I was going to fit it in. His reply was a little short on answers, but it was long on perspective; that was itself very useful.

May 30, 1986

My dear Tim,

I know you are pushing hard right now to complete all requirements before graduation and to prepare for your move to Florida. It is no surprise that you are overextended and have little time for casual chatting. If there is anything my wife and I can do to speed you on your way, please let us know. We will miss you and Ginny next year, more than we can say.

I remember you telling me some years ago that you had read some edition or other of Richard Baxter's *The Reformed Pastor*. Baxter had a philosophy on how to deal with distortions of the gospel. If someone came into his area preaching what he judged to be a faulty approach to justification, his first resort, he said, was not to preach *against* the error, but to "preach up" justification better than the other preacher.

So if there is some dominant emphasis in popular religion that is in your view harming the flock over which the Lord appoints you as "shepherd," you might think through just what is making this aberration so popular. Of course, it might owe a great deal to the influence of the surrounding culture, but it might also owe something to a deficiency in the churches. Many a heresy is nothing more than an exclusivist overemphasis on something that is missing from the mainstream. And then your own teaching and preaching and pastoral care must constantly bear in mind the perceived lack so that your own people will not find the aberration so attractive.

Within such a framework then let me suggest a way of looking at some of the developments you are describing. From your New Testament courses at Yale and Trinity, you are doubtless aware that the Christian lives in a certain kind of eschatological tension, the tension between the "already" and the "not yet." *Already* we have been justified, *already* we have received the Spirit, *already* we have become the children of God, *already* we live under the promised saving reign of God—while we are *not yet* what we ought to be, *not yet* do we see everything under Christ's feet, *not yet* do we have resurrection bodies, *not yet* is the saving kingdom of God consummated in the promised perfection of the new heaven and the new earth. In one form or another, this tension repeatedly surfaces in the New Testament books.

If one side of this tension is emphasized at the expense of the other, the result is always catastrophic, not only for doctrinal stability but for the long-range good of the church. An *under*-realized eschatology—that is, one that does not adequately appreciate what we already have in Christ, but simply moans and groans its way through life, waiting restlessly for the return of Christ—will find itself robbed of the joy of New Testament Christians, of the power of the Spirit in life and witness, of any sense of indebtedness to God who has already "rescued us from the dominion of darkness and brought us into the kingdom of the Son he loves" (Colossians 1:13).

On the other hand, an *over*-realized eschatology will so emphasize the blessings that we already enjoy in Jesus Christ that it may not adequately stress what is reserved for the future, nor appreciate the darkness of the world in which we live, nor grasp the fact that faithful Christian living in this fallen world means self-denial under the constraints and freedom of the cross. Christians afflicted with over-realized eschatology will *expect* to be healed, to be wealthy, to be powerful, to be wise. They are children of the King, they say, and therefore they should live like princes and princesses—forgetting that the King of Kings Himself died in shame on a cross and demands that we take up our cross daily and follow Him.

In the New Testament, the Christians with the most palpably over-realized eschatology are the Corinthians. Meditate at length on 1 Corinthians 4:8-13 and its thematic ties not only with 1 Corinthians, but with 2 Corinthians as well (especially 2 Corinthians 10-13).

In my view, part of the triumphalism of the modern charismatic movement, and for that matter of part of the religious right outside the charismatic movement, depends on over-realized eschatology. It has not seriously thought through what it means to live in a world that crucified the Master—the Master who demands the crucifixion of His followers as well. It has no theology of suffering (unless a penchant for escapism can be dubbed a theology of suffering), no theology of death, no theology of discipline, no sense of the mystery of providence.

Worse, this over-realized eschatology has coalesced with a lot of pent-up feelings in the American public that cry out for expression. After the shame of Watergate and Vietnam, of rising taxes and stagflation, we *want* to feel good about ourselves; we *want* to feel that certain things are our due. This has been a significant part, for good or ill, of Reagan's legacy. He has taught us to feel good about ourselves again. And preachers, consciously or unconsciously, have capitalized on this change. It is not hard to use theological arguments to move people along a kind of Christianized version of a path they'd rather like to take anyway. In the worst streams of this movement, the ones that openly argue you *ought* to be healthy and wealthy and powerful, the shallow theological arguments are being aligned with the sin of envy. Meditate long on Psalm 37, and remember that Paul labels covetousness idolatry.

In this sense, over-realized eschatology is profoundly compromised and must be opposed. Even in the more moderate streams of contemporary over-realized eschatology we see things that are worrying. The issue is not really whether some people get healed at some particular meetings or not—in itself that wouldn't prove anything anyway (see Matthew 7:21-23)—but the entire framework of Christian thought and expectation, the balance of things in the light of the Word. This does *not* mean, as you know, that I side with those who argue that miracles have ceased. My concern is not "cessationism" (as it is called), but with the balance and proportion of Biblical Christianity.

But there is another sense in which these movements are reaching out to people and giving them a sense of spiritual reality often missing in formally orthodox but rather dead churches. In no country in the English-speaking world are churches fuller and the sermons emptier than in America. Of course, there are magnificent exceptions. But I am not surprised by the flight from evangelical orthodoxy into high-church ritual on the one hand (Webber's *Evangelicals on the Canterbury Trail*—at least they have aesthetics) and into the Vineyard movement on the other. If people are not nurtured by the spirituality of the Word, they will try to locate "spirituality" elsewhere. A desperate hunger for spiritual experience is abroad in the land. It is not altogether surprising that in this day of fast food, microwave ovens, ten-minute tune-ups and drive-up banks, many will opt for what they perceive to be the fastest, most efficient doses of spiritual experience available. Nevertheless I judge that the strongest impetus for such movements lies in the spiritual anemia of so many evangelical churches.

So "preach up" and live out full-bodied Christianity without fear or favor. It is better than all substitutes, which are inevitably reductionistic. Insist on the spirituality of the Word; insist that Christianity be public as well as private, corporate as well as personal, pious as well as doctrinal, self-denying as well as orthodox, passionate as well as thoughtful, evangelistic as well as Biblical, spiritual as well as credal, joyful as well as serious, worshipful as well as enjoyable. And in this day of over-realized eschatology, work hard at making people homesick for Heaven, for only then will they be of much use on earth.

If I were you, I would not worry too much about the popularity of this or that movement. I will probably sound old when I say it, but I have seen a lot of movements come and go. The ones currently with us will be around for quite a while, but I suspect they will crest rather soon. Just as the political liberalism of the '60s triumphed in 1968 and immediately crashed, losing the confidence of the American people and giving Nixon his strongest majority, so the rising profile of evangelicalism during the past few years is cresting, and in its moment of triumph (a charismatic TV evangelist running for President!) it is about to crash. There is simply not enough substance to sustain it.

But always remember that what endures after various movements come and go is the local church. At this stage in your life and ministry, do not worry too much about what is happening at the national level. Simply build the people to whom God has called you. Feed people the Word of God, pray for them, love them, convey the reality of God's presence to them by word and deed. What is important at the end of the day is the church—ordinary churches trying to live faithfully in a rapidly changing society. Ordinary churches pastored by ordinary people like you and me, knowing that we cannot do everything, but trying to do what we can and seeking God's face for His presence and blessing so that His dear Son might be honored and His people strengthened.

Please keep in touch. Do not let graduation from seminary become a reason for weakening the links between us.

Love in the bonds of Christ,
Paul

37

*E*d. note: We have excluded a number of brief letters exchanged
between Journeyman and Woodson in the fall of 1986. The letters contained details about the "new" old home that Tim and Ginny
purchased in the Orlando area, an invitation of the Journeymans to
the Woodsons to visit them whenever they could (visits to Disney
World and the Epcot Center were alluringly cited by Journeyman as
additional reasons to do so), and Tim's banter about how cold
Chicago is compared to balmy Orlando during the winter months.
However, in February 1987, the correspondence between
Journeyman and Woodson took a more serious turn.)

My initial fears of not being accepted by the members of my
church began to subside somewhat as my first year in the pastorate
wore on. The members gave this rookie minister a much warmer
welcome than he deserved. Ginny seemed to connect with the people especially well. They apparently saw in her the kind of authentic
Christian faith that is genuinely attractive and needs no self-adver-
tisement. Most folks seemed encouraged that several newcomers
were joining our membership each month. And how I love to preach
the Word of God. What a privilege!

But by no means did I feel totally at ease. I frankly felt unprepared
for the avalanche of things I was supposed to do as pastor. I had
imagined that I would have more hours to spend in my study reading books and working on sermon preparation. In reality, my daily
study period was fractured repeatedly by telephone calls. My "to do"
list kept expanding at a rate that exceeded any possibility of com-
pletion. I began to wonder how one person could do all the things
that cried out for attention—hospital visitation, meetings with the
elders, the youth ministry, unexpected family emergencies—and
always the press of preparation for one more sermon. Especially
after the rush of all the Christmas meetings, I became irritable and
sometimes quite impatient. Ginny noticed this and suggested that I

just "kick back" for a few days and relax. I didn't know how to do that in this situation.

One of my elders, James Olssen, must have also sensed that I was feeling overwhelmed. Early in January he took me aside after a Sunday morning service and asked if we could meet for breakfast one morning the following week. Mr. Olssen was in his mid-seventies and had moved from Minneapolis to Orlando five years earlier to retire. Much like Dr. Woodson, he had befriended Ginny and me. By his demeanor, you just knew James Olssen was a wise Christian, the quiet encourager type who sought the advancement of the kingdom rather than his own interests. He did not have "I" printed anywhere on his forehead, as some people so noticeably do.

I agreed to meet with him the next Thursday morning. It was an eventful breakfast. Mr. Olssen said to me something like this: "Tim, you give the impression that you are frustrated by the burden of your responsibilities. But if people sense your agitated spirit, you will be less effective in providing the congregation with the calm pastoral direction it needs. You may begin to scold the congregation rather than preach the Word of God in a warm, winsome way. I think the Lord has given you a wonderful servant heart for Him and the ministry; I would hate to see you become downcast and less effective in ministry. That is why I am so bold as to raise this issue with you in your first year here in Orlando."

At first I was dismayed. I felt defensive. But then I looked into Mr. Olssen's eyes and knew that he had not intended to wound me. What was I to do? James Olssen had read me like a book. I was beginning to wonder how to survive. I was a "servant" all right, but one who was getting crushed by "service." At least theoretically, the elders were to share in the responsibilities of running the church. But in that first year of ministry I had foolishly determined to put my stamp on each phase of the ministry. For whatever reason, the elders seemed ready to let me assume the lion's share of the work. Mr. Olssen's words were the first I had heard from any elder about the problem.

Moreover, another of the elders, let's call him "George," drove me to distraction. "George" was a young lawyer who had a profitable practice in town. The first time I went out to breakfast with him, he said to me, "Pastor Journeyman, I have come to an understanding of Revelation 20 which, according to my research, no one in the history of the church has ever entertained before. But I am certain my interpretation is the correct one. I feel God gave it to me." He then went on to explain in remarkable detail what the interpretation was.

After listening intently to his explanation, I could understand why no one else had ever thought of this interpretation.

As gently as possible, I tried to point out a few deficiencies in his interpretation. His face became red, his blood pressure rising. Apparently he was not used to anyone contradicting him. He blurted out, "Is it not the right of each believer to interpret the Word of God according to his or her conscience? How do you know that your interpretation is the right one and mine is not?" My heart sank. Not only had I alienated one of my elders, but he had directly challenged my own capacity to understand Scripture. I couldn't finish my breakfast that morning, so knotted up was my stomach.

When I reached the office, I immediately went to the computer and pounded out a letter to Dr. Woodson. While not minimizing all the wonderful things happening in the church, I did emphasize my woes. I suppose I was awash in self-pity, and I wanted Dr. Woodson to know what I was experiencing. I missed talking with him so much. I could have picked up the phone that morning, but I figured that he would be teaching at that hour.

Here I was, a seminary graduate with what I thought had been a good training, beset by problems I could not have imagined overtaking me. I, Tim Journeyman, seemed incapable of coping with my pastoral duties even in my first year of ministry. I had alienated an elder in less time than it takes to finish a breakfast. And I was already beginning to feel lonely in ministry.

Dr. Woodson did not let me down. When his letter arrived, I was greatly relieved.

March 3, 1987

My dear brother Tim,

When your letter arrived, I thought how nice it would be if Elizabeth and I could simply board a plane and fly down to Orlando to see you folks. Would it not be a delight simply to go out with you and Ginny to one of your favorite haunts and sit and drink coffee and chat for an afternoon. But life does not always allow us to do what we really want to. There are these minor encumbrances in the way known as responsibilities.

I was so pleased to learn about Mr. Olssen. He sounds like a wise gentleman. How gracious the Lord is to have given you an elder like him! May I suggest that you get to know him well? He could serve as a remarkable friend to you in days ahead when you need to pour out your heart about the life of the church or any other matter. Unfortunately, many pastors have no resource persons like Mr. Olssen. These pastors sometimes bottle up their anxieties and frustrations internally, remain unchecked in their mistakes, indulge in huge rounds of self-pity, and become very lonely. This is harmful to themselves, their families, and their churches.

Tim, we need one another in ministry. You should not try to be an evangelical superman and by yourself direct all the principal tasks of the church. This posture will lead to disenchantment for both you and your people. Mr. Olssen's advice is sound. The fact of the matter is that you need the laypeople in ministry and they need you.

At Trinity did you happen to read Jacob Spener's *Pia Desideria* ("Pious Longings"—1675)? To my mind this work remains one of the great classics on the life of the church. You may recall that Spener warns that pastors sometimes forget that the laypeople are spiritual priests, just as pastors are (in line with the Bible's teaching on "the priesthood of believers," a doctrine Martin Luther greatly emphasized). When pastors forget this doctrine, they tend to take on themselves the whole responsibility of running the church and thereby lose the fellowship, support, shared vision, and cooperation of others. Fatigue sets in rapidly. Intriguingly, this can easily happen with gifted pastors who can do everything (at least for a while!) but shouldn't.

In *Pia Desideria* (Fortress, 1980, pp. 92-93) Spener highlights the wisdom of Luther's counsel:

> Nobody can read Luther's writings with some care without observing how earnestly the sainted man advocated this spiritual priesthood, according to which not only ministers but all Christians are made priests by their Savior, are anointed by the Holy Spirit, and are dedicated to perform spiritual-priestly acts. Peter was not addressing preachers alone when he wrote, "You are a chosen race, a royal priesthood, a holy nation, God's own people, that you may declare the wonderful deeds of him who called you out of darkness into his marvelous light."

Then Spener offers his own solution to what we today call pastoral burnout: reliance upon laypeople in ministry. He writes:

> No damage will be done to the ministry by a proper use of this priesthood. In fact, one of the principal reasons why the ministry

cannot accomplish all that it ought is that it is too weak without the help of the universal priesthood. One man is incapable of doing all that is necessary for the edification of the many persons who are generally entrusted to his pastoral care. However, if the priests do their duty, the minister, as director and oldest brother, has splendid assistance in the performance of his duties and his public and private acts, and thus his burden will not be too heavy. (pp. 94-95)

When laypeople are taught that they are spiritual priests and understand their duties and opportunities, then the burdens and joys of the local church are shared more equitably and the church prospers. When laypeople are taught that they have spiritual gifts to exercise in the church, then they begin to realize how important their own contributions are to the ongoing work of Christ. Tim, your laypeople can do things you can never do. Many of them have spiritual gifts different from your own. The spiritual health of the church depends on laypeople working together with you in a common ministry.

Why do laypeople frequently not assume their God-given roles? Often we clerics are to blame for this failure. Sometimes we have seized everything ourselves; more commonly we have simply neglected to teach them about their position and functions in the church as spiritual priests. We have failed to lead them to the joy of discovering what their spiritual gifts are and how to exercise them.

Without this instruction, laypeople will often assume that their principal task is to pay the preacher and the staff whom they have hired as "professionals" to do the work of the church. It is the preacher's job to put on a "program" for the church. If they, the laypeople, like the program, they will keep the preacher. If they do not, then they will force him out, or they may leave the church in a huff to find another with a better program. Fearful that laypeople will vote with their feet and with their pocketbooks if they do not like the program, pastors will often feel harried and hurried. They will go along with these spiritually enervating "rules of the game." Thus a cycle is set up by which clerics and laypeople corrupt each other.

To put the matter another way—often in our suburban churches, "professionals" in ministry (i.e., pastors) encounter professionals from the workplace, and neither group has a genuine commitment to the premise that all parties are spiritual priests. The professionals from the laity apply business standards to evaluate the "success" of the church; the pastor and staff largely accept these same standards in order to keep the good will of the laypeople. In this context church life is often assessed as "very successful" because the program runs well and attendance is good, even though spiritual power may be lacking, prayer is not deemed a priority, and very few people are finding Christ as Savior and Lord. The church becomes a comfortable place where few demands are placed on anybody but the pastoral staff which *must* produce an excellent *program*.

I wonder what the Apostle Paul would think about contemporary evangelical churches that have fallen into this pattern. Do you recall the characteristics of the Thessalonian church Paul recommended as a model for others? "We always thank God for all of you, mentioning you in our prayers. We continually remember before our God and Father your work produced by faith, your labor prompted by love, and your endurance inspired by hope in our Lord Jesus Christ. For we know, brothers loved by God, that he has chosen you, because our gospel came to you not simply with words, but also with power, with the Holy Spirit and with deep conviction. You know how we lived among you for your sake. You became imitators of us and of the Lord; in spite of severe suffering, you welcomed the message with the joy given by the Holy Spirit. And so you became a model to all the believers in Macedonia and Achaia. The Lord's message rang out from you not only in Macedonia and Achaia . . . your faith in God has become known everywhere" (1 Thessalonians 1:2-8a).

Tim, I long for you and your people that your church will become a "Thessalonian" church, one in which all its members share in "work produced by faith," "labor prompted by love," "endurance inspired by hope." What a joy it would be for someone to write about your church the way Paul wrote about the Thessalonians. But a church like this involves everyone—all the spiritual priests with their diverse gifts working together as the Body of Christ.

Even your elder "George" needs to use his gifts in the church. May I suggest that you invite him out for breakfast again and get to know him as a person? If he brings up his "unique" interpretation of Revelation 20, just listen to him. Then move on to another topic. Perhaps after you have gained his friendship, you could suggest to him that in the history of Christian doctrine and Biblical interpretation, it is rare for someone to emerge with a sound viewpoint that no one has ever proposed before. Then you might provide him with a mini-course in hermeneutics. He will listen more carefully if he sees you as a friend rather than as an authority figure pulling rank over him with your expertise in the Biblical languages and theology. And if instead he turns out to be one of those obstreperous people who simply cannot be taught anything, then at least you will have assurance that you did everything possible to win your brother.

Elizabeth and I send our warmest greetings to you. Your letter has prompted us to pray more fervently for you. Please remember, Tim, God is faithful. He will take care of you and Ginny and your church through this rough patch. He certainly has proven His faithfulness to Elizabeth and me over these many decades.

With love and prayers,
Paul

38

Ed. note: The frequency of letters between Tim Journeyman and Professor Woodson diminishes somewhat during the spring and summer of 1987. At the most three were exchanged, all having to do with personal news and encouragement. Ginny did send Dr. and Mrs. Woodson a few postcards from Florida and one from Camp of the Woods in Speculator, New York, where the Journeymans spent their vacation during the month of August.)

On September 15, 1987, Ginny and I celebrated our first year of ministry in our church in Orlando. Several of the elders, including the Olssens, took us out to dinner at a fairly posh restaurant. What a lovely evening! We had come to appreciate each other and to work together more as a team. Old Tim Journeyman had decided that he did not need to have an answer for every question or be the principal architect of every committee meeting. The elders were beginning to take more ownership of the church and to share in the joys and sorrows of the people.

What's more, even "George" and his lovely wife attended the outing at the restaurant. I had begun to see "George" in a different light after we had talked further and prayed together. It turned out that "George's" desire always to be right stemmed from feelings of insecurity. Now he was beginning to use his spiritual gifts to encourage others. What a work of God's grace in a man's heart!

Dr. Woodson's letter of March 3, 1987, had been the cause of the turn-around in my own attitudes. In the fall of 1986 I had been caught up in the fantasy that the church in Orlando was *my* church and that its success depended on what I did. I had completely lost sight of my earlier vision of the ministry.

Dr. Woodson had asked in his letter whether I had read Spener's classic work, Pia Desideria, on spiritual renewal. Not only had I read the book, but I had written a paper on German Pietism and Spener for a Church History II class at Trinity. And yet Spener's emphasis on the "spiritual priesthood," which sounded so salutary in semi-nary, had dropped away from my consciousness. Rather I had become wrapped up in an egotistic desire to please "my" laypeople by showing them how hard I could work.

Mr. Olssen was the first to sense a change in my attitude. We went out for another breakfast, and I had the opportunity of telling him about the letter and about Dr. Woodson. Mr. Olssen's eyes moistened as he listened to his rookie pastor describe a 1 Thessalonians 1 vision for what our church could become in the Orlando area. After we left the restaurant, we had a wonderful time of prayer in his parked car.

By the fall of 1987 the church was growing quite rapidly. The elders were pitching in with the increased work load. Their own enthusiasm for ministry was growing. At their meetings they set aside more time to pray. They earnestly sought the Lord's guidance and power as they planned evangelistic and social outreach into the com-munity.

But even with the elders' increased involvement, my own sched-ule became more crowded—even worse than it had been when I thought I had to do everything. In October 1987, I wrote to Dr. Woodson and described the Lord's blessings upon our church. I also mentioned that now my problem was how to manage my time given the multiple responsibilities the Lord had graciously given to me. In passing, I mentioned that my correspondence with him had dropped off because of these time pressures. In the return mail arrived the fol-lowing letter.

October 12, 1987

Dear Tim,

Please do not apologize for not writing more frequently. From my point of view if I hear from you only periodically, I will simply assume that the ministry is going well and that you are prospering in the Lord. I have full confidence in your maturity in Christ. Or to state it more properly, I have every confidence that God is able to per-fect His work in you (Philippians 1:6), and I detect many signs of His sanctifying grace in your life. What a wonderful Savior is this Christ whom we trust with our very lives. He is so faithful.

You asked if I had any suggestions for sorting out how to live when there is "too much to do." Elizabeth chuckled when she heard that you had requested advice from Paul Woodson on time management. Do you remember when you, Ginny, and I were at Baker's Square in Libertyville, and I suddenly exited the restaurant at a wild gallop? I had completely forgotten about a committee meeting at Trinity and had double booked a coffee outing with you two. Well, Elizabeth knows of many other such incidents which completely compromise any claims of efficiency I make.

With the preface in mind that the "preacher practiceth not what he preacheth," here are a few thoughts:

1) *It is better to do fewer things well than many things poorly.* My father was once conversing with me about how he had lived his life. Almost poignantly, he said: "Son, I wish I had done fewer things better." I was young then, and I did not really understand what he meant.

Young men have a way of becoming old men. Among the most surprised people in the world is the young man who discovers that he is becoming old. I have gone through my surprise stage. Now that I am old, I understand what my father was trying to tell me. Life can become a blur of unremitting activity. We can live it without thinking about what we are doing. Far better is it to pause, think, and then choose to do fewer things better.

2) *For the Christian walking with the Lord there will always be too many things to do.* This should come as no revelation. We live in a hurting world in which our "neighbors" have endless physical and spiritual needs. That you should in one sense feel overwhelmed by what you perceive to be needs in the church and in the world around us is a normal Christian experience.

3) *The Christian is not able to do all the good and worthy things known to him or her.* We cannot right every wrong or bind up every wound. This realization may frustrate us. But we must confess that we are not all-powerful and that there are limits to our human resources. In this context we must learn how to say no even to some very worthy causes.

4) *Generally speaking, we should choose to do those things that are in line with our gifts.* If I have the gift of teaching but cannot keep my checkbook in order, then I should teach and not try to be an administrator or church treasurer. Effectiveness in ministry is enhanced enormously if a person's area of service matches his or her gifts. Other people in the Body of Christ will have the gifts to do the things I cannot do well.

5) *We should try to avoid living "what-if" lives.* I have encountered senior Christian leaders who tended in their later years to ask themselves, "What if I had tried harder when I was doing this or

doing that?" As they reminisce, they focus inordinate attention on the "what ifs." Far better when you do something to do it with all your might. Then you will not be prone to say later, "What if I had really tried." In point of fact, you know that you really did try. The same principle applies to the choices you make. Work out your priorities as thoughtfully and as prayerfully as you can, and then do not keep trying to second-guess yourself. God is still sovereign, and only He has the right to keep the books. Meditate on 1 Corinthians 4:1-7.

6) *When all is said and done, a pastor should remember what his principal roles are—to preach and to teach and to care tenderly for the flock.* If you get caught up in a CEO mentality (your essential goal is to direct a smoothly running church), and yet the Word of God is not preached with knowledge and the Spirit's power, the ordinances are not faithfully administered, worship and prayer and evangelism are no longer central (protestations notwithstanding), and there is neither deep and growing knowledge of God nor any church discipline, then you have become the leader of a slick organization rather than a pastor in Christ's church. Keep focused on your calling.

7) *We must learn to relax in the Lord and rest in the assurance that He is building His church.* I have met many frustrated pastors who are exhausted in the Lord's service. Somehow they have converted that sense of exhaustion into a sign that they are following Christ as true disciples. At the same time, they may confess that they are irritable and frustrated. I do not believe that this pattern of existence is what the Lord generally intends for His servants. How encouraging on the other hand to encounter a pastor who, despite all the challenges and difficulties of the ministry, possesses a serenity of spirit. From what does this serenity spring? You know that he spends time with the Master and meditates on the Word of God. He is following the lifestyle set forth in Psalm 1.

8) *At a purely practical level, make lists of the things you must do, prioritize them, and work through the lists, checking off the completed tasks as you go.* Crossing things off not only helps you to see where you are, but shows you what you have accomplished. After a few weeks or months of such discipline, you tend to estimate more accurately how long a task will take. If something is not completed (perhaps because of an unforeseen emergency), it will be among the lowest items on the list if you have prioritized the tasks. And once you start working through your list, do not lightly turn aside from it (for example, because the mail has just arrived). Slot in time for

such tasks, but do not continually sacrifice the important on the altar of the urgent.

Tim, I realize that these suggestions are neither original nor profound. Nonetheless, they are fundamental, and they may have some value for you. Certainly I myself have reflected on each one quite a bit. But the preacher practiceth not always what he preacheth!

Elizabeth and I are hoping that an occasion will arise in the near future when we can see you folks again. You know that you are always welcome to stay at our home should you visit the Chicago area. We pray for you regularly and are so pleased that the Lord seems to have His hand of blessing upon the church.

Warmly,
Paul

39

*G*inny and I went to her parents' home for a few days between Christmas and New Year's Day, and we managed to route our flight back to Orlando through Chicago without having to pay too much extra. That gave us a delightful two days with the Woodsons.

Among the things we talked about at some length was the impact of the moral scandals then erupting in the lives of several televangelists. Dr. Woodson saw the Bakker scandal (for instance) as both cause and effect. It was the effect of declining moral standards in the nation and the church and the painful result of "ministry" tied more to image and success than to reverence, holy fear of the Lord, deep God-centeredness, and a passionate concern to preserve balanced, Biblical Christianity. But Dr. Woodson feared that this moral failure would cause endless jeering by the press and a subtle reinforcing of cynicism, even within the church. Already many reputable mission agencies were feeling an economic squeeze as people refused to give to the work of the Lord, apparently on the ground that there are a lot of hypocrites. Hypocrites there are, and always have been—all that means is that Christians must learn to distinguish the true from the false and not be too surprised by human sin.

The Swaggart scandal involved some new dimensions, and in the first two months of 1988 these had a bearing on our own church. One of our deacons was caught in an adulterous relationship that had been going on for two years. He immediately repented and as far as I could see was really torn up. What sort of church discipline should be applied? Granted the genuineness of this brother's repentance, granted that God forgives the sins of believers who confess their sin (1 John 1:7, 9), what right does the church have to mete out any punishment?

On the other hand, I was deeply uneasy about applying the same reasoning to Swaggart. I had to be honest with myself. I had never liked his ministry, his incessant showmanship, his simplistic authoritarianism, but I could not quite decide how much of my reserve sprang from cultural differences and how much from considered theological differences. In any case, when the Assemblies of God suggested (according to the press) that Mr. Swaggart should be debarred from public ministry for a period of at least six months while he was undergoing counseling, I felt the "sentence" was much too light. And then, suddenly, it became less than clear that Swaggart would submit even to that minimum restraint.

So when I wrote to Dr. Woodson toward the end of February, I was looking for some guidelines in church discipline. Of course, this subject had been treated at seminary, but the hard cases, I felt, did not get the attention they deserved. When, if ever, should a minister of the gospel who has fallen into scandalous sin be restored to public ministry? I did not have Jim Bakker and Jimmy Swaggart in my congregation, but I did have a deacon discovered in an adulterous relationship.

March 5, 1988

My dear Tim,

I am sorry you are facing such a difficult and sensitive issue. I wish I could say your experience is exceptional, but it is not. Any pastor who stays in the ministry for a few years and is involved with growing numbers of people is going to face something like the problem in front of you.

Before I try to answer your question directly, let me insist on four points where (I feel sure) we would be in agreement, but which nevertheless need to be articulated to ensure there is no misunderstanding over what I'll say next. First, sexual sin is not blasphemy against the Spirit; it is not the unforgivable sin. Second, in a church, discipline rightly begins with mutual admonition, thoughtful and caring and prayerful warning, encouragement, and so forth, right up to the extreme sanction, which is excommunication. In other words, we should never think of church discipline solely in terms of excommunication. Third, this final sanction is applied to only three kinds of sin in the New Testament—major doctrinal deviation, especially among those who are teaching others; major moral delinquency (like that described in 1 Corinthians 5); and persistent, divisive lovelessness (cf. Titus 3:10). Finally, if this extreme sanction is required, it must be administered with tears and brokenness, not self-righteous ham-fistedness. Even then, the purpose of the exercise, in addition to keeping the church as pure as possible, is to bring back the erring brother or sister.

Up to this point, I think, many would agree. Moreover, if a brother or sister caught in grievous sexual sin (to stay with the immediate cause of your letter) persists in that sin and shows no repentance or remorse, then the church has no choice, sooner or later, but to go through with the ultimate discipline.

Division of opinion erupts, however, when we deal with the brother or sister who admits the sexual violation, repents, and vows not to let it happen again. Let us assume that in the opinion of the leaders of the church this repentance is genuine. What happens in that case? Does one go through with the excommunication, or not?

Throughout much of the patristic period, believers in this condition would be exhorted to attend the meetings of the church, but would be forbidden the Lord's Table—sometimes for years at a time. I think most of us would agree that there is no clearly indicated Biblical warrant for this sort of sanction (though in some cases there may be pastoral wisdom, if not Biblical warrant!).

But the real division of opinion comes over whether the restoration of such a person to church fellowship entails reinstatement to any position of leadership he or she enjoyed before the sin took place. Here opinion is sharply divided. Some insist, in the strongest terms, that fallen leaders are not "damaged goods" (as one recent writer in *Christianity Today* put it [Ed. note: *CT*, December 11, 1987]). Others take the opposite line. Leaders (especially pastors) who fall into sexual sin should never be allowed into the pulpit again.

I understand that a conservative denomination has recently passed an extraordinarily strict code. From now on, no minister will be admitted to its ministerial if either marriage partner has ever been through a divorce (even before they were Christians). I can appreciate the desire to take a stand against the drift, especially common in California, where some ministers are into their third and fourth marriages. But the reasoning here is less than persuasive.

Because the Levitical priests were to be pure and without blemish, so (it has been argued) the ministers of the gospel must be pure and without blemish. Yet surely the antitype of the Levitical priesthood is either the entire people of God under the new covenant (cf. 1 Peter 2:9) or Jesus Himself, the great High Priest (Hebrews)—not ministers in the Christian church. What this position is saying—or not saying—about grace, one shudders to think. It is a typical case of overreaction. In theory, someone could commit a murder, get sent away for twenty years, become a Christian in prison, emerge from incarceration, grow as a Christian, attend seminary, and eventually become an accepted pastor—all without impediment—while the person who divorced his alcoholic and promiscuous wife at age twenty-one, while still an utter stranger to grace, would be perpetually debarred. Curiouser and curiouser!

On the other hand, the appeal Swaggart makes to the primal place of forgiveness in the Christian way entirely mistakes the issue at hand. The critical point, I think, is this—restoration and forgiveness, as foundational as they are, do not necessarily entail *instant restoration to leadership*. Restoration to church membership and all the means of grace is one thing; restoration to leadership is another. If Swaggart has truly repented, I would like to think that his church would accept him as a fellow Christian in need of God's forgiving grace and would embrace him as a brother with both compassion and gentleness. Most emphatically, however, this does *not* mean that he should be restored to leadership any time soon.

When the New Testament deals with qualifications for Christian leaders (e.g., 1 Timothy 3:1ff.), the emphasis is on integrity. The New Testament is quite happy to accept as Christian leaders those who have led a pretty raunchy life up to the moment of conversion, but who have then turned around and over a period of time demonstrated integrity, humility, meekness, gentleness, and a growing grasp of Christian truth. Where reports of alleged misconduct circulate against Christian "elders," the New Testament says that such reports should be treated with healthy skepticism; gossip and slander were not unknown in the ancient world. But when a charge is proved, the New Testament insists that the Christian leader caught in such a circumstance is to be publicly reproved so that other leaders may fear. In other words, part of the function of the discipline should be to make an example of him (1 Timothy 5:19-20). A slap on the wrist does not accomplish that. More important yet, because of the New Testament emphasis on integrity, because of its insistence that leaders be "above reproach" (even in the eyes of outsiders!), a publicly fallen leader has disqualified himself for, at very least, a considerable period of time.

It seems to me that the authorities in the Assemblies of God have displayed compassion, but have not adequately considered some of these principles. "Outsiders" can understand, however begrudgingly, how a person of less than wholesome morality who genuinely gets converted and turns his or her life around may rise to a position of leadership. Someone like Chuck Colson comes to mind. What is far harder to respect, both within and outside the Christian church, is the person who has been preaching morality in the strongest terms while living a lie. If Swaggart gets up to preach in three months or some similarly short period, there will be a national snicker. The church can withstand persecution, slander, intellectual struggles, and various forms of legal and personal opposition; it cannot withstand snickers.

The credibility issue is even more significant in this instance than if Swaggart had been guilty of a one-night stand. The principles would have been the same; but those principles are all the more forceful when we remember that, according to news reports, Swaggart's sexual sins have been of long standing. During the time he was berating Bakker he himself was living a double life, and he had such wide influence. Add to this the fact that Swaggart raised about twelve million dollars annually, approximately 25 percent of the AOG annual missions budget (at least, according to news reports), and it becomes clear that the AOG itself *ought* to feel the pressure to go out of the way to maintain its own reputation. What might be a pathetic national snicker at Swaggart's expense is in danger of becoming a national snicker at the expense, not only of the AOG, but of Christianity that genuinely seeks to live in quiet submission to the Bible. (Ed. note: It is important to consider the end of the story. Swaggart broke away from the AOG, refusing to accept even their restrictions. At one point he spoke of keeping himself out of the pulpit for three months; in reality, it was about a month. To their credit, the AOG has not restored his credentials.)

The argument that Swaggart has done so much good that he ought to be restored to public ministry as rapidly as possible does not stand up very well. However much good or evil he has done, one of the first things Christians ought to learn is that sin should not be dismissed as mere peccadillo on the basis of the sinner's status. Sustained hypocrisy should not be reclassified as merely personal foible. It reminds me of the old line, "Yes, Mrs. Lincoln, but apart from the shot, how did you enjoy the play?" Christian preachers and leaders and thinkers must be stamped by integrity.

This does not mean that Mr. Swaggart should not under any circumstances be restored to public ministry. But he should be permitted to regain public ministry only by regaining public credibility, a reputation for being "above reproach." He can do this only if two points are observed—first, it is going to take a great deal of time; and second, he is going to have to start at the bottom and build a reputation for faithfulness in small matters before he can be trusted with much. He needs to start by driving a bus to pick up school kids and elderly pensioners, teaching a Sunday school class for ten-year-olds, and demonstrating over five or ten or more years that he is willing to serve Christ in lowly places, regaining his reputation for integrity, demonstrating that he is broken and reformed because he has come to hate sin, not because he got caught. In time, it is possible, just possible, that he could eventually regain a national pulpit without a national snicker. Failing these steps, he should never be permitted to preach under the auspices of any responsible evangelical body again. If that means we are impoverished by the loss of his talents, so be it.

But suppose the person caught in such a sin is a sixteen-year-old girl without any leadership or prominence in the church. What then?

In many conservative churches, the girl would be made an example, and the youth minister who made her pregnant would be allowed to resign quietly and move away, complete with three months' pay. This is a rank double standard.

The *only* time a leader in such a situation should not be brought before the entire church is when to do so would damage even more people (for instance, if he has slept with two or three married women whose husbands do not yet know what occurred). Then the discipline might have to be firm, but discreet.

But where these sins are public, the general rule ought to be that the confession must also be public, before the church. There ought to be public remorse, transparent confession, and the establishment of some kind of accountability. In such an environment, there ought to be no impediment to restoration to membership. Indeed, if repentance is prompt and excommunication has not taken place, there is no reason why it should. But the person should be immediately removed from all leadership positions. With time, if there is clear accountability, spiritual growth, fruit demonstrating repentance, restitution where possible, incremental steps in responsibility and leadership, and a sense of personal call confirmed by the church itself, it may be possible to restore such a person to significant leadership as well. Otherwise, no way.

As ever,
Paul

40

*O*ne evening in April 1988, Ginny and I were loading the dishwasher and chatting after a late supper. Suddenly, like a lightning bolt, it crashed home to me that ten years earlier at Princeton University I had confessed Christ as Lord and Savior. Little did I know in 1978 what a difference coming to Christ would make in the unfolding of my life.

If you had asked me before my conversion where I would be a decade later, I could never have guessed pastoring a middle-sized evangelical church in the Orlando area and married to a wonderful Christian woman named Ginny. Rather I would have speculated that I would be trying to make a go of an academic career in history or else living on Long Island, commuting to Manhattan each morning, and making a concerted effort to scramble up the corporate ladder in the insurance business. I would have remained single, not wanting to get involved in a long-term commitment to any one woman. My basic egoism would not have permitted that.

But the Lord had other plans for my life. For this I am so grateful. Ginny and I were—and are—deeply in love. We wanted to start a family. The church was beginning to prosper in terms of its spiritual health. Mr. Olssen continued to meet with me whenever I needed someone to talk to in confidence about particular problems in the church.

One thing I noticed about some of the people in our church, especially the younger ones, was that their lives were desperately busy. When the weekends came, they wanted to head to the beaches and enjoy the out-of-doors as an escape from their hard-driving Monday through Friday jobs. I could not fault their need for relaxation, but I began to wonder whether their interest in spiritual things and the work of the church was suffering.

I recalled that at Trinity one professor had talked about what he called "California Christianity." As a native of New Jersey, I had no idea what he was describing. But now, perched in a church outside of Orlando with Disney World in the neighborhood, I began to wonder whether or not there was such a thing as "Florida Christianity"—that is, people had so many opportunities for entertainment and recreation that inadvertently their commitment to spiritual things took a distant second place.

Not wanting to be a geographical determinist, I pushed this thought out of my mind. Moreover, I had come to know some fine Christians from Florida and California. But in a letter I wrote to Dr. Woodson in May of 1988, in which I reminisced about my Christian pilgrimage during the previous decade, I mentioned in a jocular fashion my musings about "California" and "Florida Christianity."

His response was rather revealing.

May 11, 1988

Dear Tim,

Your letter recounting how the Lord has led you during the last ten years warmed my heart. The Lord has been very faithful to you, Timothy.

It seems like only yesterday that I received your first letter. If I recall correctly, you told me about the passing of your father as well as your conversion to Christ. I was deeply saddened by the news regarding your father but overjoyed by your own personal news. What mixed feelings! I just wish that your dad had lived to see what a fine young man you have become.

The attraction of sports and recreation for some of the people in your church is understandable. There is something wonderful about enjoying God's creation. How relaxing it is to walk along a beach at sunset, watching the waves pile up on the shoreline, only to beat a hasty retreat. There is something exhilarating in participating in a fierce athletic competition. The Bible employs references to sports as a metaphor related to living out the Christian life. Often love of recreation and sports is a blessing—participation can build character and discipline, and being a spectator can be relaxing and enjoyable—part of the good gifts of our Heavenly Father.

But this same love can be a bane. I love to watch sports; college or professional makes little difference. This is no revelation to you. Sometimes I get so caught up in a game that the outcome affects my entire demeanor. When the Bears lose a close one, I find myself in a surly mood.

What I am about to tell you is nothing I am proud of, but my own failure may provide a useful illustration. Once I was asked to preach at a church on the Sunday evening that the Super Bowl was going to take place. The winds were howling outside as they sometimes do in Chicago in January. The temperature was plummeting so far below zero that TV and radio announcers were warning folks to stay in. That seemed like an excellent idea. I called up a layperson responsible for the evening service at the church and asked if he thought it was a wise idea to hold the service in such weather. The layperson agreed with my "concern" for the welfare of the people (maybe he was a football fan too!). He indicated that he would postpone the service until the next Sunday evening. My heart leaped for joy. I could stay at home and watch the Super Bowl.

Upon more sober reflection, however, I realized what had happened. My interests in sports had pushed aside my commitment to Christian ministry. The next day I was terribly stricken in conscience, and in tears I confessed my sin to the Lord. On occasion my love of sports is a blessing; at other times it is a curse.

Another illustration comes to mind. I visited a Christian youth camp in California one summer after graduating from college. I dropped by the campground just in time to watch a camper-staff basketball game. To my amazement, along the sidelines stood Larry Davidson—the head counselor, athlete *extraordinaire,* and permanent fixture at the camp. I walked up to him and asked why he was not playing on the staff team as he had when I had been on staff two summers before. He said, "Paul, I used to get so caught up in the intensity of the game that I would say and do things that as a Christian I just should not have, and that with campers looking on. I decided before God that my testimony as a Christian was more important than my very real craving for sports. I quit playing competitively a year ago for that reason." Larry had come to grips with his problem of letting his love of sports throw his walk with the Lord off kilter.

For millions of people throughout the world there has been no such corrective. They live for the days when their favorite teams play. A victory means the heady heights of ecstasy, a defeat the lowly dregs of despair.

Recently, I heard a commentator on the radio say in all seriousness that this country has no national religion except baseball, with Cooperstown, Ohio, the site of the national shrine. This claim sends chills through my soul because I have the feeling it is not just a joke; for many people it is the pathetic truth. If you define religion as that which commands our ultimate attention or is our ultimate concern, then being a fan of baseball, football, and basketball (or whatever) is the religion of many people. They live and die by the fortunes of their heroes and heroines; their gods and goddesses are contemporary sports figures.

How then might you lead your people on this matter? May I suggest that you begin by highlighting the very real delights of sports and recreation and relaxation? But then you might show that these can become diversions or distractions leading us to take our eyes off Christ. Pascal long ago warned that people fill their lives with activities (he calls them "diversions") to escape thinking about God, life, and death. I imagine some of your people have never assessed the power of diversions in their own lives. You might prompt them to reflect about this by asking if they have ever hoped that a sermon would end before 12:00 noon so that they might rush home to watch the NFL on television. My own experience of hoping that a church service would be canceled on a Super Bowl Sunday evening was the wake-up call that forced me to deal with my own attitudes.

I would be very interested in knowing what you think about these issues. Moreover, should you broach this delicate topic with your people, I would be intrigued to learn how they respond to your gentle admonitions. My guess is that a few members in your congregation will find it genuinely liberating to reduce sport from the realm of religion to the realm of wholesome fun.

Once again please give our best regards to Ginny. Elizabeth is well. She prays for you regularly.

With our love,
Paul and Elizabeth

41

In the late summer as I planned ahead for services throughout the fall, I became increasingly restless over what we were doing in the area of worship. The church was young enough that I had been able to introduce a number of innovations, but quite frankly services frequently were suffused with a sense of unreality. Some enjoyed the Scripture choruses and the guitars we used in some of our services; others did not. We tried corporate readings, printing in the bulletin the entire text of Scripture to be read because too many English versions were present in the congregation to achieve a consensus any other way. We toyed with some liturgical responses; we tried open times of praying and sharing. Once or twice we put on a skit to illustrate some point in the sermon. But I could not escape the feeling of unreality stamped on much that we did. Once in a while the glory of the Lord seemed to shine through. But I thought that there had to be a way of improving what we were doing.

September 1, 1988

My dear Tim,

You have expressed the problem very well—a feeling of unreality. And so you have tried to change things. I believe it was C. S. Lewis who said that he could enjoy any kind of liturgical style at all, except one that changed too often. In his view, frequent changes draw attention to themselves or to the clever people who are making them, and therefore away from God. On the other hand, when a form is very bad or very musty or clearly doing nothing but enhancing boredom, something must be done.

But what? And is changing this or that the real solution? I sometimes feel that evangelical churches in the liturgical traditions are busily trying to free themselves up from these encumbrances, while those in the "free" traditions are busily trying to adopt a more liturgical style.

The fundamental question to decide, of course, is what worship is. At a rudimentary level, it is nothing but the ascription of worth to God. But more can be said if we try to look at the Biblical-theological structures that define a proper approach to worship.

In the Old Testament, although there is certainly a large place for private devotion, the central place for worship is the temple and the entire "cultic" apparatus that goes with it. Here one *serves* the Lord and *worships* the Lord and *praises* the Lord. But under the new covenant, it is astonishing how the "cultic" terminology of the Old Testament is transmuted. Christian worship is not associated with a temple, but tied to all of Christian living. To go no farther than Romans 12:1-2, our offering of ourselves to God is our "spiritual worship." This pattern (as several writers have pointed out) is a constant feature of New Testament "worship" language (e.g., *leitourgia* and cognates, etc.).

On the other hand, the conclusion sometimes drawn from this valid observation has missed the mark. It has been argued that if Christian worship involves all of life, then what we do when we come together for corporate meetings cannot properly be called "worship"; it must be something else. This "something" has variously been tagged fellowship, instruction, mutual exhortation, or the like.

It is surely better to argue that, just as our entire life is to be lived out in worship to God in an attitude and a style and a faithfulness that is *constantly* ascribing praise to Him and giving thanks to Him (after all, the church can almost be defined as those everywhere who call on the name of the Lord, 1 Corinthians 1:2), so also our coming together is supremely marked by such worship. In this view, the other things that enter into our services are part of worship. It is not that we worship for a few minutes (for instance, in singing) and then have a time of sharing that cannot be considered worship or listen to a sermon that should be dubbed "instruction" but not "worship." Rather, all that we do in our corporate meetings, as in all of our lives when we are on our own, must be offered up to God as an offering to Him, a service, worship. We are doing corporately and with total concentration what we should have been doing on our own all week—we are worshiping the living God.

If this is where we begin, then what we will go after when we think about improving our "worship services" is not the manipulation of this or that bit of liturgy, the addition or subtraction of choruses, or some decision about guitars or pipe organs, but a deeper knowledge of God. That simply can't be faked. I think it was George Burns who said that the key to his success was first learning honesty; and when he could fake that, he could achieve anything. We smile; but in our more rueful moments we have to admit we sometimes fake a real knowledge of God, and then try to go through the motions as if no one can tell.

But of course they can. That is why it is possible to attend a "Free" Church of Scotland service, without instruments, singing only metrical psalms, and join in profound worship—while another Free church, singing the same psalms, is as dead as a dodo. That is why it is possible to attend a service with a small orchestra, lots of hand-clapping, many Scripture choruses, and the like and know the Spirit's presence—while a church organized along similar lines seems nothing more than cheap entertainment and shoddy display.

I am not saying that the mechanics are unimportant. But more important than anything else is the preparation of your own heart and the heart of everyone else who has anything to do with the public, corporate leading of the people of God. In other words, our corporate worship should be the overflow of the worship that characterizes all our lives all the time.

If we grant that this is the right approach, Biblically speaking, to the challenge of improving our worship, there are still some practical points worth observing.

People have disputed the significance and power of music for years. In my view, there is nothing intrinsically moral or immoral about notes, musical styles, instruments. There is nothing intrinsically more reverent about, say, a guitar, than an organ. For some strange reason, we have had more guitars on the quarterly "day of prayer" at TEDS in the last few years than on any other day; is the guitar more calculated to induce prayer than the Cassavante pipe organ?

The truth of the matter, I think, is that each of us maintains mental and emotional associations between certain instruments and certain attitudes, between certain kinds of music and certain kinds of response. For middle-aged Christians from a conservative background, the organ has far more associations of reverence than the guitar, let alone drums. For young people converted at university and nurtured there in the local chapter of IVCF or Campus Crusade, the organ may have overtones of stuffiness, of traditional hypocrisy. And if you want things to really swing, pay a few visits to a first-class African-American church!

That means that we need to tolerate one another. In a culturally diverse church, we need to do more—we need to accommodate one another and learn from one another. When some people pursue, say, more liturgy, I suspect they are feeding their rising sense of aesthetics more than anything else. Liturgical worship can be wonderful; so can a freer style. But the ultimate criteria have very little to do with form.

They do have a great deal to do with content. Musical pieces should be chosen first and foremost for their lyrics, not for their beat. Many a service would be greatly improved if whoever is leading would simply keep quiet and stop the endless talking. Let the prayers and readings and songs and testimonies carry themselves; or, if you must say something, plan in careful and prayerful detail what you will say, constantly remembering that the aim is to glorify God, not enhance your reputation.

More generally, I think that our corporate meetings must at some point strive to achieve a note of massive dignity, and at another point strive to achieve profound intimacy. I do not mean to manipulate people by wording things like this; I mean, rather, that our meetings need to reflect both the vertical relationship we have with God and the horizontal relationship we have (or ought to have!) with each other because we are Christians. Very few of us can achieve both in one service, let alone in each service. That means, at the practical level, that in different services you might self-consciously strike a tone a little different from that of another service—but complementary to it in the whole life of the church.

Do I need to say that in my view, proper preaching is not something undertaken in addition to worship, but it is an integral part of worship? As it represents God's living Word to His covenant people, it calls all to offer themselves to Him and is itself, both in the delivery and the hearing of that Word, an act of homage.

A hundred other matters clamor for attention, but I sound like I am lecturing. I'd love to come down and spend some time with you folks.

Love in Christ Jesus,
Paul

42

At the end of September, a man and his wife in our church became ill. The diagnosis—they both had AIDS. And their two children, ages three and five, though still clinically clear, tested HIV-positive.

The shock to our congregation was palpable. Despite our education efforts, some parents were deeply worried about letting their children come to Sunday school and the like. Another question surfaced in whispers in corridors before one of the deacons put it to me privately, speaking for quite a number in the church.

Everyone learned that the man had engaged in bisexual activity seven or eight years before. He met and married his wife and, after their first child was born, they decided they ought to come to church. That is when both of them were converted, not too long before I became their pastor. How, then, should the church handle this? "Men committed indecent acts with other men, and received in themselves the due penalty for their perversion" (Romans 1:27)—the passage was quoted at me with some vehemence. But the wife and the children were innocent victims; surely they should be treated a little differently from the man whose callous disregard for moral standards had in effect sentenced not only himself but his wife and two children to a premature and horrible death?

This analysis cannot be right. Yet I confess I am uneasy about relinquishing all connections between AIDS and moral conduct. I asked Prof. Woodson how he would articulate the relationship and what pastoral judgments would follow.

November 7, 1988

My dear Tim,

You are certainly facing all the difficult questions early on in your ministry. Many is the comfortable suburban church where AIDS is still entirely unknown, except as an item on the news and in *Time* magazine. But the challenge before you is not the worst. A TEDS graduate serving a church in a farming community in the next state wrote the other day to say that a stalwart family with six children in his congregation is facing a horrible future. Four of the six are hemophiliacs. Two have already died of AIDS, doubtless contracted before 1985 when the nation's blood supply was cleaned up. One tests HIV-positive. The oldest child, now a man of about thirty with two children of his own, both hemophiliacs, refuses to be tested and refuses to test his children.

I have no easy answers.

You know as well as I do that HIV is not a tough virus. It can be communicated only by sexual activity or through a mingling of blood. In practice, the latter means that you can get the disease by using a needle contaminated by someone else or by a blood transfusion from a contaminated supply. It is just possible for a doctor or dentist to become infected from a contaminated patient through some miniscule wound with which the doctor or dentist is afflicted, but this is exceedingly rare and can usually be avoided by such elementary means as wearing protective gloves. Babies can be born with HIV if their mothers are carriers.

Certainly the way the disease spread in its early stages was through sexual transmission and drug abuse. And most of the earliest sexual transmission in this country was homosexual. In America, the risk of infection from one sexual encounter with a carrier is far higher if the intercourse is homosexual than if it is heterosexual. Some think this is because the anal wall, never designed for the rough treatment of intercourse, is more likely to bleed, thereby increasing the likelihood of infection. In Africa, where accurate statistics are harder to come by, the disease seems to be multiplying as quickly through the heterosexual population as elsewhere, primarily through prostitution. The reasons for this are not certain, though several theories have been advanced.

When various agencies tell us that this is a plague and that any of us could contract this disease, they are lying. If you do not take intravenous drugs with someone else's needle, and if you are not promiscuous, the chances of being infected, now that the blood supply has been cleaned up, are infinitesimally small. That does not mean there are no victims in other categories. For example, the spouses of those who have been promiscuous are at risk; the prenatal children of HIV carriers are at extreme risk.

I suppose this means I should say something about homosexuality. I do not remember if you took any advanced courses in ethics at TEDS. Despite warped efforts to show that the Bible condemns only promiscuous homosexuality, but not covenantal homosexuality (that is, a monogamous homosexual union), the fact of the matter is that the Bible condemns homosexuality, period. Scientific attempts to link homosexuality to an organic root have (so far as I am aware) proved ambiguous. Apparently some physical factors are more frequent in homosexuals than in heterosexuals, but there is no infallible causal relationship (i.e., if you have such-and-such a factor, you will turn out to be a homosexual). If you are white, your whiteness is genetically determined; you cannot repent and become black (or vice versa). But I have known a number of practicing homosexuals who are homosexuals no longer.

What repeated studies have shown, however, is that about 67 percent of homosexual males come from one stereotypical background—a weak father (or no father present) and a bullying mother. Another 30 percent or so come from another background—a brutal father and a mother who is abused by him. The remaining few percent were usually seduced in their youth, often by a homosexual relative, and set along a certain pattern. Somewhat similar figures have been put forward for lesbians, but with the obverse family problems; and so far as I know, the research is less secure in their case.

Among the inferences to be drawn from these studies is the fact that not a little sin has social effects. These families are unbiblical in structure and priorities; and the effects on the children are grim. Doubtless practicing homosexuals are willing participants and therefore share the responsibility; but much of the blame must be laid at the door of the previous generation or generations, where the families simply broke down, and abuse of one kind or another prevailed.

Most expositors will tell you that Romans 1:27, which you cited in your letter, does not make AIDS or any other venereal disease the "due penalty of their perversion." Rather, it is homosexuality itself that is the due penalty of the perversion of constantly unrequited but nurtured lust. There were no barriers, no moral restraints, Paul says; and finally these people discover they are enslaved by passions they cannot possibly break by themselves.

But although the Bible condemns homosexuality, it must also be said with the loudest voice that it condemns all fornication, all lasciviousness. There is no reason to think that heterosexual licentiousness is cute or attractive or normal and should be used to sell cars and soap, while homosexual licentiousness is either debased or the target of specially "sensitive" plays. What we have, rather, is the nation reaping the whirlwind for the abandonment of moral resolve, the loss of the center, the sacrifice of moral law above its own constitution. And the end is not yet in sight. We can talk about "alternative lifestyles" instead of homosexual sin; we can comment on sexual partners instead of referring to them as adulterers and fornicators, but all that does is indicate how far we are from looking at things from God's perspective.

But does this mean, in the pastoral need you have before you, that you should treat this man and his wife differently? Surely not in the kind and quality of care you give! When God unleashes the terrible judgment of war, both the "just" and the "unjust" get bombed and maimed. Now this terrible scourge of AIDS afflicts the world. It is important to say that it is the result of sin and that the most common means of contracting it are doing things that God forbids. But it is important to say this with tears in your eyes and to recognize that we live in a sex-crazed society, and to some extent we are all participants, all contaminated by the sheer ubiquity of the temptations. Just as Christians ought to help those who suffer in time of war, so should they help those who suffer from AIDS. Here, if anywhere, the church has the opportunity to serve, to display compassion, to prove that we are aware we are all poor sinners in need of grace—and to display that grace even as we insist that God is not mocked and that the only final hope is a return to Him for the pardon and cleansing only He can give.

If a distinction should be made any place between this man and his wife, it should not be in the quality of care given them, but in the precise nature of the counsel given. That man is going to face terrible pangs of guilt; that woman, unless she is altogether extraordinary, is going to combat the deepest bitterness and resentments—and her own brand of guilt because of her children.

(Ed. note: The letter turns to personal matters and greetings.)

As ever,
Paul

43

A t the end of the year, I resolved to improve the quality of my prayer life, and I wrote to ask if Paul had any tips in time for New Year's resolutions.

December 30, 1988

My dear Tim,

I found your letter moving and refreshing. It called me back to priorities I too quickly neglect myself.

We seem to be living in a day of renewed interest in "spirituality." Unfortunately, that rubric seems to cover an awful lot of ground, some of it silly, some of it dangerous. The New Age movement is interpreted by many as the recovery of spirituality. Since its structure is profoundly monistic, this reduces to mystical experiences in which the self is "actualized" or "realized" or the like. It has almost nothing to do with the spiritual pursuit of the personal/transcendent God and Father of our Lord Jesus Christ.

Even within Christendom, there is a return to Catholic mystics and to one form or another of the "New Pietism" instead of to the "spirituality of the Word." If these categories are strange to you, I urge you to read the brief work by Peter Adam, *Roots of Contemporary Evangelical Spirituality* (Grove Books #24; 1988).

The sheer, frenetic pace of life is daunting. We have all these labor-saving devices, and we simply program ourselves to run faster, do more things, take on one more load. But the danger is that we do not have time to think, let alone to pray. The unexamined life is scarcely worth living; for the Christian, the prayerless life can signify rebellion to boot.

So for what it is worth, here is a miscellany of advice about praying. I wish I always put all of this into practice.

Plan to pray. I do not mean to say the obvious. I mean, rather, that you will not drift into prayer, and so unless you plan to pray and set aside time to pray, you will not pray, except very cursorily now and then. You have to budget time to pray.

Copy out the prayers of Paul, memorize them, and pray your way through them, regularly, thoughtfully—asking God for the petitionary content in those prayers not only for yourself, but for the people over whom He has made you overseer. That will keep you busy for a long time. If you run out of material, start working through the prayers of Moses and the prayers of David.

Use helps to keep your mind from wandering. Verbalize your prayers; use lists; pray through certain sections of the better hymnbooks.

Regularly pray through your list of members and adherents and their families. (You will also find this ensures that you learn their names!)

Mingle praise and petition. Learn to tie your petitions to the priorities of Scripture (e.g., as far as God is concerned, it is far more important that we be holy than healthy).

Make sure you set aside time to pray with your wife.

Try to set up a small circle of prayer warriors who will meet regularly, at least once a week, to do nothing but read Scripture and pray with you. They may transform your ministry.

Ensure that your list of prayer concerns enables you to keep in mind the whole world. Do not lower your gaze so that all you can think of is your own parish, no matter how important it is to you.

When there are challenges or difficulties or pastoral needs, learn to make prayer the *first* recourse, not the last.

Consider keeping some sort of prayer diary—not simply a list of things to pray for, but a kind of honest spiritual autobiography. That was a Puritan technique, and some find it helpful today. I confess it is not something I do myself; but some find it a powerful way of keeping honest.

And pray for me, please. I need it.

Happy New Year!

Yours in Christ's service,
Paul

44

*I*n January 1989 Ginny and I had no idea the world was plunging
into a momentous year of revolutionary drama. We could guess
that on July 14 the French would inevitably celebrate the two hun-
dredth anniversary of the fall of the Bastille. But to celebrate, the
French would party in the streets, not actually storm the government
buildings of President François Mitterand. However, in Germany the
Berlin Wall would tumble down and a social and political revolution
of the greatest magnitude would rock Eastern Europe—of that we
had no idea.

In the early months of 1989 Ginny and I continued our work in
the church. Ginny was also holding a part-time job to help defray
the costs of our home mortgage. Technically, we were "home owners," but we did not know which 22 percent of our house actually
belonged to us.

In March of 1989 Dr. Woodson wrote and extended an invitation
to me to come to a conference entitled "Evangelical Affirmations
'89" to be held at Trinity Evangelical Divinity School in May. Dr.
Woodson indicated that the conference would be co-chaired by Dr.
Carl F. H. Henry and Dr. Kenneth S. Kantzer, two evangelical stal-
warts whom he greatly admired. Hundreds of evangelicals were
expected to gather together to draw up a set of affirmations upon
which they could agree. It was hoped that the conference would
enhance evangelical unity. The conference was to be sponsored by
the National Association of Evangelicals and Trinity. Dr. Woodson
thought I might enjoy attending and suggested that Ginny and I
could stay in the extra bedroom of the Woodsons' home in Highland
Park.

When I told Ginny about this invitation, her immediate response
was, "Let's go." Then a cold wave of reality hit us. We looked at our
checkbook and realized we could not afford a trip of this kind. Our
mortgage payments were eating up much of my salary.

I wrote to Dr. Woodson and thanked him for his gracious invitation which sadly we had to decline. The idea of meeting with Christians from various denominations was very attractive to me. But I really did not understand why such a conference was needed. I asked Dr. Woodson if he knew more about its rationale. As a faculty member at Trinity, he had probably spoken with Dr. Kantzer and others about this.

Dr. Woodson's response to my letter was an eye-opener.

May 10, 1989

Dear Tim,

Thank you for your gracious letter. Elizabeth and I understand very well why you are unable to attend the conference. Please be assured that if you are ever in Chicago, you have a standing invitation to make our home your home.

I'd be glad to outline the reasons why those who are planning "Evangelical Affirmations '89" believe that such a conference is propitious. There is a pervasive perception that the post-World-War-II evangelical movement has been fractured into so many pieces that unity within the movement is unattainable. Indeed in some recent literature the motif that evangelicalism is nothing more than a mosaic of diverse Christian groups is receiving considerable play.

In one sense the concept of a mosaic is useful. Christians do differ from one another and have varying doctrinal emphases. But a number of proponents of the mosaic analogy argue that there is no design in the mosaic; it consists merely of unrelated pieces of chipped glass. The inference is that no common core doctrines or practices exist to unite evangelicals.

But your experience and my own tell us that there is a unity in Christ that overcomes denominational barriers and distinctives. When you meet with an evangelical Methodist, you sense that he or she is a fine Christian even if not a Presbyterian like yourself. Those individuals who abuse the mosaic motif by making each Christian group completely different from any other really do not have a grasp of evangelical ecclesiology. True believers, whether Congregational, Episcopalian, Presbyterian, Baptist, Methodist (or whatever), charismatic or noncharismatic—whether they are black, yellow, brown, or white—whether rich or poor, belong to the same church, for there is only one church. It is Christ's church, the community of the redeemed.

The aim at "Evangelical Affirmations '89," is to make the unity of the evangelical churches more manifest. I am absolutely convinced that critics have overemphasized the disunity of the evangelical movement.

Some would say that actual evangelical unity is now a pipe dream. How can the evangelical movement which in 1975 Dr. Martin Marty argued upheld the doctrine of Biblical inerrancy as a *sine qua non* be put back together when profound differences now exist among evangelicals regarding this pivotal doctrine? This is not an easy question to answer.

Moreover, has not the evangelical community been wounded so severely by the TV scandals that it will not be able to recover its balance as a force for righteousness in this land? This too is not an easy question to answer.

When I asked one of the conference planners for a more explicit listing of the reasons for the conference, he cited some of these same points:

1) Moral improprieties—the troubling realization that a number of evangelical leaders have become ensnared in gross sins and that the cause of Christ is being brought into disrepute by these deviations from God's standards of righteousness.

2) A doctrinal identity crisis—the loss of commitment to a number of important beliefs of Biblical faith is occurring within evangelical circles.

In a major review of James D. Hunter's *Evangelicalism: The Coming Generation,* Carl F. H. Henry has written:

> Even with allowance for weaknesses in sampling and possible excessive inferences, there can be little doubt that theological and ethical slippage on evangelical campuses outruns constituency assurances given by public relations departments, administrators, and trustees. The 15 mainstream evangelical campuses probed by Hunter profess to espouse the core theology of the evangelical worldview. But the day is gone, he concludes, when the evangelical establishment—ecclesiastical, editorial, evangelistic or humanitarian—can take for granted that graduates of evangelical schools are religiously "safe."

Perhaps more startling than Hunter's findings were observations made last year by Professor George Marsden of Duke University. He proposed that those who advocate what he calls "Open Evangelicalism" should be wary not to succumb to Protestant liberalism. In reviewing a book on Protestant liberalism, Marsden commented that two contributors to the volume, William Hutchison and Leonard Sweet, "suggest that liberal Protestantism may be alive and well in left-wing evangelicalism." Marsden continues, "It is, of course, a fair warning, or a fair promise (depending on whether it comes from Sweet or Hutchison) that Open Evangelicalism could drift into Protestant liberalism. Modern religious institutions seem usually to drift to the left" (*Fides et historia*, 20:1 [January, 1988]: 49). This warning is particularly pungent because on many fronts Professor Marsden is himself a proponent of "Open Evangelicalism."

3) A revisionary sociological perception of evangelicalism—a reduction of "evangelicalism" to merely sociological categories. Several noted scholars, such as Professor Donald Dayton, have pronounced obituaries for the evangelical movement because its alleged components ostensibly lack any common bonding traits. Dayton has called for a moratorium on the use of the term *evangelical*—a term which, he says, has lost meaning. Others have declared flatly that evangelicalism lacks any doctrinal core; rather, the movement consists of a loose affiliation of voluntary societies.

Those who are planning "Evangelical Affirmations '89" want to address these issues and foster a salutary evangelical ecumenism. For this reason invitations have been extended to Christians from a very wide background. Nonetheless, the planners realize that unity bought at any price is a pyrrhic victory. Just as in the Early Church, Christians drew up "rules of faith" with the goal of clearly defining what the faith is, so at the conference it is hoped that those in attendance will draw up affirmations that will bring about the widest agreement upon core evangelical doctrines and practices.

Personally, I applaud any effort by anyone to build up Christians in the faith. Today, we need people who will throw themselves into the work of building up the saints. Unfortunately, some of our brightest young evangelicals have apparently given themselves to the work of criticism. Criticism is easy; building up others takes self-denying commitment.

I sometimes have the distinct impression that the most stringent criticism of evangelicals, oddly enough, comes from other evangelicals bent on winning the favor of a nonevangelical audience. By this I mean that some young evangelicals feel that they must criticize their own religious tradition in order to gain acceptance in an academic community hostile to that tradition. Evangelicals should by all means be self-critical—but for the right motivations and with a sense of ownership and compassion.

Tim, even as I write these words, I feel that I am becoming too critical. Jonathan Edwards's admonition about criticism has long rested in my mind and makes me wary of the emergence of my own critical spirit. Edwards argues that spiritual pride is "the main door by which the devil comes into the hearts of those that are zealous for the advancement of religion. . . . " He continues:

> Spiritual pride disposes us to speak of other persons' sins, their enmity against God and His people, the miserable delusion of hypocrites and their enmity against vital piety, and the deadness of some saints, with bitterness, or with laughter and levity, and an air of contempt; whereas pure Christian humility rather disposes, either to be silent about them, or to speak of them with grief and pity.
>
> Spiritual pride is very apt to suspect others; whereas a humble saint is most jealous of himself; he is so suspicious of nothing in the world as he is of his own heart. The spiritually proud person is apt to find fault with other saints, that they are low in grace, and to be much in observing how cold and dead they be, and crying out of them for it; and to be quick to discern and take notice of their deficiencies: but the eminently humble Christian has so much to do at home, and sees so much evil in his own heart, and is so concerned about it, that he is not apt to be very busy with others' hearts; he complains most of himself, and cries out of his own coldness and lowness in grace, and is apt to esteem others better than himself.

These words are some of the best that I have ever read on spiritual pride, other than in Scripture itself. Calvin says that even poking fun at others in jest often wounds them more than we know. If I had my life to live over again, I would try with the Lord's grace to be much more careful in my speech. The Lord hates a proud heart and a critical spirit.

Again, should you ever be headed this way, please let us know. Elizabeth and I really would like to see you again. We miss you very much.

And should it cross your mind, please pray for the Evangelical Affirmations conference. We really do need to pray that the Lord will have mercy upon us as and pour out His spirit in power on the church. Our disunity certainly does not please Him.

As ever,
Paul

45

In late 1989 the sight of Berliners and other Germans singing and dancing on top of the Berlin Wall sent chills up and down my spine. Ginny and I were thrilled. We sat before our TV screen transfixed. As the year 1990 progressed, we watched in amazement as the people of Central and Eastern Europe took to the streets and then threw out their Communist leaders one after the other. Why were the Russians not calling on the troops at their disposition in their satellite states to quash the democratic movement? It simply did not make sense; the Russian bear, a huge superpower, was letting its empire slip away.

In mid-1990, after several casual exchanges of letters during the previous year, I wrote to Dr. Woodson about another matter of a confidential sort. I also happened to mention my utter surprise at events taking place in Europe. It seemed as if I and many other Americans were watching "history in the making" without a context for understanding the dynamics of the revolutionary upheaval.

In his reply Dr. Woodson shed a little light on the meaning of the dramatic events of 1989 and 1990.

July 14, 1990

Dear Tim,

(Ed. note: We have excluded a lengthy segment of Dr. Woodson's letter owing to its very personal nature. In his letter Tim had indicated to Dr. Woodson that he and Ginny had been trying to start a family for some time but without success. A physician had told the two of them that they might not be able to have children. Tim and Ginny were reeling before this news. Dr. Woodson's counsel was as touching as it was encouraging. Tim Journeyman has given us permission to make this editorial comment.)

Now let me comment briefly on revolutionary events in Eastern Europe. Your amazement is obviously shared by millions of other people around the world. Apparently some academics did surmise that trouble was brewing for the Soviets. One of my friends who is a historian at a university in France recently explained to me that Marxism as an ideology had been losing adherents on both sides of the Iron Curtain long before 1989. During the late 1970s and 1980s François Furet, a leading French historian, launched a devastating attack on the Marxist construction of European history, especially Marx's analysis of the transition from feudalism to a capitalistic society during the French Revolution (you might want to glance at Furet's *Penser la révolution française,* for example). My friend also indicated that, as judged by papers delivered in May of 1989 at the International Congress on the History of the French Revolution (held at Georgetown University), the Marxist analysis was in rapid retreat among many intellectuals, whether they came from this side of the Iron Curtain or the other, and that before the Wall fell.

This may mean that what looked like a spontaneous reaction against Soviet repression in Eastern Europe was in fact more like a slowly building active volcano finally blowing its top. Many intellectuals behind the Iron Curtain had privately given up Communist ideology years earlier. This was particularly true in Poland where the Roman Catholic church has been so powerful. I myself remember meeting a Polish historian in Paris years ago. He was a member of the Communist Party in Poland, but he told me privately that he did not really believe party doctrine.

But no one expected the changes to come this fast. As a Christian, I should have recalled that God holds the nations in His mighty hands and that they rise and fall at His good pleasure. But I must confess I thought that the Soviet system was so muscle-bound and awesome it simply could not be challenged, at least in my lifetime. My unbelief has prompted me to return to Isaiah 40 with renewed understanding and deep awe at the sovereign power of God.

Events taking place in Central and Eastern Europe may create remarkable open doors for evangelism in that part of the world and for learning from our brothers and sisters in Christ who have been schooled and purified in the fires of persecution. I do hope that Christians will not miss these opportunities for spreading the gospel of Jesus Christ and for establishing enduring ties of fellowship.

Both of you have very important and difficult concerns on your minds. Please be assured that Elizabeth and I will be praying for you in days ahead. If Ginny would like to call Elizabeth, please encour-

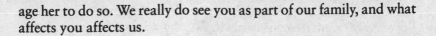

age her to do so. We really do see you as part of our family, and what affects you affects us.

As ever,
Paul

46

*G*inny and I were delighted with the way the lay people in the church were taking on more and more responsibilities. A genuine spirit of camaraderie and common purpose seemed to pervade the elders' meetings. On occasion as Ginny and I talked and prayed together in the evening, we could only marvel at the change in the life of our church and in our own lives. What a joy it was to watch the Lord working in the lives of many people. Parents were becoming reconciled with children, and adults who had not spoken together for years found ways to end their feuds. The women's Bible study and men's breakfast group were flourishing. And prayer was beginning to be the heartbeat of our church.

But all was not peace and light. Despite the brave face she put on, Ginny had to wrestle with her feelings when she was around younger couples with children. And I had grown much more uneasy about our community after some of the high schoolers at an ice-cream social told me about Satanic rituals allegedly performed by a few of their classmates. Then again, we were having more people join our church coming directly out of sexual promiscuity and the drug culture. It seemed to me as if there were two different Americas emerging and clashing with each other—one upholding traditional Judeo-Christian values and another determined to challenge those values to the hilt in the name of unharnessed freedom and a quest for self-fulfillment.

In late 1990, I wrote to Dr. Woodson and asked how he and Elizabeth were doing. Obviously, I was corresponding with them less now—not because of any loss of affection or respect but because Ginny and I were simply too consumed by church activities to keep up a concerted correspondence of long letters.

In my letter I gave Dr. Woodson an update about our personal situation. Then I asked him what he thought about the continued dra-

matic developments in the world order and the unraveling of traditional values at home.

December 18, 1990

Dear Tim,

Thank you for your fine letter. We were so pleased to hear from you once again. Elizabeth and I rejoice that your church is spiritually alive, evidenced by the fact people are coming to know the Lord and that a healing of relationships among Christians is much in evidence. We were obviously interested in your personal news as well.

We do trust that this will be a wonderful Christmas season for you and that the year 1991 will be your best ever in the Lord.

I agree with you wholeheartedly. We are watching events I could not have dreamed would take place, at least in my lifetime—the apparent unraveling of the Soviet order, the isolation of Cuba. . . . Doubtless other chapters will be added to the saga.

As the idol of Marxism totters and falls, so the idols of naturalistic Darwinism and Freudianism may fall as well. To propose this hypothesis seems at present as ludicrous as it would have been to predict in 1980 that the Soviet Union would fall apart by the early 1990s. But there are signs that naturalistic Darwinism and Freudianism are much more vulnerable to telling criticism today than they have been in the last three or four decades.

Consequently, when we analyze the contemporary cultural scene, we should not automatically assume a gloomy posture. Alarmist evangelical commentators can sometimes give the public the wrong impression and feed a pessimistic spirit. It is true that the evil one is unleashing tremendous havoc in this world. But we recall Luther's good word of perspective, "One little word [the name of Jesus] will fell him."

Christians need to be instructed and warned about the dangers of the New Paganism, the New Age movement, the cults and multiple "isms" out there. But Christians also need to be taught that the evil one who is the ultimate sponsor of these movements has already been defeated at the cross. And every Christian should be informed about the spiritual armor available to him or her in the warfare in which each of us is engaged (Ephesians 6:10-18).

So I am not as pessimistic about the present situation as some evangelical writers are. At one level things are very dark; but God is sovereign, and the impending collapse of Marxism, and the potential collapse of naturalistic evolution and Freudianism—three idols of contemporary secularism—may signal a time of tremendous opportunity for Christian witness.

If in God's mercy these monstrous idols are destroyed, the question would really be this: Who or what will rush into the void when atheistic secularism seems less attractive? Will the nations be swamped by a tide of spiritualism? And how will evangelicals respond to the opportunity of living in a world where people are spiritually hungry? Will evangelicals meet the challenge of counteracting the siren calls of the Shirley MacLaines and other New Agers? Will they send missionaries to Eastern Europe, Russia, and to China? Right now missionaries from a number of world religions such as Islam, not to mention the major cults and various New Age ideologies, are hard at work bidding for the loyalties of our neighbors here in the United States and of peoples around the world.

We Christians need to reach out to our neighbors with the gospel in this time when an ideological vacuum seems to be opening up. More than ever we will need to be people of prayer. Our foes are powerful and will not yield ground easily. In one sense we may be approaching a time similar to the one the early Christians faced when it cost people much to name the name of Christ.

Elizabeth and I are very grateful that we remain basically healthy. The bones do creak a little bit more now and then, and on occasion I am short of breath climbing the stairs, but otherwise I seem to be fine.

Elizabeth likes to go on walks around the neighborhood. She gently urges me to join her on these jaunts insisting that it would be good for me. She is right. But the Bulls are playing well this season, and I enjoy watching other people exercise more than I enjoy exercising myself. Elizabeth finds this somewhat annoying. But around play-off time, if the Bulls are still alive in the competition, my guess is that she will join me in front of the TV set. This may sound a touch triumphalistic on my part. In reality, I wish I watched sporting events less frequently.

Again, thank you so much for writing. We really would like to hear from you more, but we understand that you are frightfully busy. In any case, whether you write soon or not, be assured that you and Ginny are in our thoughts and prayers.

Grace and peace,
Paul

47

*B*y the kindness of a friend on the faculty of Trinity Evangelical Divinity School, Prof. John Woodbridge, I managed to get hold of an early copy of the book by Phillip Johnson, Darwin on Trial (Washington: Regnery Gateway, 1991). Although I have never had scientific training, my courses a decade earlier in the history and philosophy of science spurred me on to read a few books in the area now and then. Pastoral experience had exposed me to wide divergences of opinion among Christians about the subject of origins—whether at the lay level or among Christian leaders. On the one hand, Henry Morris and those with him hold to a young earth and a high view of Scripture, but the most acerbic scholars in this camp adamantly insist that any other interpretation is both flawed and compromised. Despite their zeal and activism, they exercise little influence in the culture at large.

On the other end of the evangelical spectrum, usually with an equally high view of Scripture, countless evangelical thinkers have bought into some form of theistic evolution. Many of them are responsible scientists, but their exegesis of Scripture sometimes strikes me as weak and unconvincing. Moreover, as far as I can see, these people are equally without influence in the culture at large; atheists and naturalists do not see why they should learn anything from this group.

Into this potpourri of opinion, Johnson's book came as a bit of a jolt. I found it refreshing and stimulating, but I could not quite put my finger on why. Read at a certain level, it was saying things that had been said before. I wrote to Prof. Woodson asking if he had read the work and what he thought of it (mentioning that he could probably obtain a copy from Dr. Woodbridge).

March 23, 1991

My dear Tim,

(Ed. note: Woodson's letter begins with a number of personal items, good wishes to the Journeymans, and a discrete inquiry as to whether any medical progress has been made in the Journeymans' quest to start a family.)

My delay in replying stems from the fact that I had not read the book before reading your letter. I have now read it carefully, parts of it twice. I doubt if what I have to say will tell you anything you don't know, but you are more than welcome to a few random reflections.

First, even where the scientific material Johnson presents is not new, it is packaged in a novel way. The only similar book I can think of is one by a fellow called Macbeth, written a couple of decades ago, called *Darwin Retried*. Johnson's work is far superior. As you know, he is by training a lawyer—a lawyer on the faculty of a prestigious law school (Ed. note: at Berkeley). What he sets out to do is at one level quite modest. He assesses the quality of the argumentation in many of the standard works on evolution.

Thus, although he frankly admits he is not a scientist, this fact is scarcely a limitation on the enterprise. He has read himself into the relevant literature (even his critics concede the point), and now, like a good courtroom lawyer, he sifts the kinds of arguments and the calibre of evidence that evolutionists adduce, and in his assessment they are found wanting. This is important, for it puts the evolutionists on the defensive.

Second, this book is going to receive attention because of its author. I am not referring to the fact that Johnson is a lawyer; rather, I mean that he cannot be dismissed as an inferior mind connected with some second-class separatist school (however fair or unfair such a charge might be if leveled against someone else). Like a number of other scholars I could mention—I am thinking of a chemist in Georgia who has Nobel potential, of a psychiatrist at Harvard, and several others—Johnson is simultaneously a notable scholar in his own field and a Christian willing to tackle unbelief and wrong-headed thinking in the university. His friends say that one of his most delightful features is that he is not bothered by what people think of him. That stance reduces timidity, encourages boldness, and makes a scholar willing to make mistakes and risk opprobrium.

Third, Johnson limits his aim. He does not try to cover everything. For instance, he does not pretend to be a Biblical scholar or to have all the answers to the complexities of Biblical interpretation. From his perspective, it is more important to tackle naturalistic philosophy than to resolve every related dispute among believers. In terms of his own influence and mission, that stance is undoubtedly the part of wisdom.

So his point is not that he can prove theism; his purpose is not to prove the Bible is true. His point is narrow, but extremely well aimed. He argues that in terms of the hard evidence and the valid arguments, science supports no more than modest conclusions about how biological types can vary, within fairly limited boundaries, once they are already in existence. But the textbooks on evolution, almost all of which are written by philosophical naturalists, not by theistic evolutionists, extrapolate this slim body of evidence to make enormous claims about the power of mutation and the origin of life itself. The evidence is simply not there to support their claims. These scientists are like the preacher who kept penning "AWYH" in the margin of his sermons— "argument weak, yell here." The ultimate reason why so many of these scientists adopt this stance lies not in the evidence or in the power of the argumentation, but in their commitment to naturalism.

In fact, Johnson has nicely documented how often atheistic naturalists have frankly insisted (conceded?) that something like Darwinism has to be true, regardless of the state of the evidence, because the only alternative to a self-guided evolutionary process is a supernatural Creator—and for them such a conclusion is unthinkable. But that, of course, is a religious conclusion.

Fourth, implicitly Johnson is also tackling Christian thinkers who have too easily bought into some form or other of theistic evolution. At the very moment when a mounting pile of evidence threatens to overturn the evolutionary framework (and Johnson documents how a small but significant number of evolutionists now admit as much), not a few Christian academics, several decades behind, think they are being avant garde and sophisticated to board the sinking ship.

I could say more, but I think I have said enough. I wish Johnson well; may the Lord sustain him in boldness and humility as he challenges the gods of the age in the modern temples of Reason.

Tim, I cannot close this letter without assuring you that Elizabeth and I continue to pray for you and Ginny, not least that the God who answered Hannah's prayer will also answer yours.

With much love,
Paul

48

Early in November 1991, while preparing a series of sermons on Romans, I began to do some serious theological reading in the area of justification. I read Bannerman's old standard, worked my way through various dictionary articles, and then sampled some of the more modern treatments, including those of Ernst Käsemann and E. P. Sanders.

I did not read far enough into the most recent literature to gain a grasp of all the nuances, but I did see that the field was hotly debated and thoroughly confusing. At the same time, my love of history ensured that I knew how important justification by faith was during the magisterial Reformation, during the Puritan period, and in the Great Awakening. I could not help feeling that it was seriously neglected and perhaps misunderstood in our own times. I asked Dr. Woodson what he thought.

November 24, 1991

Dear Tim,

The topic you are raising is one of the largest and most complex of our day, at least in theological circles, and certainly one of the most important. But I thought I would get back to you with a few random reflections before I leave for two weeks of lecturing in the Far East.

I should perhaps begin by confessing my limitations. By training and experience, I am a systematician with considerable amateur interest in the history of doctrine. I am not a New Testament scholar. For fair comment on the technicalities of the more recent discussion, you should write to one of your old teachers in the New Testament department.

Your concern, I think, is well placed. In the modern discussion, although there have been some insightful contributions, there is rather more confusion than consensus. At the popular level, these confusions have not filtered down directly, but they probably have an indirect effect by stifling preachers from saying too much lest they be out of step with the latest research! The result is that they say nothing. I am referring, of course, only to pastors who, like yourself, have graduated fairly recently. Those who went through twenty years ago are in most instances blissfully unaware of the current debate. Even so, among many of them there is also a loss of proportion and clarity in their grasp of justification, and this affects not least their evangelistic preaching, but indeed what they mean by something as basic as "preaching the gospel."

Debates on the issue have not been at the academic level only. The ongoing Anglican/Roman Catholic dialogue has made justification and related matters its central topic for the past few years, issuing in ARCIC II—a notoriously fuzzy document, in my view. Then of course there was the discussion between Lutherans and Catholics, published under John Reumann's capable editing ten years ago. Alister McGrath has written a magisterial two-volume history of the doctrine, *Iustitia Dei*, published four or five years ago at a ridiculously expensive price by Cambridge University Press.

If I had to indicate where I think discussion should go, or, more accurately, if I had to reveal my biases by commenting a bit on recent discussions, I think that in the few minutes now at my disposal I should say five things.

First, the issue needs to be extended beyond Paul to embrace a discussion of the theology of the entire Bible. Among those who think that there is no such unity to the Bible's documents, of course, this suggestion will prove unpalatable. But for me, the issue is how God accepts sinful men and women, and that issue is as broad as the entire Biblical canvas. The topic has been too narrowly tied to one corpus (Paul's) and to one word group.

Second, contemporary discussion as to whether or not justification is the "center" of Paul's theology is bedeviled by ambiguity as to what "center" means. If you mean something like "that which holds it all together," it is hard to see how you could prove the point unless Paul himself structured his thought that way—and, quite transparently, he doesn't. If you mean something like "that which is of supreme importance," it appears that other things are made correspondingly *un*important—and that seems a bit harsh on Paul's

Christology, say, or his teaching on the Spirit, or half a dozen other things.

But I would be prepared to argue that for Paul justification is fundamental and foundational in that it marks the entrance point of a person into the new covenant, into the life of the Spirit, into acceptance before God. It is foundational in that in the life of the believer every other blessing flows out of this initial step. For that reason, it is essential that we try to get our understanding of it right.

Third, much of the contemporary debate was kicked off by the important book by E. P. Sanders, *Paul and Palestinian Judaism* (Ed. note: 1977). Arguing primarily against Lutheran (especially German) scholars, Sanders said that the picture they painted of first-century Judaism was badly skewed. Jews in Jesus' day were not narrow legalists who thought salvation could be earned by having more good points than bad points. Protestants had come to that position, he argued, partly by reading Reformation debates back into the first century and partly by reading fifth-century A.D. Jewish texts back into the first century. Sanders argues that all the relevant forms of first-century Judaism adhered to "covenantal nomism": Jews recognized that they were "saved" by grace, but that they kept themselves by works. And Paul, Sanders insists, is no different. He, too, espouses covenantal nomism. The fundamental difference between him and his opponents is not over legalism and the nature of saving faith, but over Christology. Paul and Christians like him accepted that Jesus was the promised Messiah, while most Jews denied the point. Obviously, if this view prevails, then it is bound to have some important bearing on how we read what Paul says about justification by faith (and not according to the works of the law).

By now I am quite sure that some of this is coming back to you from your days at Trinity! There is no doubt in my mind that you were introduced to Sanders in one of your courses on Paul. Sanders has set the agenda for contemporary Pauline studies, and many have bought into him. I am no expert on the Jewish literature of the Second Temple period (Ed. note: i.e., around the time of Jesus and the first four decades of the Early Church), but a couple of my colleagues in the New Testament department think that Sanders has 1) rightly protested against some terrible caricatures of Judaism, but 2) deployed an indefensible reductionism by lumping together all the forms of first-century Judaism under the one banner, "covenantal nomism," 3) clearly misread some important texts (for example, although Josephus, the first-century Jewish historian, constantly appeals to God's grace, he repeatedly treats God's grace as something earned by faithfulness and obedience—a stance far removed from Paul), and 4) his exegesis of Paul, though clever, is simply not very convincing.

Fourth, building on the work of Sanders, James D. G. Dunn, both in a two-volume Romans commentary and in several articles, has argued that Jews were not so concerned about law in any of the dominant legalist senses; rather, they were worried about tribal markers, the things that marked them off as Jews, the covenant people of God—circumcision, eating kosher food, and the like. Along the same lines, N. T. Wright has recently argued that for Paul, justification does not mark God's declaration that we are *just*, but rather God's declaration that we belong to the covenant community.

But note what this does. It makes the fundamental issue a question of self-identity—to what group do we belong? I cannot here enter into a lengthy study of particular passages in Romans, Galatians, and Philippians, but I am persuaded that this is deeply mistaken. Our fundamental need, according to Paul (and the rest of the Biblical writers!), is our alienation from and rebellion against God. What we need is to be cleared by Him; what we need is to be declared just by Him. Justification is thus tied to the fundamental question: How shall any man or woman be declared just in God's eyes? Meditate long on Romans 3:20ff. The answer, God's answer, is the cross. That same cross seems vaguely peripheral if what we really need is to be declared a member of the right group, rather than just before God.

Finally, I should perhaps mention the position of E. K. Käsemann. He argues that the expression "the righteousness of God" and its background in the Old Testament show that for Paul "righteousness" (or "justification"—the one Greek word can mean either) does not have to do with God declaring guilty people just, but with God keeping His promises; He is just, and therefore He does what He says. If He promises to vindicate His people, He will do so, because He is just. Clearly, this approach to justification also removes the cross from center stage.

On this subject, one of the most helpful articles I have read is by S. K. Williams. It was published in *Journal of Biblical Literature*, 99 (1980): 241-290, and is narrowly focused. Williams takes up the two expressions *dikaiosyne* and *dikaiosyne theou* (Ed. note: either "righteousness" and "righteousness of God" respectively, or "justification" and "justification of God" respectively). In almost all discussion, people have argued for a certain meaning to *dikaiosyne* and then proceeded to argue that *dikaiosyne theou* is a subset of that meaning, simply God's righteousness or justification or whatever. Williams has shown, in my judgment convincingly, that this is not linguistically justifiable and that the resulting interpretations are wrong. He argues that *dikaiosyne theou* in Paul invariably refers to God's faithfulness to His covenant promises to Abraham; God is righteous (*theou*, "of God," taken as a subjective genitive, i.e., "God's righteousness") to maintain and fulfill those promises. By contrast, *dikaiosyne* refers to the free gift of righteousness declared to belong to the person who trusts in this God who is faithful to His covenant promises. The concerns of the Reformers are safeguarded under this latter category; the Reformers are judged wrong in their handling of the longer expression. Take a concordance and work through the relevant passages and see if this begins to make good contextual sense.

This letter is getting too long and technical. My chief point, I think, is that it is essential to tie justification to the cross, to a true estimate of sin, to the question of Christian assurance, to the nature of the gospel. Disputes in this area are not merely theoretical; they have enormous practical implications for the way we conceive of and discharge our ministry and therefore for the way many Christians who hear us will think of their salvation and rest their confidence, their faith (and therefore their assurance!) in the God who justifies them.

I'm off in on December 10 for two weeks of ministry in Japan. Take care!

As ever,
Paul

49

*P*rofessor Woodson never reached Japan.

On December 9, 1991, we telephoned the Woodsons to tell them the wonderful news—Ginny was pregnant. We were absolutely ecstatic. At the same time I wanted to wish Dr. Woodson the best on his trip to Japan and to assure him of my prayers. That's when he mentioned he had been forced to cancel the trip. Within a day or two of sending off his last letter to me, he had begun to feel unaccountably weak. He waited a couple of days and then went to his doctor. At first the doctor had moved rather slowly and then with increasing alarm. The verdict had been reached that morning—Dr. Woodson had contracted a vicious melanoma and did not have long to live. This disease can so quickly devastate the body.

I simply did not know what to say. I was utterly stunned. It suddenly dawned on me that while I was wondering if Dr. Woodson had been looking on me as the son he never had, I had been relying on him as the father I had lost. Fathers aren't supposed to die; they're supposed to be there for you.

When I phoned the next afternoon (December 10), no one was home. I kept dialing every hour or so and finally reached Mrs. Woodson later in the evening. Her husband had checked into Highland Park Hospital; she had spent most of the day with him.

Five days later, he checked out again. There was nothing medicine could do for him except keep him comfortable. A nurse started visiting the Woodsons twice a day. Ginny and I talked it over, and we decided that I would fly up to Chicago December 26 or 27—right after Christmas, with all its responsibilities at our church. Mrs. Woodson assured me that she thought that would be plenty of time. Ginny would stay in Orlando. Her morning sickness was so awful she couldn't face the flight.

I phoned the Woodsons every couple of days. I never once heard Dr. Woodson complain. His voice seemed weaker and his breathing

shallower, but in the Lord's mercy he knew exactly what he was say-
ing. He kept asking how Ginny and the baby were doing. Every time
I talked with him he quietly told me he was ready to go "home."

On December 24, Mrs. Woodson phoned. Paul had gone to be
with the Lord very early that morning.

Mrs. Woodson asked me to read the eulogy at the funeral. During
the service she somehow managed to weep and be brave at the same
time, to grieve and to be grateful to her Heavenly Father for all the
years she had enjoyed with Paul.

To be frank, I felt numb, both at the funeral and in the weeks that
followed. The suddenness and the personal magnitude of this event
were too much for me to absorb. I did not properly grieve over Dr.
Woodson's death until mid-February when I received the following
letter, handwritten and slightly quavering, from Mrs. Woodson.

February 10, 1992

My dear Tim and Ginny,

It has been so kind of you to keep in touch with me by phone and
letter since my dear Paul was promoted to glory. I am more grateful
than I can say. When I've sorted out a few things here, I intend to
take you up on your invitation and come and visit you. Perhaps by
the time I come, Ginny, the worst of your sickness will be over. If not,
perhaps you'll let me mother you just a little.

A couple of evenings ago I found myself weeping in the bedroom,
and my mind went from my loss to your baby, and to the fact that we
never had one, and then back to Paul and to all the students we "par-
ented" over the years. I couldn't figure out how many of my tears
were from pain and loss and loneliness, and how many were out of
quiet gratitude, especially for you. It has been a very confusing time.

When I was young, I somehow thought that when old people die,
the people around them sort of expected it. But you never expect it,
and bereavement hurts terribly at every age. How grateful I am that
the Lord has drawn very close to me in my deep need. For the first
time I am beginning to appreciate the many passages where God
declares Himself to be the One who comforts the widow and the
orphan.

While going through Paul's papers, I read through a diary he
started to keep when he found out he did not have long to live. I am
astonished how much he wrote. When I come down to see you, I'll

bring it with me so you can read it. But I thought I would copy out a few paragraphs from here and there and send them to you right away.

December 11, 1991

There is nothing like imminent death to concentrate the mind. Yet we are all, all, under sentence of death. Why do we take so long to think about it so hard?

So far as I know myself, I am not afraid of death. I know whom I have believed and am convinced that he is able to guard what I have entrusted to him for that day (Ed. note: 2 Timothy 1:12). I have some fear of pain, of losing control. I earnestly pray for grace to endure with gratitude to the end, to say and do only those things that will bring honor to Christ, to avoid all things that would bring reproach upon Him.

December 12, 1991

A year or so ago Don Carson (Ed. note: in the New Testament department at TEDS) gave me a copy of his book *How Long, O Lord? Reflections on Suffering and Evil.* I scarcely glanced at it at the time; I have read it through during the last ten days. I wept with joy when I read again the old hymn by James Montgomery (Ed. note: 1771-1854).

> *Forever with the Lord!*
> *Amen, so let it be!*
> *Life from the dead is in that word,*
> *'Tis immortality.*
> *Here in the body pent,*
> *Absent from Him I roam,*
> *Yet nightly pitch my moving tent*
> *A day's march nearer home.*
>
> *My Father's house on high,*
> *Home of my soul, how near*
> *At times to faith's foreseeing eye*
> *The golden gates appear!*
> *Ah! then my spirit faints*
> *To reach the land I love,*
> *The bright inheritance of saints,*
> *Jerusalem above.*

Forever with the Lord!
Father, if 'tis Thy will,
The promise of that faithful word
E'en here to me fulfil.
Be Thou at my right hand,
Then I can never fail;
Uphold Thou me and I shall stand;
Fight and I must prevail.

So when my latest breath
Shall rend the veil in twain,
By death I shall escape from death
And life eternal gain.
That resurrection-word,
That shout of victory;
Once more, Forever with the Lord!
Amen! So let it be!

December 14, 1991

Of the various projects I wish I could have completed, only two really stand out. I wish I could have finished my work on Calvin's doctrine of God. I have so many notes and rough drafts of chapters that perhaps someone at Trinity will take the project on.

But the other one is perhaps even nearer my heart, though I am not as far along. In recent years I have sought out invitations to speak evangelistically to the completely unchurched—to men and women who have never held a Bible, who have no idea what it says, whose concept of God (if they think there is a God) is likely to be vague, ill-defined, perhaps monistic or deistic. I have learned much from these opportunities, and I think an evangelistic book that lays out the Bible's principal story-line needs to be written for unbelievers. Almost all our evangelistic booklets and books presuppose that the reader has some sort of basic Christian heritage, even though for a growing number of Americans and other Westerners nothing could be farther from the truth.

I remember a meeting about four months ago when a Hindu student heard me speak on the direction of history toward the end, toward Heaven and Hell, toward genuine accountability toward God, toward the prospect of uncontested pardon or irretrievable guilt. In the discussion afterward, he commented, "But if this is true, it must change the way we live!" I nodded and smiled, but before I could say anything he rushed on. "Most of us, when we tell others

282

what our goals are, think about the period of time until we are sixty or sixty-five. After that we retire. But if we must formulate our goals both for this life and for the life to come, those goals will determine how we live now." I concurred completely and read him some verses from the Sermon on the Mount to confirm this perspective.

Who could make use of my notes from these talks and turn them into a useful evangelistic book? I wonder if Tim would do it.

December 18, 1991

I can feel myself getting weaker. My only regret is that I am leaving my dearest Elizabeth behind. God, be merciful to her and comfort her, and make the joy of the Lord her strength. Surround her with people who will cherish her and give her room, yet who will sustain her.

Dearest God, I would have so many, many more regrets were it not for the pardon secured by Your dear Son.

> *Who is a pard'ning God like Thee?*
> *And who has grace so rich and free?*

December 21, 1991

What a privilege it has been all these years to be a follower of "the Way," and of Him who is the Way, the Truth, and the Life.

Lord God, have mercy on my dear son in the faith, Tim Journeyman.

"I have fought the good fight, I have finished the race, I have kept the faith. Now there is in store for me the crown of righteousness, which the Lord, the righteous Judge, will award to me on that day—and not only to me, but also to all who have longed for his appearing."

What a friend we have in Jesus! I read Psalm 23, and John 11, and 1 Corinthians 15 with new eyes.

You are constantly in my prayers.

With all my love,
Elizabeth